DEPRESSION:
From Psychology to Brain State

DEPRESSION:
From Psychology to Brain State

by
PAUL GILBERT

LAWRENCE ERLBAUM ASSOCIATES, PUBLISHERS
London   Hillsdale, New Jersey

Lawrence Erlbaum Associates, Ltd., Publishers
Chancery House
319 City Road
London EC1V 1LJ

L.Erlb. 29.95 1/31/85

British Library Cataloguing in Publication Data

Gilbert, Paul
    Depression.
    1. Depression, Mental
    I. Title
    616.85'27   RC537

    ISBN 0-86377-007-X

Typeset in Great Britain at The Pitman Press, Bath,
printed and bound by A. Wheaton & Co. Ltd, Exeter.

CONTENTS

1

Controversies Old and New

INTRODUCTION

Depression has been labeled the common cold of psychopathology. This comparison is an unfortunate one for it conveys the impression of a frequent but mild complaint. In reality some forms of depression are serious and deadly. Depression is responsible for the majority of suicide deaths; those most vulnerable to suicide are those who are depressed and have lost hope (Minkoff et al., 1973; Wetzel, 1976). Various figures for various countries and age groups can be presented (de Catanzaro, 1980). A general idea of the scale of the problem can be seen from the fact that in many developed countries suicide is in the top ten most frequent causes of death. Less easy to calculate, and only recently a subject of study, are those biological correlates of depression which appear to inhibit the capacity to combat physical disorder (via a cortisol $\rightarrow$ immune system feedback process). Moreover, depression may well reduce life expectancy in certain physical disorders, e.g., cancer (Whitlock & Siskind, 1979).

Outside these physical and life-threatening aspects, depression significantly affects family life. Parents who are depressed or who use various mechanisms to defend against a depression, can have a disturbing influence on their children's attitudes and subsequent vulnerability. For all these and other reasons, depression is not only the most frequent encounter in psychiatry, but in some cases it is among the most serious.

There is reason for some optimism, however. Since the turn of the century data have steadily been accumulated. Great progress has been made toward understanding the biological bases of the disorder, and developing new drugs and treatments. The psychological aspects are also better known than at any time previously. As we shall see, there is no shortage of competing theories. Thus, although frequent and potentially very serious, for the most part depression is a very treatable disorder. To advance our knowledge still further, new ways must be found to develop multidisciplinary and psychobiological theories. If not, we will end up with an ever-increasing number of theories. In such a world, debate tends to center on trivia and not on major points of agreement or disagreement.

1

The importance of understanding the causes of depression can hardly be overstated. In this book we tackle this problem from a psychobiological perspective. An endeavor is made to indicate how psychological processes influence biological processes and to highlight the need for psychobiological models capable of making these inter-reactions more understandable. It is hoped this will help counteract the growing fragmentation of approaches and models which are often based on faulty conceptions of mind–body distinctions. In view of the fact that many of our current controversies are products of ages past, brief regard is given to historical and philosophical aspects. This is followed by a review of the major psychological theories of depression. In the second part of the book a psychobiological approach, building from the psychological perspective, is presented. Chapters 6 and 7 constitute the more original and speculative basis of this work.

HISTORICAL AND PHILOSOPHICAL INFLUENCES

The phenomenon of depression has been recognized for over 2000 years. In the fourth century BC Hippocrates labeled it "melancholia." It is from these early times that one of the major disputes surrounding the classification of depression has its origins. Hippocrates, as a physician, argued that illness manifests as a quantitative variation from normal. The concern was very much the study of the individual. The Platonic approach to illness, however, arose from a particular philosophical orientation, "the doctrine of universals." This approach suggested that illness was a qualitative variation from normal, and concern was very much on the illness or disease itself and less on the individual. As Kendell (1975) makes clear, considerable controversy has embellished these positions. Indeed, the study of diseases in psychiatry is still an area of heated debate (Akiskal & McKinney, 1973a; Kräupl Taylor, 1980; Scadding, 1980).

As complex and problematic as the qualitative versus quantitative debate is, it is not the only philosophical stumbling block in psychiatry. When Descartes formalized the distinction between mind and body (Blakemore, 1977), it was in the very nature of psychiatry that this was to become a second major arena for debate. In spite of major efforts (Hill, 1981; Popper & Eccles, 1977), dualism remains a controversy in its own right and continues to plague psychiatric discussion. Indeed, it is only by maintaining a very strict dualistic approach that Szasz (1974) can argue: "The notion of mental illness derives its main support from such phenomena as syphilis of the brain or delirious conditions—intoxications, for instance—in which persons may manifest certain disorders of thinking and behavior. Correctly speaking these are diseases of the brain, not the mind [pp. 12–13]."

Dualism lies at the heart of the neurotic–psychotic controversy (Hill, 1968). Moreover, as Engle (1977) suggests, to dissociate mind from body provides the rationale for a mechanistic approach to suffering. The mechanistic approach fits neatly with Platonic disease entities. It must be said that the Platonic approach, in spite of its questionable corrupting influence on the sensitivities of the physician, has proved enormously useful, especially for the infectious diseases. Indeed, as Kendell (1975) makes clear, so successful was this approach in revealing the secrets of many disorders which had plagued man for centuries, that psychiatry could hardly resist similar endeavors with a similar philosophy. Hence, in the middle of the last century a new age in psychiatry was born out of Platonic successes in physical medicine. Yet psychiatry was to enter this era with the two outstanding controversies (qualitative versus quantitative and mind–body) far from resolved. Because it is from this time that present-day controversies in depressive illness begin to take recognizable shape, we can examine this era in more detail.

The Search for Disease Entities in Psychiatry

Emil Kraepelin (1855–1926) was born during this Platonic orientation in medicine. It was an orientation whose interest lay not so much in the patient as in the clinical phenomenon itself. For all Kraepelin's abilities, he reflected the spirit of his age in that his interest in the individual patient was, more often than not, notably absent. As Zilboorg & Henry (1941) put it, Kraepelin was "greatly interested in humanity but comparatively little in man." Kraepelin collected data from a number of sources and by careful analysis attempted to impose an ordered system of classification based on the assumption that mental illness could be categorized in terms of a distinct and finite number of disease entities.

The major distinction Kraepelin put forward for psychosis was in terms of dementia praecox and manic-depressive insanity. Kraepelin argued that manic-depressive insanity runs a cyclic course where the patient suffers from attacks of elation and depression, often with returns to normal in between attacks. The prognosis was considered favorable, in that these patients recovered. Dementia praecox was characterized by symptoms of catatonia and hebephrenia, often accompanied by auditory hallucinations. Prognosis for such patients was not good, since it was thought that dementia praecox would eventually terminate in a state of dementia proper. Diagnosis was by prognosis; if the prognosis was correct then the diagnosis was correct. This, unfortunately, led to a rather deterministic attitude to treatment; if the patient suffered from manic-depressive psychosis, the patient would recover. If, however, he or she suffered from dementia praecox, the individual would eventually deteriorate into dementia.

Although ideas concerning dementia praecox (or schizophrenia as Bleuler renamed it later) had been forming for over 40 years, Kraepelin's system did not receive uncontested support. Fifty years earlier Griesinger and also Zeller had scorned any attempt to subdivide mental illness, asserting that although mental illness could have different manifestations it was essentially a unitary phenomenon. Fifty years after Kraepelin, Menninger (1963) offered the same rebuke to the Kraepelinian system. Even in Kraepelin's own day many did not accept the Kraepelinian classificatory system. Hoche argued that there was no evidence that these "well-formed, self-contained, disease entities" actually existed in any pure form (see Lewis, 1967). Hoche viewed Kraepelin's distinct disease entities as no more than convenient symptom clusters. There also appeared to be factual discrepancies in the Kraepelinian system. Sometime earlier Kahlbaum, who had contributed enormously to the development of dementia praecox being labeled as a disease entity, had reported cycles in catatonia. Three years before Kraepelin published *Lehrbuch* in 1899, Mendel had argued that neurasthenia could also be cyclical in its course. Thus, as Zilboorg & Henry (1941) argue, these facts, among others, had to be overlooked in order to preserve the sense of solidity and correctness in the new nosological system. Consequently, Kraepelin's system, even from the time of its first emergence, showed certain characteristics of artificiality.

From an historical point of view it seems that the acceptance of the Kraepelinian system by psychiatry was a product of the age. First, as mentioned earlier, the concept of dementia praecox had been forming for over 40 years, with notable aid from Kahlbaum. Secondly, it offered psychiatry a fairly concrete paradigm, which had great potential as an integrating framework. Thirdly, the developments and achievements in general medicine placed considerable pressure on psychiatry to produce similar results. The Kraepelinian system seemed to answer the call on behalf of psychiatry.

In a sense Hippocrates won a great victory with the inauguration of the Kraepelinian system; mental illness was firmly in the hands of medicine. Yet paradoxically, in so doing, it had slipped the principles of Hippocrates and had taken up with Plato. Investigations into mental illness became more centered on the "disease entity" and its characteristics, rather than on the individual patient. Schule's Hippocratic-style warning to psychiatrists to remember that they were treating sick people, not merely sick brains, went unheeded. As Zilboorg & Henry (1941) put it, "this principle clashed too much with the newly established harmonious relationship between medicine and psychiatry."

One of the obvious consequences of Kraepelin's classificatory system, which became so dominant in European psychiatry, was that it had a significant effect on the orientation of future research. This orientation was based on the philosophy of discontinuities between disorders. Depressive illness was significantly affected by this approach. Unfortunately, Kraepelin left many pitfalls for subsequent researchers. First, Kraepelin's category of manic-depressive psychosis was a very inclusive category. Lewis (1967) points out that Hoche, in 1910, seized on this problem in his argument with Kraepelin over the existence of disease entities. Hoche argued that by the time of Kraepelin's eighth edition (1909), Kraepelin had relegated "melancholia" (involutional depression) from a disease to a clinical picture: "and that it no longer mattered whether there was mania or melancholia, occurrence once in a life or many times, at regular or irregular intervals, whether late or early with predominance of these or those symptoms, it was still manic-depressive insanity."

However, it was not only the overinclusiveness of the manic-depressive complex that presented problems for future research. Another major confusion arose from the use of terms and distinctions, such as exogenous/endogenous, reactive/psychotic, which crept into psychiatry at the turn of the century.

The Establishment of the Exogenous/Endogenous Position

The exogenous/endogenous causal distinction has had a major influence on psychiatry in general, and depression in particular (Lewis, 1971). It was introduced into psychiatry by Mobius (1893),[1] the concept being borrowed directly from the botanist Caudelle (1813).[1] This fact is of more than historic interest, however, since the botanist's exogenous/endogenous distinction rested totally on a physical discrimination. Similarly, the original psychiatric use of the exogenous/endogenous distinction was to discriminate between different "physical causes" of mental illness. Mobius labeled those illnesses considered to be due to degenerative or hereditary factors (i.e., internal causes) as "endogenous disorders." Those illnesses considered to be due to bacterial, chemical, or other toxic agents (i.e., external causes) were labeled as "exogenous disorders." As Beck (1973) points out, such definitions left no room for other causal factors, namely social or psychogenic.

Both Kraepelin and Bonhoeffer accepted Mobius' exogenous/endogenous distinction, although Kraepelin did not accept it as a classificatory system, since it was based totally on etiological considerations. However, Bonhoeffer developed the distinction further and put forward his own concept of exogenous disorders. To Bonhoeffer (1909), exogenous reactions were also of a totally physical origin. They were "modes of response by the

---

[1] As quoted by Zilboorg & Henry (1941).

brain to injury" (see Lewis, 1971). If no direct relationship between a toxin or injury and mental illness could be found, it was suggested that these toxins and/or injuries had produced intermediary products in the body, and it was these intermediary products which were responsible for the mental illness. Thus Bonhoeffer not only maintained the exogenous/endogenous discrimination as a purely "physical" distinction, but also allowed for exogenous reactions to be of a psychotic magnitude. In contrast to some modern discriminations, which on occasions have loosely equated exogenous with neurotic and endogenous with psychotic, Bonhoeffer's use of these terms was clear. For Bonhoeffer, exogenous and endogenous distinctions referred to differences in physical etiologies, whereas the term "psychotic" referred to the severity of the illness, though definitions of psychosis remained vague. However, subsequent semantic confusions were to arise in the use of these terms. At the very time psychiatry was celebrating its strengthened union with medicine, with the delineation of the disease entities dementia praecox and manic-depressive insanity, work was being conducted (notably in France) which was to intrude into this neat nosological system and raise a host of thorny philosophical problems. These problems presented many conceptual difficulties for Kraepelin's classifications.

   Psychogenesis as a problem for the exogenous/endogenous dichotomy, and the Platonic concept of disease. Through the work of Charcot (1825–1893) and later Freud (1856–1939), the importance of psychological processes as the major etiological factors in neurosis became established. But the actual concept of "neurosis" was vague and its relationship to psychosis even vaguer. It appears that at the turn of this century, the only illness considered to be of true psychogenic origin was hysteria. For example, in 1911 Bonhoeffer wrote an important paper entitled "How far should all psychogenic illnesses be regarded as hysterical?" In this paper Bonhoeffer stated: ". . . many psychiatrists would today assume that an illness must be hysterical if in its origin and development it can be seen to depend to a marked degree on psychological causes [p. 54, see Hirsch & Shepherd, 1974]."

   This statement offers some interesting insight into the current attitude of the day toward the role of psychological factors in mental illness. However, it was not a position which Bonhoeffer himself advocated. In the same paper he put forward the view that psychogenesis could play a major role in the development of other disorders besides hysteria. With regard to depressive illness Bonhoeffer argued (see Hirsch & Shepherd, 1974):

   There is, however, a group of depressive illnesses in which the psychological impetus is of prime importance. We are indebted to Reiss for drawing our attention to this group, which he called "reactive depressions." These depressive states are constitutionally based: they occur in individuals who from youth onwards are inclined to take things badly, whose depressive reaction is generally severe and of more than average duration. Severe psychological upsets can be followed by depressive exacerbations of psychotic intensity which are clearly psychogenic since frequently, although not always, when the psychological cause is removed the depressive exacerbation likewise disappears [p. 57].

(The view that "these depressive states are constitutionally based" may imply that Bonhoeffer believed that "reactivity" was an endogenous predisposition, thus placing reactivity within the concept of endogenous factors.)

Bonhoeffer further argued that some forms of epilepsy, paranoia, and mania could also be psychologically determined. Bonhoeffer believed that these illnesses could be ascertained by considering precipitating events. He labeled all such forms of illness as "reactive disorders."

Kraepelin accepted Mobius' and Bonhoeffer's exogenous/endogenous etiological distinction. He further accepted the possibility that psychogenic factors could play a role in certain mental disorders. However, unlike Bonhoeffer, Kraepelin placed psychogenic factors within the concept of exogenous causes, and did not distinguish them from physical exogenous causes, ignoring the concept of reactivity (see Lewis, 1971). This destroyed the purely physical characteristics of the original exogenous/endogenous distinction. In so doing, Kraepelin introduced into his own nosological system the old philosophical problem over the existence of a dualism between mind and body.

Prior to the absorption of psychogensis into the exogenous concept of causality, exogenous illness was regarded as physically determined, e.g., through bacteria, toxin, and/or injury. The inclusion of nonphysical factors within the exogenous concept presented considerable problems since it implied that psychological, nonphysical factors could interact with the (physical) disease process. But this position is essentially incompatible with the Platonic concept of a "disease entity." Indeed it is at this point in history that we see the mind/body and the qualitative/quantitative problems becoming entwined within the same sources of reference. If mental illness is a disease entity, it is a disease in a bodily (physical) sense, brought about by either organic injury, toxins, or other physical entities (Bonhoeffer's definition of exogenous), or through an inherent (endogenous) weakness in the physical (genetic) make-up of the individual. A disease "entity" in this sense cannot be influenced by nonphysical factors. Thus if mental illness is a disease entity (or a number of disease entities), then it follows that mind and body should be regarded as similar (i.e., physical entities), in other words dissolving the dualism between mind and body. But if such is the case, if there are no grounds for separating mind and body, if they are both to be regarded as physical entities, how can nonphysical, psychological factors affect a physical mind and induce or influence a physical disease process? On the other hand, if the principle of a mind–body dualism is maintained, then the concept of mental illness as a disease entity begins to become strained, since it is not logically consistent to have a (physical) disease entity of a "nonphysical" mind in the same way as a physical disease entity of a physical body. It is indeed a confusing issue and, as mentioned earlier, it has been this type of problem which has prompted Szasz to adopt his somewhat extreme position.

Various attempts have been made to save the disease entity concept of mental illness, by separating all illnesses of psychogenic origin from the endogenous (physical) illnesses. Thus, as Fish (1974) points out, Schneider argued that neuroses, psychogenic reactions, personality developments, and abnormal personalities are not illnesses in a sense of there being a morbid process in the nervous system, while the functional psychoses are illnesses in this sense. But this solution still leaves the problem of clearly specifying the dividing line between "physical" mental illness and "nonphysical" mental illness. The attempts to identify this dividing line have been at the heart of many of the controversies regarding mental illness, especially those concerning a meaningful classification of depression. It is a view which is unprofitable and probably incorrect, since even the so-called "neurotic" conditions can be shown to have physiological correlates. Moreover, some so-called "neurotic" depressions respond well to drugs.

MODERN APPROACHES TO CLASSIFICATION

Ever since the development of the Kraepelinian nosology, much was written about the "exogenous" disorders, with their identifiable external etiological characteristics, but very little appeared concerning the endogenous disorders. This situation was particularly noticeable for depression. The endogenous depressive disorders existed as "hypothetical, intangible, elusive predispositions, constitutional or hereditary forces which could be conjectured but not demonstrated (Lewis, 1971)." Thus, classification in terms of etiology was dubious since endogenous disorders were by definition simply those disorders for which no precipitatory (or exogenous) factors could be found. Consequently, the diagnosis of an endogenous disorder rested on the assumption that if no exogenous event presented itself as the cause of the illness, then the illness must be the product of a morbid disease process in the central nervous system. Partly as a result of this dilemma, various methods have been used to try to identify the natural boundaries between the subtypes of depression. In general three alternative approaches have been used (e.g., see Becker, 1974).

1. The cross-sectional approach which seeks consistent groups of signs and symptoms (syndromes).
2. The longitudinal, natural history approach which examines inter-relationships between various factors such as family history, age of onset, duration, severity, periodicity, and outcome.
3. The treatment-response approach which seeks to identify subgroups by examining different responses to various forms of therapeutic intervention.

Unfortunately, the semantic definitions of the subgroups studied have presented many confusions. For example, Bowman & Rose (1951) suggested that the neurotic/psychotic distinction usually refers to no more than vague differences in severity of illness. For reasons outlined above, the exogenous/endogenous distinction used by Kraepelin presented logical problems (Lewis, 1971). Realizing the confusion produced by the inclusion of psychogenesis in a definition of exogenicity, Ewald (1948; see Lewis, 1971) argued for a trichotomy of exogenous, endogenous, and psychogenic. While the logicality of these distinctions was accepted at the time, they have not become an established classificatory system. To confuse matters further, many writers have used terms concerning etiology and terms concerning severity synonymously. Thus, as Kendell (1976) points out, some authors, including himself, have:

. . . regarded "psychotic" and "endogenous" as synonymous, and "neurotic" and "reactive" likewise, using either pair of terms to denote two contrasting syndromes—the one consisting of severe, unvarying depressions, often with an acute onset, and accompanied by retardation, guilt, diurnal variation of mood and severe insomnia and weight loss; the other consisting of milder illnesses, often accompanied by anxiety, prone to vary from day to day, with self pity and histrionic outbursts rather than guilt, and complaints of anorexia rather than weight loss [p. 17].

On the other hand, some authors, notably those from North America, have been more specific in the use of these terms. For them, the distinction between "neurotic" and "psychotic" referred only to a consideration of severity, whilst the reactive (exogenous)/endogenous distinction referred only to etiological considerations. According to this use of these psychiatric terms, reactive psychotic illness and neurotic endogenous illness would be quite meaningful clinical descriptions. Thus, considerable confusion has been generated over the differential use of certain psychiatric terms, often resulting in misconceptions regarding the types of patient who have been placed in one subgroup or another. Furthermore, although various early studies often used etiological terms and distinctions as descriptions of their "classified groups," these studies were not directly concerned with etiological considerations. Rather, as Becker (1974) pointed out:

> ... they are chiefly concerned with whether depression is unitary or binary, that is, a single syndrome or two syndromes (endogenous and reactive), and whether the syndrome or syndromes is/are categorical or dimensional, that is, whether they are discrete entities (categorical) or whether they are normally distributed and occur in varying combination with each other or with other syndromes (dimensional) [p. 38].

These disputes are still very much with us, and reflect a failure to solve the Platonic (qualitative, categorical) versus the Hippocratic (quantitative, dimensional) concept of disease, assuming, of course, that a resolution is desirable and possible. At the heart of these disputes remain the fundamental problems of the philosophical orientation to the concept of disease. Eysenck (1970) argued that in the study of depressive illness, each of these two philosophical approaches (Platonic versus Hippocratic) has two basic positions. For the Platonic qualitative concept of a disease entity, depression can be either unitary categorical or binary categorical. For the Hippocratic concept of disease, depression can be either unitary dimensional or binary dimensional. A further complication is the view that some depressions are of the mind while others are the direct result of a primary (body) biochemical dysfunction.

The recent history of the search for a meaningful nosology of depression has provided advocates for each of the four positions. Eysenck (1970) has argued that Mapother & Lewis both held a unitary categorical view of depression. While Lewis was certainly against the subdivision of depression, it is unclear whether he believed depression to be a well-delimited, clearly separable illness, distinct from all other illnesses. Yet a necessary condition for both the unitary and binary categorical views of depression is that depression is a disease which is clearly distinguishable and separable from all others (e.g., schizophrenia). The history of the confusion over cross-Atlantic diagnostic practices casts some doubt on the evidence for such a view (Beck, 1967; Kendell, 1975). Moreover, Kendell's stipulation for the demonstration of a zone of rarity between supposed disease entities has not yet been provided. Most recently, Kendell & Brockington (1980) used a nonlinear method of analysis in an attempt to show a zone of rarity between affective psychosis and schizophrenia. They were unable to offer any support to the disease entity view. They concluded that the necessary evidence to distinguish the psychoses into Platonic-like disease entities has not been provided, but rather the evidence favors a dimensional classification. In fact little has changed since Kendell (1975) argued that there is no clear evidence for categorically distinguishing affective illness from either anxiety or schizophrenia. Indeed he suggests there is, as yet, no clear evidence to establish the existence of any functional disease entity in psychiatry. Kendell's arguments are, of course, fundamental. However, recent research on the classification problem has shown more concern with developing research methods for classification, allowing reproducibility, and searching for subdivisions "within" the broad spectrum of the depressive disturbance. This work seems to have partially replaced the search for the natural boundaries between depression and other disorders.

For both the unitary categorical and the binary categorical views, a demonstration of the distinctiveness of depression is required. In other words, depression as an "entity" must be shown to be different from other "entities," i.e., anxiety and schizophrenia. In the mid-1960s and early 1970s Roth and his co-workers from Newcastle suggested that they had obtained evidence for distinguishing neurotic from endogenous depressive disorders (Carney et al., 1965; Kiloh & Garside, 1963) and for distinguishing depressive illness from anxiety states. Their position is basically a binary categorical one.

Early attempts to replicate these findings produced variable evidence (e.g., see Mendels & Cochrane, 1968). Prusoff & Klerman (1974) used a discriminate function analysis to try to separate depressed and anxious patients. They suggested this was possible despite 25–40% of their patients being misclassified. For Kendell's concept of the necessity for a zone of rarity, this percentage of cases would seem far too high to suggest a categorical representation. There are many difficulties in evaluating some of this early work. Major differences in procedure and data gathering have not lent themselves to a consistency of approach or evidence, and it is not surprising, therefore, that evidence is often unclear or contradictory. Moreover, in spite of the errors and questionable assumptions of factor analysis, Kendell (1968, 1975, 1976) argues that factor analysis tends to favor a dimensional, rather than a categorical classification system. He suggests that a dimensional approach more accurately forecasts treatment and outcome than the traditional categorical (disease entity) position. Eysenck (1970) agrees with Kendell but argues that two dimensions, neurotic and psychotic, are required if substantial information is not to be lost. Kendell (1976) rejoins this by suggesting that the same argument can be made for any number of dimensions. The number of dimensions really depends on the purpose for which the classification is designed.

As we turn to examine some of the more recent evidence for various classifications, this argument regarding the number of possible dimensions will become apparent.

Recent Perspectives on Classification

A plethora of approaches and nosologies has grown up around the depressive disorders. Here we briefly examine some of these. 1. *Statistical approaches*. The statistical approach to classification has a long history. Although some workers remain sceptical of the usefulness of this endeavor, it has thrown up important data. An oft-used technique has been factor analysis (see Fowles & Gersh, 1979a,b; Kendell, 1976; Mendels & Cochrane, 1968; Nelson & Charney, 1981). In general, factor analysis has provided some support for neurotic/psychotic and neurotic/endogenous distinctions.

Cluster analysis as explored by Paykel (1971) suggested four subgroups of depression: (a) psychotic depression; (b) anxious depression; (c) hostile depression; (d) depression associated with personality disorder (see also Depue & Monroe, 1978a). Paykel & Henderson (1977), in a replication study, produced only three clusters; hostile depressives failed to separate clearly. On the other hand, Overall & Zisook (1980) suggested that (a) anxious, (b) hostile, and (c) agitated and retarded depressives can be reproduced as meaningful subgroups. Cooke (1980a) used a complex statistical procedure to investigate subtypes of depression in a normal population. He reported the existence of four syndromes: (a) vegetative; (b) anxious; (c) cognitive; with the fourth consisting of the more classical endogenous symptom profile. Cooke suggests that people can experience differing levels of each syndrome and a dimensional rather than categorical approach best fits the data.

2. *The theoretical approach.* Klein (1974) offered an interesting, theoretical discussion on the question of endogenous depression (endogenomorphic depression). Klein suggests that endogenomorphic depressives have a dysfunction of the pleasure areas of the brain. Hence they may share common symptoms with neurotic depressives, but only endogenomorphic depressives experience a pervasive loss of pleasure at all levels. The implication of Klein's analysis is that only specific key symptoms are of value in attempting to distinguish between endogenous and neurotic symptoms. This, he suggests, is because the few qualitative distinction symptoms of the endogenomorphic patient may be entirely swamped by being embedded in the enormous array of common, overlapping symptoms which are produced secondary to demoralization. Since Klein's distinction rests on assumed neurophysiological differentiation, the validity of the distinction remains to be seen. The effectiveness of tricyclic drugs in both endogenous depressive disorders and other neurotic complaints (e.g., panic attacks) may be difficult to fit with Klein's proposals.
    Other theoretical approaches can be derived from psychoanalytic

approaches but in general they throw little light on classification. Seligman (1975) suggests his model of learned helplessness may be a model for reactive depression, but others have suggested that (in some respects) it best fits the endogenous disorders (Depue & Monroe, 1978a).

3. *The treatment outcome approach.* There have been numerous attempts to classify depression via treatment response (e.g., Rao & Coppen, 1979; Raskin et al., 1970; Raskin & Crook, 1976). Generally the more severe the depression, especially if psychotic, the greater the indication for physical therapy. However, Raskin & Crook (1976), in a comparison of chlorpromazine, imipramine and placebo, make the point that the active treatment affects symptoms, and not patient types. (See Fowles & Gersh, 1979a, for a discussion of Raskin & Crook's findings.)

4. *The unipolar–bipolar distinction.* Following the distinction first put forward by Leonhard (1959) and Perris (1966), the unipolar–bipolar system has become of major importance. This classification, to some extent, avoids the controversies engendered by mind–body and qualitative–quantitative issues. More recently, differentiation of the bipolar disorders has been suggested. Bipolar I patients are those with a positive family history of bipolar illness and who have required hospitalization for both mania and depression. Bipolar II patients have a positive family history of bipolar illness, but have only been hospitalized for depression. Bipolar III patients also have a positive family history for bipolar illness, but have only experienced one depressive episode. These more complex distinctions have yet to be proven (Depue & Monroe, 1978b).

One of the difficulties with this system is that the unipolar depressions remain a very mixed and heterogeneous group. Unipolar depression may in practice be little more than a diagnosis of depression in the absence of a bipolar component. Hence, a number of problems still surround this system (Depue & Monroe, 1978b, 1979; Kendell, 1976), including the use of drugs like lithium, which have been found effective for some of the schizophrenias (Hirschowitz et al., 1980).

5. *The primary–secondary distinction.* Primary depression is not preceded by any other psychiatric or physical disorder. Primary depression may be either unipolar or bipolar, the unipolar depressions being further subdivided into "pure depressive disease" and "depressive spectrum disease." Secondary depression is preceded by and may accompany other psychiatric disorders (e.g., anxiety neurosis, alcoholism, personality disorder, etc.) or a physical disorder (Robins et al., 1972). This distinction has the advantage of being accompanied by useful research diagnostic criteria (Feighner et al., 1972). As neat as this nosology appears, it is not without its difficulties (Akiskal et al., 1978; Kendell, 1976).

6. *The hierarchical model.* The hierarchical classification of depression arises from the work of Foulds (1973) and Foulds & Bedford (1975,

1976). According to this model (which applies to the large spectrum of psychiatric disorders), symptoms can be arranged with regard to the disturbances in personal functioning. The hierarchy consists of four classes of symptoms: (a) dysthymic states—anxiety, depression, and elation; (b) neurotic symptoms—phobic conversion, dissociative, compulsive, and ruminative; (c) integrated delusions—delusions of contrition, grandeur, and/or persecution; (d) delusions of disintegration—primarily of the schizophrenias. Patients with symptoms in higher classes may have symptoms of lower classes, but the reverse does not hold true.

Foulds & Bedford (1976) suggest distinctions of depression along the dimensions of (a) depression versus not depression; (b) psychopathological versus not psychopathological; and (c) psychotic versus neurotic. This classification is of interest for a number of reasons. It allows for psychotic depressives having neurotic symptoms. In this sense it bears some similarity to Klein's ideas of the existence of embedded or core symptoms in certain disorders. It allows for the possibility that patients may shift between neurosis and psychosis (Akiskal et al., 1978) or indeed, show instability of diagnosis over time (Kendell, 1974). There is some support for this system (e.g., Bagshaw, 1977), but it has not attracted much research. Moreover, Surtees & Kendell (1979) failed to demonstrate that psychotics can exhibit significant neurotic symptoms as the model predicts.

7. *The biological approaches.* The biological approach to classification has accelerated considerably in recent years. Maas (1975) and Schildkraut (1976) have suggested two types of depression based on possible changes in neurochemical parameters: type A depressions have a deficit in norepinephrine pathways, and type B depressions have a deficit in 5-HT pathways (see also Akiskal, 1979).

Schildkraut and his colleagues have published two important papers outlining potential biochemical differences between depressive subgroups (Schildkraut et al., 1978a,b). These researchers have investigated urinary output of the metabolite of norepinephrine, 3-methoxy-4 hydroxy-phenylglycol (MHPG). In addition they also obtained measures of the following biochemical variables: norepinephrine (NE), epinephrine (E), metanephrine (MN), normetanephrine (NMN), and vanillylmandelic acid (VMA). Using a standard least squares regression analysis, they generated an equation which produced a score for the dependent variable. This dependent variable they called D, the depression type score.

While the analysis is complex the data they obtained point to the possibility of distinguishing subgroups of depression according to catecholamine metabolic differences. Using the D score as the dependent variable, they suggest a discrimination between three subtypes of depression which fit the following clinically derived syndromes:

1. Bipolar manic-depressive disorder, schizoaffective and some unipolar endogenous depressive disorders: These share the biochemical characteristics of low urinary MHPG, a low D score, and low urinary epinephrine.
2. Unipolar nonendogenous plus some endogenous depressions: These share the biochemical characteristics of high urinary MHPG and high D scores.
3. Schizophrenia-related depressions (with chronic asocial behavior): These share the biochemical characteristics of low urinary MHPG, low urinary epinephrine, and low urinary metanephrine but have a high D score and high platelet monoamine oxidase activity.

The known dysfunction of cortisol production in depressives (Depue & Kleiman, 1979) is another fascinating avenue of research. More recently, Carroll et al. (1981) have extended their work to devise a specific test for depression (melancholia). The test depends upon the use of dexamethasone. This substance, in specific doses, is able to inhibit cortisol for up to 24 hours in normal subjects. However, disturbance of the hypothalamic-pituitary-adrenocortical axis (HPA), as occurs in some depressions, enables these patients to demonstrate early escape from dexamethasone inhibition. Thus, it is possible to differentiate those depressives who demonstrate dexamethasone escape from those who do not.

Psychophysiological differences between depressed subjects have also been investigated. In his review of the data, Lader (1975) concludes that depression is primarily a disorder of biological retardation. Any anxiety or agitation present in a depression is superimposed on a basic biological retardation component.

8. *The longitudinal approach.*   Finally, special attention is given to an example of the longitudinal approach. This work has important implications for the systems of classification discussed.

In one of the most useful studies of the 1970s, Akiskal et al. (1978) used a longitudinal approach to investigate the heterogeneity of neurotic depression. Using a standard psychiatric diagnostic procedure (DSM 11), these authors argued that neurotic (nonpsychotic) depression was the only appropriate diagnosis for each of the 100 cases studied. Patients with other diagnoses, e.g., manic-depressive illness; anxiety, obsessional, and phobic neuroses; and organic brain damage, were excluded.

In 22% of cases depression appeared to be clearly related to situational events, but for the other 78% situational events tended to act as a trigger mechanism for the depressive episode. On the question of reactivity of neurotic depression these authors argue that: ". . . neurotic depression was viewed as a functional illness, representing a psychological, understandable reaction to adverse environmental contingencies in both vulnerable and nonvulnerable personalities [p. 759]."

At the index episode, symptoms were generally mild, i.e., a clear absence of psychoses (as required by selection criteria) plus a relative absence of major vegetative disturbances (e.g., sleep, appetite, and libido) and psychomotor (retardation and agitation) disturbance. Symptomatology presented largely on the subjective (psychological) level, with few clinical signs of endogenous depression. In 90% of cases other symptoms of non-affective neuroses were evident, e.g., obsessional, anxiety, and phobic symptoms; 24% of cases showed a characterological difficulty, designated as a life-long tendency to overreact to normative stress. The overall impression then is of a very mixed group of individuals and symptoms.

Akiskal et al. (1978) present many important points for consideration, only some of which can be summarized here. Their findings include:

1. Of the 100 patients studied, 36% went on to develop depressions with an endogenous profile of symptoms. Given the authors' initial exclusion criteria and the mild, reactive nature of the neurotic depressed state at the indexed episode, they are led to agree with others (e.g., Klein, 1974) that the endogenous concept of depression should be divorced from considerations of severity or cause. In their view mild, nonpsychotic, endogenomorphic depressions, which may be either precipitated or not, do indeed exist.

2. These researchers were unable to demonstrate a relationship between a neurotic episode and a subsequent psychotic one, i.e., some patients having been diagnosed as neurotically depressed had subsequent episodes of psychotic depression, or moved into a depression of psychotic depth via a neurotic depression. These researchers do not mention the possibility that specific life events, e.g., childbirth, may play some role in these transitions. Clinical observations suggest, however, that women who suffer a psychotic, puerperal episode can be left with a neurosis which may take longer to clear. In any event Akiskal et al. believe that their data support a hierarchical conceptualization of illness as advocated by Foulds (1973) and Foulds & Bedford (1976). This evidence seriously undermines the idea that neurotic and psychotic depression are qualitatively separate or are different diseases. The neurotic–psychotic distinction may hold little validity for predicting the course of an individual's illness over time, or for the development of a meaningful nosology. A further interesting point not discussed by these researchers is that a treatment not effective at one time in the subject's history (i.e., neurotic depressive condition) may become effective at a later point (psychotic depressive condition). Furthermore, the person may (or may not) make a complete recovery with physical treatment when psychotic, but the same treatment may be less effective when neurotic symptoms dominate presentation. This seems one of the puzzling but important questions for both the classification and treatment-response studies. It would, however, seem to echo Raskin & Crook's (1976) findings

that drugs affect symptoms, not people or illness types. At the very least it warrants further research.

3. The view that neurotic depression is equivalent to secondary depression (Winokur, 1973) was found to be true for only 50% of cases. Moreover, one-fifth of those studied went on to develop bipolar illness, which also casts doubt on the view that neurotic depression is a subgroup of unipolar depression. Nevertheless these researchers still believe that a primary–secondary distinction has some usefulness for depressions that arise in the course of a nonaffective disorder.

4. The presence of a characterological disorder significantly affected outcome. They suggest that these patients may overlap with Paykel and co-workers' clusters of hostile and personality disorder patients. They point out that:

. . . a patient may suffer from a pure primary affective illness or primary affective illness in the context of severe characterological disorder (in which instance it will have poor prognosis). Conversely, a patient may suffer from a character disorder (such as hysteria, sociopathy, or related disorders) with concomitant alcohol and drug abuse as well as depressive symptoms [p. 764].

In later work Akiskal et al. (1980) have suggested that characterological depressions may be subdivided into "subaffective dysthymias" and "character spectrum disorders." The subaffective dysthymias are a heterogeneous group with individuals approximating to either a unipolar or bipolar pattern of symptom presentation. Generally, these are considered potentially good (physical) treatment responders. The character spectrum disorders are less good (physical) treatment responders. They tend to show less physiological similarity to true depression (e.g., on REM latency, and the cortisol dexamethasone escape test) and more traits traditionally associated with personality disorder. It is hypothesized that the chronic depression of this latter group is related to an adverse development history (e.g., alcoholic parents, social deprivation, etc.).

CONCLUDING COMMENTS

This chapter has outlined some of the historical debates and controversies surrounding the classification of depression. It is clear that although progress is being made, there is still considerable confusion and debate in the area. Blumenthal (1971) points out that heterogeneity of depression resides at a number of levels, e.g., symptom presentation, treatment response, and etiology. Keller & Shapiro (1982) have made the important observation that acute episodes of depression may arise against a background of chronic depression, labeled "double depression." Weissman & Klerman (1977b) also raised the issue of the relationship between acute and chronic depression. There are notable gender differences in prevalence and presentation of depression (Byrne, 1981; Weissman & Klerman, 1977a). Furthermore, various disorders may share common biological mechanisms (e.g., Horrobin & Manku, 1980).

One of the problems for classification is the extent to which individual experiences of discontinuity in subjective state may be grouped together. For example, catastrophe theory (Postle, 1980; Zeeman, 1977; see Chapter 7) allows deeper insight into how the brain may function in a discontinuous manner. But whether these changes can be investigated from a group perspective is uncertain. The lack of stability of some pathological states (Akiskal et al., 1978; Kendell, 1974) raises problems with the use of crosssectional data analysis. Furthermore, the assumption that similar disturbances in neurochemical processes will give rise to similar psychological changes is also in doubt (Mendels & Frazer, 1974).

In spite of these many difficulties the pursuit of meaningful classifications of depression promises to throw up important sources of data. However, to approach the problem from a psychological point of view, the classification issues are puzzling. As Beck (1967) and Beck et al. (1979) make clear, the cognitive themes of the depressive are remarkably similar regardless of subtype. Moreover, apart from excluding psychotic and bipolar depressives, those engaged in the nonphysical treatment of depression have shown an almost complete disregard for classification issues. It would seem that whether depressed patients are anxious or retarded, hypochondriacal or hysterical, psychological therapies are relatively effective (Weissman, 1979). This is not to say that there is no attempt to discover which therapies are most effective for which patients. Rather it would seem that for the unipolar depressives at least (who make up the vast majority of cases), distinctions as they exist at present do not seem particularly helpful to the psychotherapist. Understandably, psychotherapists tend to put forward their own systems of classifications (e.g., Blatt et al., 1982) based on psychological mechanisms. These, at present, do not fit neatly with the more medically orientated nosologies. Hence, as Kendell (1975) suggests, for the majority of cases classification usefulness depends upon the use to which it is to be put. Data that might guide physical treatment decisions may not always be useful for psychological treatment decisions. Unlike the medical approach, which only has a limited number of choices bound by the availability of drugs, psychotherapists are more flexible in their ability to tailor treatment to the patient's needs.

There is no doubt, however, that the presence of hypomania and the question of endogenous symptoms remain of major significance. It is unclear to what extent the endogenous profile can be more readily equated with a specific depressive disease. It may be that endogenous symptoms reflect specific central nervous system characteristics. Just as some patients with Cushing's disease can manifest major depressive symptoms while others manifest different symptoms, the same may be true of those suffering from depression. Whether such characteristics are innate or learned is unknown. There is little evidence to suggest that endogenous depressives do not benefit from psychotherapy (Bishop, 1980; Blackburn, et al., 1981). Rather it may be a question of severity. The more severe the disorder, the greater the disturbance in biological processes and the greater the difficulty in orientating the patient along psychotherapeutic lines.

2

Psychoanalytic Theories of Depression

The interaction between psychological and biological processes became especially problematic with the emergence of psychoanalysis. Although many of the concepts utilized by the psychoanalytic movement had existed as isolated ideas for some time, Freud secured himself a place in history with his ability to bring such ideas together and develop them into a comprehensive theory of mind. Hence, for the first time, a systematic theory was established which was able to explain mental pathology as the interplay of psychological processes on physiological ones, and, Freud hoped, one day vice versa.

Psychoanalysis and Freud were very much a consequence of Darwin's development of evolution theory. With Darwin came the greater certainty that man is an evolved animal whose superiority (if it be such) lies in his history and not in the hands of God. This allowed Freud to suggest that the study of the disordered mind (via psychoanalytic theory) was biological psychiatry. For, in the neurosis of man, Freud believed the interplay between the preservation of the individual and the preservation of the species was central. As evolution is important to all early analytic theories, attention must be given to it here.

Darwin's influence on psychology and psychopathology was immense but indirect. In suggesting and substantiating the view that humans and animals share a common history, shaped by the forces of evolution, the classical discontinuity view of man and animals, proposed by Descartes, could no longer exist. Man had finally lost his soul. For psychology, three major implications of Darwinian theory became evident. Atkinson (1964) and Weiner (1972) outlined these as follows:

1. Darwin and later researchers demonstrated the existence of intra-individual differences in the ability of organisms to adapt to their environment. Thus, the study of individual differences in terms of psychological ability (e.g., IQ and personality) and physical ability became of major importance. Indeed, the study of the causes of individual differences (the nature–nurture debates) has been a cornerstone of much work in clinical psychology and psychiatry. The genetic versus the environmentalist con-

troversies in the classification debates owe much to this concept of intra-individual differences in the adaptive ability of a species.
2. Darwinian principles reaffirmed the idea that laws of adaptation and learning exist in other species apart from humans. Such a view provided the theoretical rationale to study the laws of learning in animals, both for their own intrinsic interest and as a means for offering insights into learning mechanisms in humans. Weiner (1972) suggests that this led directly to Thorndike's experiments and the operant principles of the laws of effect. Also, of course, the study of physiological and anatomical mechanisms of learning in animals rests squarely on this principle. Should it have been shown that the monkey brain (say) operates radically differently from the human brain, this line of research would have been much less interesting and useful and, of course, would have challenged Darwinian principles. As it is, many of the neuroanatomical and biochemical insights (including the mapping of neurotransmitter pathways in the brain and the development of many drugs) have been possible as a result of the study of non-human brains.
3. Darwin's view of a continuity between humans and animals lent itself very directly to the idea that humans, like animals, are (to some extent) driven by instincts which are primarily concerned with survival rather than rationality. Rationality will develop if it bestows advantage in the struggle for survival.

This third implication leads directly to Freud's id psychology and indirectly to various drive reduction theories of learning. Even today, this area of psychology remains one of the most conceptually complex and controversial. Some modern theories of psychopathology ignore the difficulty of inherited psychobiological response patterns completely and suggest that it is only the laws governing the development of beliefs and attitudes that are necessary for understanding psychopathology.

At the turn of the century, however, this would have been considered naive indeed. For this was a time when questions of how man could deal with his (then accepted) primitive and savage past abounded. It was a time when Nietzsche was at his most popular. Although Freud apparently put off reading Nietzsche directly for some time, as Ellenberger (1970) points out, Nietzsche was so well discussed at the time of Freud's early maturity that it was not necessary to have read him directly to be permeated with his ideas. To be able to appreciate some of the parallels of Freudian thought with Nietzsche's ideas, it is well worth quoting Ellenberger (1970) at length. He points out the following interesting parallels:

> Psychoanalysis evidently belongs to that "unmasking" trend, that search for hidden unconscious motivations characteristic of the 1880s and 1890s. In Freud as in Nietzsche, words and deeds are viewed as manifestations of

unconscious motivations, mainly of instincts and conflicts of instincts. For both men the unconscious is the realm of the wild, brutish instincts that cannot find permissible outlets, derive from earlier stages of the individual and of mankind, and find expression in passion, dreams, and mental illness. Even the term "id" (das Es) originates from Nietzsche. The dynamic concept of mind, with the notions of mental energy, quanta of latent or inhibited energy, or release of energy or transfer from one drive to another, is also to be found in Nietzsche. Before Freud, Nietzsche conceived the mind as a system of drives that can collide or be fused into each other. In contrast to Freud, however, Nietzsche did not give prevalence to the sexual drive (whose importance he duly acknowledged), but to aggressive and self-destructive drives. Nietzsche well understood those processes that have been called defence mechanisms by Freud, particularly sublimation (a term that appears at least a dozen times in Nietzsche's works), repression (under the name inhibition), and the turning of instincts toward oneself. The concepts of the imago of father and mother is also implicit in Nietzsche. The description of resentment, false conscience, and false morality anticipated Freud's descriptions of neurotic guilt and of the superego. Freud's "Civilization and Its Discontent" also shows a noteworthy parallelism with Nietzsche's "Genealogy of Morals." Both give a new expression to Diderot's old assumption that modern man is afflicted with a peculiar illness bound up with civilization, because civilization demands of man that he renounce the gratification of his instincts. Scattered throughout Nietzsche's works are countless ideas or phrases whose parallels are to be found in Freud. Nietzsche taught that no one will complain or accuse himself without a secret desire for vengeance, thus "Every complaint (Klagen) is accusation (Anklagen)." The same idea with the same play on words is to be found in Freud's celebrated paper "Mourning and Melancholia": "Their 'complaints' are actually 'plaints' in the older sense of the word" [p. 277].

Outlining the parallels between Nietzsche and Freud does help to put Freud in some philosophical and historical perspective. It is clear that social Darwinism and Nietzsche's philosophy did have an enormous impact on Western thought at this time, and Freud could not have avoided being influenced by it. Jung (1963), for example, unlike Freud, clearly outlined the influence Nietzsche had had on his thinking. There were many other influences, of course, and the above does not detract from Freud's originality.

Today these influences on our thinking are less acute, and perhaps our models of human behavior are more influenced by current developments in the technical fields. Thus, computerization has brought with it psychological ideas of information processing, feedback systems, circuit loops, and the like. It would seem unfair, however, to introduce analytic ideas without some recognition of the background from which they emerged. It is with these thoughts in mind that Freud's ideas on depression are introduced.

THE INFLUENCE OF FREUD

As we have seen, Kraepelin was the first to systematize the distinction between dementia praecox (schizophrenia) and manic-depressive psychosis. The phenomenonology of the manic-depressive complex changed throughout the course of Kraepelin's publications. Indeed, it was this tendency to broaden the concept which enabled Hoche and others to accuse Kraepelin of making woolly and ill defined distinctions. Although these disputes raged in the background, it seems that Freud generally accepted Kraepelin's classification system, despite the fact that it managed psychogenic disorders poorly or not at all. Of major importance was Freud's apparent belief (in which he was not always consistent) that psychoanalytic theory should address itself to mild and severe forms of the disorder, including manic-depressive illness. That this is so can be seen from the following extract taken from *Mourning and Melancholia*, first published in 1917. Here Freud makes clear his concern with the manic episode:

> The most remarkable characteristic of melancholia, and the one most in need of explanation, is its tendency to change round into mania—a state which is the opposite of it in its symptoms. As we know, this does not happen to every melancholia. Some cases run their course in periodic relapses, during the intervals between which signs of mania may be entirely absent or only very slight. Others show the regular alteration of melancholic and manic phases which has led to the hypothesis of a circular insanity. One would be tempted to regard these cases as non-psychogenic, if it were not for the fact that the psycho–analytic method has succeeded in arriving at a solution and effecting a therapeutic improvement in several cases precisely of this kind. It is not merely permissible, therefore, but incumbent upon us to extend an analytic explanation of melancholia to mania as well [p. 253].

There are a number of elements in this passage which should be considered. If Freud is talking about true manic-depressive illness, then he may have had psychoses in mind. However, it is unclear how familiar Freud was with the true psychoses. For example, his analysis of paranoia did not arise from directly observed data, but was derived from Schreber's book on the subject. On the other hand, Abraham (1911) clearly stated his concern with depressive psychoses and offered an account of a case which today would most probably be considered a bipolar affective illness. Abraham postulated a connection between obsessional neurosis and depression, and in regard to the manic-depressive cycle he argued that: "Psychoanalysis shows, however, that both phases are dominated by the same complexes, and that it is only the patient's attitudes towards these complexes which is different [p. 149]."

It seems fair to conclude, then, that early psychoanalytic views had a rather inclusive notion of depression and were not simply concerned with mild neurotic states. It is interesting to note Freud's rejection of the "cyclical insanity" view of manic-depressive illness on the basis of the reported efficacy of psychoanalytic treatment for some cases. The possibility that spontaneous remission may have played a role is not considered. However, he does consider a role for biological factors later in the paper, which suggests some lack of consistency in his approach. Moreover, a certain element of doubt about the generality of an analytic explanation is also evident in *Mourning and Melancholia*. Freud wrote: "Our material, . . . is limited to a small number of cases whose psychogenic nature was indisputable. We shall, therefore, from the outset drop all claim to general validity for our conclusions . . . [p. 243]."

This was to create a problem for subsequent psychoanalytic proposals, for having acknowledged a probable lack of generality, the phenomenology to which Freud addressed his theory was very wide indeed. In general, the limiting factor was a kind of diagnosis by prognosis. If manic-depressive insanity responded to psychoanalytic therapy, then it was psychogenic. If a case did not respond to such treatment, few conclusions were drawn regarding etiology. More recently, some psychoanalysts have agreed that even in severe depression psychogenic elements are of the utmost importance (Arieti, 1977, 1978).

The problem for any science, of course, is that if we are to understand "X" we must also know what is "not X." To some extent it was the failure to designate those depressions for which psychoanalytic theory and therapy were not applicable that has sown the seeds for many heated disputes. Knowledge that might rescue this difficulty (e.g., concepts of multi-causality, vulnerability, and psychobiological perspectives) were some years away. Adolf Meyer in America, however, did much to ignite a psychobiological approach to psychopathology and his impact on clinical practice has been great. Unfortunately, as Klerman (1979) observes, for one reason or another Meyer's impact on research has been disappointing by its absence.

There is much that can be written on the various aspects of the generality of psychoanalytic theory and the patients from whom the ideas developed. Such considerations should be borne in mind when considering Freud's view of melancholia.

Mourning and Melancholia

Mourning and Melancholia was undoubtedly a landmark in psychological theorizing on depression. By the time of its publication in 1917, many events in the history of the psychoanalytic movement had already occurred. Jung and Adler had disaffected themselves from Freud, the First World War was well under way in all its tragedy, and Freud himself, now into his sixties, had experienced his own personal crisis. Moreover, psychoanalytic theory had erected a complex and powerful set of axioms for explaining the development and cure of neuroses. Although Abraham had offered a psychoanalytic theory of the manic-depressive complex some six years earlier (from which Freud borrowed and acknowledged), it was *Mourning and Melancholia* which was to shape many of the subsequent views on the subject. Freud had touched on the problem of periodic depression some years earlier, believing it to be a third form of anxiety (Goldberg, 1975). But it was in the comparison of mourning with melancholia that Freud directed his attentions to a systematic explanation of depression. As psychoanalytic theory was already well developed, Freud's analysis was much more than a simple comparison of these two states. Hence, *Mourning and Melancholia* is a complex work incorporating many aspects of general psychoanalytic theory, including libido theory, narcissism, ambivalence, the oral personality, regression, the process of identification, and so on. It is not surprising, therefore, that many of the subsequent debates and modifications to Freud's view of depression related as much to disputes over psychoanalytic theory in general as to depression in particular. Jung (1963), for example, notes that Freud's concern to explain all neuroses in terms of libido theory caused many problems. Jung himself believed that psychic disturbance could have a variety of causes, of which only a few may relate to libidinal difficulties. It needs to be emphasized, therefore, that a complete understanding of Freud's theory of depression requires a good, general grasp of psychoanalytic theory. Since such an exposition cannot be undertaken here, the reader interested in this approach should consult psychoanalytic literature directly (e.g., Anthony & Benedek, 1975; Wollheim, 1971). Only the central elements of Freud's position will be discussed.

In *Mourning and Melancholia*, Freud proposed that loss was central to both these states. Both are painful states of mind which focus on a lost object. However, loss may be of a more ideal kind or the patient may be unsure about what is actually lost. Thus, there is the suggestion that for some depressed individuals the object lost has been withdrawn into the unconscious. In mourning, however, the loss is very much within consciousness. Freud highlighted a further important distinction between mourning and melancholia by suggesting that in melancholia there is "an extraordinary diminution" in self-regard, which is not present in mourning. In mourning, it is the external world which has become impoverished and empty. In melancholia it is the internal world, the ego itself, which has become poor and empty. It is in the explanation of the relegation of loss to the unconscious and the lowering of self-esteem that Freud turned to psychoanalytic theory. Here we should note the distinction between "observations" of phenomena (in this case psychological events) and the "explanation" of how these events came about. Many writers agree with Freud's observations of the importance of loss and a lowering of self-esteem in depression, but disagree as to the mechanisms by which these occur.

Freud argued that ambivalence to the lost object resulted because of the high dependency needs of the patient. Such dependency needs (a characteristic of the oral phase of development) carried with them feelings of frustration and hostility. To express these would endanger the relationship, thus they are relegated to the unconscious. Unfortunately, keeping these aggressive feelings at bay requires the investment of considerable libidinal energy. When the loved object is lost, these negative feelings, powered by libidinal energy, become attached to the ego itself. This occurs through a process of identification with the lost object. As a result the hostile impulses are unleashed against the self, causing a catastrophic fall in self-esteem. The anger and hostility, fuelled by libidinal energy, are directed inward against the ego. This is sometimes conceptualized as "anger turned inward."

Mourning and Melancholia in Retrospect

Following the publication of *Mourning and Melancholia*, constant revisions, developments, and alternatives to the theory have appeared. Psychoanalytic theorists, however, nearly always start with Freud's basic statements on depression. Unfortunately, at least two serious problems exist in this work.

The first of these problems relates to Freud's noble but, at this time, mistaken efforts to maintain a close union with neurobiology and psychoanalysis. The *Project for Scientific Psychology*, written in haste in 1895 but never published, formed the neurobiological framework from which Freud was to postulate the mechanisms in the formation of psychological symptoms (Wollheim, 1971). He believed that neuronal energy was excitatory, could be diverted or repressed, but not destroyed. In consequence the idea that quantities of energy could be shunted around the central nervous system according to the vicissitudes of mental mechanisms appeared tenable. Indeed, it leads directly to the concept of symptom substitution and the importance of catharsis (the release of repressed energy) for recovery (McCarley & Hobson, 1977).

Today psychopathology is regarded as either idiosyncratic styles of information processing and learning, or as various biological dysfunctions which interfere with the brain's capacity to process and filter information. In view of the fact that few seriously believe the energy transfer model of brain–behavior interactions any more, it is remarkable how some psychoanalytic theorists continue to produce theories which require just such a model. The second major problem revolves around the importance of anger and aggression. In some theories of depression the importance of anger is almost totally ignored (e.g., Beck, 1976), but for Freud anger against the self was central to an understanding of low self-esteem and self-destructive acts. Unfortunately, psychoanalysis treats aggression as a unitary phenomenon. In reality aggression manifests in many different forms; it is under the control of different stimuli and different brain areas. Thus, aggressive behavior may manifest as rage, territorial, or predatory attack, or it may be defensive, and so on (Montagu, 1976). Aggression is certainly not unitary, and arm cutting or drug overdosing may represent quite different forms of aggression (with different biological pathways) than, say, the irritable aggressiveness noted in most depressives. Moreover, the idea that anger is turned against the self to protect the loved object from attack requires qualification (see Chapter 6). Klein (1974) argued that blaming others is a common neurotic depressive trait. Friedman (1970) and Weissman et al. (1971) found that some depressives experience a heightening of aggressive feelings and irritability. Patients' self-statements of worthlessness or hatefulness cannot be taken as aggression toward the self in any meaningful sense. Rather, they reflect particular forms of cognitive appraisal.

It is important to recognize that difficulties with the energy transfer model and the aggressive impulse notion are fundamental. They call into question the idea that it is aggressive impulses which, when unleashed against the ego (and, previously unconsciously, directly at the loved object), cause self-esteem to fall, because of the savage attacks on the ego. If the energy transfer model of brain activity is unacceptable, then the concept of libidinal energy may appear redundant. Consequently, some other process or processes must be investigated to explain low self-esteem in depression.

Before moving on to a consideration of what these processes may be, it should be noted that the Kleinian development of Freudian thinking in many ways went further, in suggesting an instinctive and aggressive impulse basis for psychopathology.

THE KLEINIAN INFLUENCE

The work of Melanie Klein came eventually to represent a major departure from Freud. In the early days, however, during the 1920s, Klein regarded her work with children as an expansion and development of libido theory. Subsequently, it became clear that the later formulations proposed by Klein constituted radical changes in psychoanalytic thinking and led to a further fragmentation of adherents, especially in Britain. Like other developments in psychiatric thinking, Kleinian ideas have influenced concepts in ways which are obscured by history. Although much of the language of Kleinian theory is highly suspect, it has had a subtle impact. Of all the individual divergences from classical psychoanalytic thinking (e.g., Jung, Adler, Reich, Rank, and so on), Kleinians have been among the foremost in advancing a therapeutic technique based on the transference relationship. Unlike the Freudian approach, which suggests the transference develops slowly, Kleinians believe that it occurs immediately, brought by the patient, at the start of therapy. This allows for early interpretations, and opens the possibility for short-term, focal psychotherapy. This appears odd to non-Kleinians because of the potential number of possible interpretations. However, Klein's system acknowledges only two fundamental forms of maladaptive mechanisms relevant to pathology. Both are related to processes which are inevitably confronted during the first months and years of life. Given this, the style of interpretation is guided by which of the two types of mechanism seems responsible for the patient's difficulty.

The mechanisms of pathology relate to two developmental stages or positions; the paranoid-schizoid position and the depressive position. The relationship between positions and mechanisms is complex. Generally, "positions" refer to developmental stages whereas "mechanisms" refer to the psychological processes used at these stages. Thus, it is possible that individuals use paranoid-schizoid mechanisms for coping with conflict even though they may be well into maturity with the cultural standards of success behind them. In regard to depression, there is sometimes the confusion that depressive illness relates to mechanisms associated with the depressive position. This is inaccurate, since severe and psychotic depression can relate to paranoid-schizoid mechanisms. In such cases the severity of the depression relates to the engagement of primitive, intense, paranoid-schizoid mechanisms associated with the very first phase of life. Mechanisms associated with the depressive position are likely to relate to milder forms of pathology. One aim of psychotherapy is to interpret and hence help the patient avoid the use of paranoid-schizoid mechanisms which can bring about detachment from reality. This system of thinking can be made clear by considering the two developmental stages or positions in more detail.

Paranoid-schizoid and Depressive Positions

Kleinians start with the hypothesis that at birth there is a complete projection of all bad feelings associated with inevitable frustration. To protect the internal world the baby is all good. Any badness must therefore have a source outside of self. Thus, aggressive impulses experienced at points of frustration are not seen as arising from self but from outside self. It is assumed that the newborn baby is totally incapable of integrating self-generated, aggressive impulses within its own ego structure. Clearly, there can be no guilt at this point since there is nothing to be guilty about; all badness and aggressiveness are outside. Thus, there is an internal splitting of good and bad. Also, it is assumed that the baby can only relate to part objects, e.g., to the breast, which are not integrated into any complete whole object, e.g., the mother. Again, through inevitable frustration, the baby experiences good part objects (e.g., the good breast, giving fulfilment and comfort) and bad part objects (e.g., the bad breast, empty, absence, non-fulfilling, frustrating, not capable of satisfying). This constitutes an external splitting of good and bad. Thus, there is an internal dichotomy or split—good inside, bad outside—and an external split—good part objects and bad part objects.

The mechanisms of the paranoid-schizoid position are of a splitting of good and bad, all or nothing, absolute dichotomies. Use of this paranoid-schizoid mechanism has the patient making absolute judgments, and projecting all the causes of badness outside of self. Where badness is identified it is outside self, threatening to destroy what is inside, and thus forming the basis of paranoia.

As the child develops (possibly at about six months and onward) there is an awareness that both the internal split, of good inside and bad outside, and the external split, of good and bad part objects, is not a reflection of reality. The child comes to realize that the good and bad part objects are actually part and parcel of the same whole object, e.g., the mother. Thus, the whole object is both loved (for being at times good) and hated (for being at times bad). In addition there is a growing realization that some of the aggressive (bad) impulses do arise from within. These two realizations, which occur at an unconscious level, set up a terrible problem. It is suggested that the baby now comes to fear the strength of its own aggressive impulses toward the bad parts of the whole object, lest in the process the good part object is also destroyed. Entry into this stage of development constitutes the depressive position. Problems at this level manifest as needs for reassurance that the good has not been destroyed. Separation anxiety originates here. In therapy patients who have not successfully negotiated this stage of development will experience intense anxiety about their own aggressiveness toward loved objects, including the therapist. It is hypothesized that patients using mechanisms relating to this position will have unconscious fantasies that they may, or have, destroyed the therapist with their own badness.

Entry into the depressive position also marks the first experiences of guilt. There is an unconscious awareness that what the self does in the world has an effect on the whole object. Thus, there are instinctive aggressive impulses both to destroy the object of badness, but also to keep it intact and put it back together. Segal (1975) states that:

> . . . his (the baby's) concern for his object modifies his instinctual aims and brings about an inhibition of instinctual drives. And as the ego becomes better organised and projections are weakened, repression takes over from splitting. Psychotic mechanisms gradually give way to neurotic mechanisms, inhibition, repression and displacement [p. 75].

While successful negotiation of the paranoid-schizoid position is possible, there is doubt whether the depressive position is ever fully overcome. As with Jung's concept of individuation, there is a movement toward it perhaps, without complete success ever being assured.

It follows from this model that mild (neurotic) depressions revolve around mechanisms of the depressive position. The patient experiences intense anxiety about his own destructiveness and capacity to be loved and wanted. The experience of internal, destructive impulses produces significant guilt and constitutes a threat to the loved object, by possibly (in unconscious fantasy) destroying what is also loved and needed. Here we see a reworking of Freud's concept of dependency needs and anger turned inward. More severe depressions, however, relate to earlier paranoid-schizoid mechanisms where internal and external, and good and bad, part objects are profoundly split up and separated. Severe depressions are different from mild depressions in their propensity to use these primitive (early) coping mechanisms.

Anyone who has tried to study Kleinian theory and ideas relating to object relations theory (which is a separate theory, though sharing some points in common with Kleinian views) will know that this summary is a gross oversimplification. As with Freud's views on depression, Kleinian theory involves a complex framework of ideas and concepts, from which the foregoing has been abstracted.

Comment

Whether or not one accepts this developmental theory, there is little doubt that in subtle and modified ways some of these ideas have filtered through to different theoretical models. Moreover, the idea that the more primitive (early) the mechanisms engaged, the more severe the disturbance, may fit with the biochemical work, which shows similarities between severe depression and schizophrenia, and also with hierarchical models of classification suggesting that psychotics also have neurotic problems (see Chapter 1).

Klein's views are far more instinct related than those of Freud. Moreover, they reflect her work with children, in that they are concerned with mechanisms which are an inevitable consequence of limited cognitive development. This, of course, is also a weakness, since there seems no objective way in which such ideas can be tested. Nevertheless, it is possible to observe patients behaving and thinking in ways which may accord with the description Klein makes. The question is, does Klein offer a testable paradigm for such observations?

Klein attempted to consider the ways a young child may work through a love–hate (aggressive) conflict. One may agree that this type of conflict, as Freud and others suggest, is often evident in psychopathology. It is also true that some theorists do not pay nearly enough attention to it. Hence, Chapter 6 it is considered from a cognitive-behavioral-ethological perspective. However, it can be suggested that behavioral theory, as advanced by Ferster (1973, 1974; see Chapter 3), and possibly Solomon (1980), offers a more rational basis for discussion of love–hate conflicts. It should also be considered that much of the difficulty the child faces has to do with attributions, that is, who or what causes this or that to happen. Thus, perhaps an attributional analysis of some of Klein's concepts would provide a more comprehensive framework for considering these issues. Indeed, the relationship between attributing a quality to someone and projecting a quality onto that person needs to be explored (see Holmes, 1978, 1981; Sherwood, 1982). As yet cognitive theory has not given the necessary attention to mechanisms such as projection.

Klein, like Freud, had a developmental view of psychopathology. That is to say, vulnerability was laid in the child's navigation of various developmental periods, or stages. Although Klein worked especially with children, while Freud did not, both argued that vulnerability arose from childhood experiences or fantasies. Jung, however, is one of the few analytic theorists who does not specifically relate vulnerability to childhood.

THE WORK OF JUNG

The work of Carl Jung has sometimes been dismissed as too mystical and obscure for serious study. Although his ideas on the inheritance of archetypal forms via repeated experience over generations are probably false, Hall & Nordby (1973) suggest the concept of the archetypes remains valid and appropriate from the Darwinian perspective.

Jung postulated that man, as an evolved species, inherits specific predispositions for thought and action. These predispositions exist as foci within the collective unconscious capable of guiding aspects of behavior and emotions autonomously. As Ellenberger (1970) suggests, Jung's theories on the archetypes have often been misunderstood. Nevertheless, Jung has had an enormous, though indirect, impact on psychology.

One of the most relevant archetypes for understanding depression, and of obtaining clear insight into the concept of an archetype, is the persona. As Hall & Nordby (1973) make clear, the persona is an inherited predisposition to behave in a way which facilitates conformity, social acceptance, and social integration. It is the archetype which motivates us to be accepted by others. More specifically, it is the mask which is exhibited to one's fellows "with the intention of presenting a favourable impression so that society will accept him [p. 44]." Since the persona is only one aspect of the self, too little or too much development of the persona can have unfortunate consequences.

In cases of "persona inflation," the individual overidentifies with his mask. He becomes too involved with conformity and too reliant on external sources of reinforcement secured from others with the use of his persona. Hall & Nordby (1973) suggest that:

. . . a persona-ridden person becomes alienated from his nature, and lives in a state of tension because of the conflict between his overdeveloped persona and the underdeveloped parts of his personality.

On the other hand the victim of inflation can also suffer feelings of inferiority and self-reproach when he is incapable of living up to the standards expected of him. He may, as a result, feel alienated from the community and experience feelings of loneliness and estrangement [p. 45].

There are a number of points here which are of importance. First, the persona is a necessary and innate aspect of psychological functioning. It derives from the evolution of man as a social animal. Without some predisposition for individual members of the group to conform, all would be havoc. Persona function may begin to develop when the infant starts to form attachments to peer-group members. From this point on, the function of developing social dominance for the group becomes plainly evident. Harlow & Mears (1979) indicate that early play between age-mates often reveals undercurrents of dominance–submissive interactions. Persona inflation or deflation, when operative in the psychological difficulties of an individual, often shows itself as problems with social dominance; that is, the person may feel inferior or superior to others.

In Jungian theory, these difficulties come about through the underdevelopment of other aspects of the personality. This is the situation where an individual learns that the outward success of his persona is the means to personal happiness. The person can only be happy if the part he is playing (parent, lover, academic, sportsman, etc.) is acceptable and is reinforced by others. In other words, the individual seeks to play his part to the full and failure must be avoided at all costs, for without the reinforcement of others self-esteem is dealt a catastrophic blow. In general terms, persona difficulties result from a learning history where success of a role is highly reinforced and failure is punished (see Chapter 4). The basic wish of the individual is to seek safety in conformity. In a persona-dominated person, the overriding problem is a high dependency on external sources of reinforcement and approval.

In Jung's view, depression not only results when the persona act fails. Depression and a sense of emotional isolation can appear when the individual begins to realize that no matter how successful the persona, happiness and contentment are short-lived and empty. This may occur when the "shadow" archetype intrudes into persona functioning. In this case individuals become aware that their act is false, it is not a true or complete reflection of the person they are or wish to be.

A conflict between archetypes can also be a source of depression. As individuals begin to realize that their act is false and life is meaningless, they are forced to acknowledge all those aspects of themselves which have been hidden by their mask. They may become aware that there is a good deal of aggression and general nastiness behind their mask, which they have hidden both from themselves and others. Thus, shadow–persona conflict can exist within many depressive disturbances. If those shadow qualities are expressed then the individual may indeed be cast out, and face the abandonment and loss of love and respect that the persona has worked so hard to secure.

Jung suggested that the shadow related to the more instinctual qualities of the mind. There seems to have been some tendency for the concept of the shadow to overlap Freud's idea of id function. But a simple equation of shadow with id is incorrect. Jung (1940) suggested that the shadow consisted of "the inferior or less commendable part of the person [p. 20]." Looked at in cognitive terms, the shadow reflects those attributes of self which are "judged to be," by individuals themselves, less commendable or inferior. Since such judgments are usually culturally determined, it is not surprising that shadow qualities are often considered more primitive and immoral. However, while this may be true, it is also the case that qualities of shadow are negative attributes based on the "person's own judgment" of good and bad. Thus, for a man with a strong male persona, qualities of self which are seen as weak, tender, or sentimental may take on shadow function. In other words, in this case the shadow and the anima (female qualities of the self) become one and the same. Thus, the strong male seeks to repress those attributes of self which he judges to be bad, overly emotional, useless, or weak. As Jung (1940) says, the anima and shadow may become largely identical.

Shadow function may be understood if matched against its opposite—

persona function. Whereas the persona deals with conformity to peer-group values, shadow function is an expression of individual wants, needs, wishes, behaviors, and so on, which might be viewed as anticonformity or threatening the reinforcement and approval from others. But Jung suggests it is a quality of shadow which gives the personality depth and individuality. Sometimes the shadow may seek expression in conformity, that is, through persona function. In these situations the individual has a strong wish to be good, loved by all, highly respected. In effect, he seeks to be a hero and may fantasize himself as a real hero. The individual comes to believe that if he can excel at some task he will become a dominant member of his peer group, able to have all the pickings of whatever his society can bestow on him. In these fantasies the workings of evolutionarily old, social dominance concerns are evident. The socially dominant animal can copulate with whom he likes, be aggressive and beat his opponents, be admired and loved by everyone, and so on. In the fantasies of neurotic patients, however, these implications are not always obvious, though they can be, especially in men.

Now there is much that could be written on this subject and I have only given a very simplified account. As Jung makes clear, however, personal development can only take place with the death of the hero ideal. (Indeed, Jung, 1963, himself encountered this conflict.) In cognitive terms we can say that the wants, wishes, and desires, primitive or otherwise, need to be acknowledged and detached from persona function. In the early stages of therapy the process of separating persona from shadow may leave the patient in limbo. Often patients have identified with the hero ideal or an overidealized perfect image for so long, that with its departure they find themselves unsure of their real self and frightened in case parts of them are less than acceptable.

Jung's approach readily allows us to observe how such conflicts arise from innate and inherited psychological predispositions. It needs to be emphasized, however, that the archetypes refer to specific psychological tendencies. Thus, although individuals may play different roles with different groups, these are all part of the same need to conform, that is, they have the same function—similarly, with the shadow. Thus, we should not make entities of these functions, for this leads to the unmanageable situation of seeing individuals as having multiple personas or multiple shadows. Just as a functional analysis can be applied to various behaviors (Ferster, 1973, 1974), we may also apply a functional analysis to the archetypes.

Hence, Jungian theory suggests depression can arise from distorted formation and inhibition of psychological processes which have their origins in evolved predispositions. The persona archetype is especially useful for understanding depression. This is because it allows consideration of the innate (psychological) basis of certain forms of psychological construction, relating to social, integrative behavior. Moreover, conflicts between the archetypes, for example the persona and shadow, may be at the heart of many depressive disturbances. Depressives have lost their way to the extent that they overvalue persona attributes: "I must be a good, loving person, successful, always hard working, be loved, be approved of by others," etc. They have not come to terms with the realities of being human; that sometimes they will be angry, unreliable, have sexual fantasies, be cowardly, etc. Although depressives feel they need others to survive, and wish to seek their support, they also fear that should others see their shadow, they will reject and abandon them. These conflicts activate and maintain psychobiological response patterns which have evolved in relation to loss of peer-group love and support. In very severe cases, depressed patients may be overwhelmed by shadow attributes and see themselves as useless, aggressive, wicked, evil, a danger to others, unloving, and unlovable. There is a complete loss of the individual's perceived capacity to become reintegrated with his peer group or form significant, loving attachments. Persona function is completely lost to the dominating shadow.

Jung in Retrospect

Jung's notion of psychic energy can be criticized in much the same manner as Freud's concept of energy. He had little idea how such energy might operate in the central nervous system. His tendency to work and write "at breakneck speed" resulted in much that was oddly written and obscure. This has probably done much to confuse issues. When synthesizing his ideas he could write with clarity (Jung, 1933), and provided interesting ideas on the relationship between the unconscious and the conscious in relation to attitudes:

> The unconscious itself does not harbour explosive materials, but it may become explosive owing to the repressions exercised by a self-sufficient, or cowardly, conscious outlook. All the more reason, then, for giving heed to that side! It should now be clear why I have made it a practical rule always to ask, before trying to interpret a dream: What conscious attitude does it compensate? [p. 21].

In the latter part of this book, special attention is given to the idea that attitudes and beliefs can amplify and modify psychobiological response patterns. The roots of these ideas are found with Jung.

Jung's theory of mind is considerably more complex and wide ranging than that of Freud. His mystical leanings and, at times, obscure style have not endeared him to the scientific community. Yet Jung's concept of the archetypes may prove among the most useful of psychobiological concepts. A major distinction between Jung and other psychoanalysts was his view that neurosis was produced in the present, not the past (Storr, 1973). In therapy, a major concern was to keep the patient in touch with reality by focusing on the here and now.

Jung was among the first to outline how personality types influence the form and nature of the individual's neurosis. His view that different personality types had different biological make-ups has been proved by Eysenck and others. For depression, the role of personality remains vague. In regard to biological treatment, personality may be important. For example, extroverts may respond better to amphetamine-related drugs, whereas introverts respond better to the more sedative drugs.

Jung was also responsible for the idea of the life process (Staude, 1981) and for noting that many depressions commence later in life. In his spiritual approach to the human, he was in total opposition to Freud. Sadly, there have been many arguments as to which one of the two was the greater. Sometimes the arguments, carried out in their names, have come down to little more than personal digressions. Which of the systems one chooses depends on the purpose to which it can be put. Both are extremely illuminating, but both are recognized, by their originators, as being just the first steps on a long journey to understanding.

ATTACHMENT LOSS AND DEPRESSION

Bowlby's (1969, 1973, 1977a,b, 1980) development of attachment theory constitutes a major advance to the understanding of psychopathology. Like Freud, Klein, and Jung, Bowlby's concern is with the activity of inherited psychobiological response patterns. But for Bowlby, the most important response patterns are those guiding the formation and development of attachment objects, not those governing aggressiveness or sexual impulses. Indeed, Bowlby (1969) offers a major criticism to Freud's energy concept of mind and presents an alternative explanation of how evolved, instinctive behavior operates.

Unlike some theories of depression, the central factors of Bowlby's theory—disturbances in the development, maintenance, and/or termination of attachments bonds—are seen to underlie a variety of psychopathological disturbances. Therefore, these are not processes which are specifically related to the etiology of affective disturbance(s), though they are important for such a theory.

The general axioms of attachment theory can be summarized as follows:

1. Attachment behavior is instinctive (goal-directed) behavior. There is an inherited predisposition to behave in a way which maintains proximity and communication with attachment figures. This inherited predisposition has survival value and, as a consequence, it has evolved in a variety of species.

2. Some systems which mediate attachment behavior may only be activated under conditions where the functions of attachment behavior (e.g., to protect) are threatened. In other words, situations which are potentially threatening to survival (e.g., aloneness, strangeness, noise, strangers) will activate a sequence of behaviors (e.g., distress calling, searching, clinging) which are designed to maintain proximity to, and protection from, the caregivers.

3. Many affective consequences are related to the making and breaking of attachment bonds. For example, uninterrupted, stable attachment may be experienced as security; threat to attachment bonds, as anger and/or anxiety; complete loss of an attachment as depression; regeneration of attachment bonds as joy. The actual affective consequences will be a function of many variables, antecedent and subsequent to the actual changes in attachment.

4. Attachment behavior is a source of varied emotional experience. It is present through all stages of life and need not be a sign of pathology or regression.

5. In addition to offering survival advantage, by protecting the young infant from predators, attachment can also provide a secure base from which to explore the environment. This ability to explore safely conveys considerable advantage in that it facilitates discrimination learning and the development of necessary skills for adaptation.

For Bowlby, early attachment behavior is the key to understanding psychopathology. More specifically it is attachment behavior toward parental figures which determines subsequent vulnerability. As Bowlby (1977a) puts it:

> The key point of my thesis is that there is a strong causal relationship between an individual's experiences with his parents and his later capacity to make affectional bonds, and that certain common variations in that capacity, manifesting themselves in marital problems and trouble with children as well as in neurotic symptoms and personality disorders, can be attributed to certain common variations in the ways that parents perform their roles [p. 206].

In describing the biological and evolutionary link between certain behaviors and the disruption of attachment bonds, Bowlby (1977a) outlines a theory of psychopathology based on maladaptive, early attachment behavioral interactions between caregiver and child. He further suggests that many psychiatric patients (especially neurotic cases) have histories which include:

> . . . one or both parents being persistently unresponsive to the child's care-eliciting behaviour and/or actively disparaging and rejecting;
>
> discontinuities of parenting, occurring more or less frequently, including periods in hospital or institution;
>
> persistent threats by parents not to love a child, used as a means of controlling him;
>
> threats by parents to abandon the family, used either as a method of disciplining the child or as a way of coercing a spouse;
>
> threats by one parent either to desert or even to kill the other or else to commit suicide (each of them commoner than might be supposed);
>
> inducing a child to feel guilty by claiming his behaviour is or will be responsible for the parent's illness or death [pp. 206–207].

All these distorted attachment relations plant the seeds for significant emotional conflict. The child may experience powerful demands for love and affection which are unrealistic and impossible. The mother may express the idea that her child(ren) is all that is important to her, thus generating considerable conflict for the child, placing it in an overly powerful position. This is often the case for children of depressed parents or where low self-esteem and marital difficulties dominate. The result is the generation of significant conflicts in later life over developing and maintaining attachment bonds.

Various early distortions of adaptive attachment behavior can have a significant effect on the organization and development of cognitive schemata relating to attachment figures. The development of attachment bonds is significantly influenced by the representational cognitive schemata of attachment. These cognitive representations (beliefs) significantly influence how information about relationships is interpreted and, therefore, shape consequent emotional reactions to disturbed attachment bonds.

To be able to understand the way Bowlby engages recent experimental work for his ideas, it is necessary to highlight briefly some of the trends in information processing that are now emerging.

Information Processing

Bowlby suggests that many processes, presumed to take place in the unconscious, can be explained using models of information processing (see also Basch, 1975; Erdelyi & Goldberg, 1979). Recent evidence would seem to support this view. For example, Shevrin & Dickman (1980) have reviewed a number of cognitive psychological experiments. They suggest that research findings to date point to the need for three fundamental propositions:

1. The initial cognitive stage for all stimuli occurs outside of consciousness.
2. This initial cognitive stage outside of conscious is psychological in nature, is active in its effect on consciousness, and can be different from conscious cognition in its principles of operation.
3. Consciousness of a stimulus is a later and optional stage in cognition [p. 431].

Each of these propositions is exceedingly important for psychopathology and requires detailed examination. However, this is not possible here since it would take us too far from the central topic of depression. It should be noted that Shevrin & Dickman suggest that the final step(s) of cognitive processes can be affected by a number of factors. These include:

1. Stimulus factors (e.g., loudness, brightness, and figural coherence, etc.).
2. State factors (e.g., level of arousal, sleep stage, fatigue, distractability, etc.).
3. Motivational factors (e.g., avoidance of anxiety, guilt, conflict, etc.) [p. 431].

There are many important issues raised by these authors and their suggestion that behaviorists should look inside the "black box" is well taken. However, there is nothing to be found in classical conditioning models, which do not allow the possibility that certain responses, either covert or overt, can be unconscious (i.e., do not enter conscious awareness). These issues move us into stormy waters and no doubt they will be debated with some heat in the not too distant future.

Bowlby suggests that there are different systems of information storage and organization. He notes the important distinctions between types of memory, especially episodic and semantic, and considers the possibility that information about attachment figures may be stored and organized in different systems. Thus, there may be specific memories of actual parenting events (episodic), but there may also be more general semantic memories relating to generalized attributes of the parent(s). There is the possibility (1) that either system may hold information which is discordant with information in the other system, and (2) that information processed by each system may come up with different interpretations of actual events. In both instances the stage is set for potential conflict. The management and consequences of this conflict are central to Bowlby's model.

The idea that information is not stored and organized in some uniform way is important. It provides one framework to explain cognitive bias and distortion (although the cognitive theory of Beck, 1976, has, as yet, made little attempt to integrate this type of cognitive data). It is also possible that a temporal conflict can exist between, and within, memory systems. Early (perhaps preverbal) memories of poor parenting may be stored at an affective level. Thus, during the helpless stage of development, the child may experience his caregiver(s) as unrewarding, rejecting, hostile, etc. As the child grows, however, the interaction between the child and parent may change. The child becomes, and is experienced as, less helpless and demanding. The child–parent interaction may then be less rejecting, especially if the child complies with parental demands. Here again, however, a source of conflict may exist between early and later memories and types of (affective versus cognitive) memory.

At present, memory is still far from well understood. As Loftus & Loftus (1980) point out, the view that memories are somehow permanently stored in the brain and remain potentially accessible and available throughout life is in some doubt. Indeed, memories may actually fuse together or become distorted. It is possible that considerable distortion can occur in this actual fusion of memory data.

Bowlby suggests that conflict can exist over what the parents tell the child about themselves as parents, and what the child actually observes to be the case. The child may experience significant rejecting, demanding, or hostile behavior from the parent, while at the same time the parent insists that (s)he be seen in a positive light. As Bowlby (1980) says: "On threat of not being loved or even of being abandoned a child is led to understand that he is not supposed to notice his parents' adverse treatment of him or, if he does, that he should regard it as being no more than the justifiable reaction of a wronged parent to his (the child's) bad behaviour [p. 71]."

As a result of this learning history there will be a tendency to "defensively exclude" negative information about the parent. They become beyond reproach. If this style of information processing continues into adult life, not only will the person be prone to make poor choices of partners (because of his tendency to exclude negative information about the potential partner), but bereavement will be exceedingly difficult and painful. In these cases anger and ambivalence are not easily worked through since the lost attachment figure has become "untouchable."

The foregoing offers some insight into the style of Bowlby's current work and the type of data on which he draws. There seems little doubt that this type of data will become increasingly important. Here, however, we have only been able to scratch the surface, although enough has been said to examine more clearly Bowlby's model of depression.

Depression

Unlike Freud, who regarded mourning and melancholia as overlapping by different processes, Bowlby relates many psychological disorders to distorted processes of mourning. In other words, vulnerability to psychopathology can actually arise from early bereavements and loss. These experiences sensitize the individual to respond to subsequent loss (especially of attachment bonds) in a pathological way. Thus, the early loss events in the child's life can sensitize to psychopathology and, Bowlby suggests, the period over which the sensitization exists can be very long, reaching into adolescence.

A major theme of Bowlby's approach to depression is that unresolved grief, and conflicts over the loss of attachment bonds in both children and adults, set up vulnerability to psychopathology. The barriers to later efforts to resolve these conflicts reside in the organization and storage of information relating to early attachment figures. In terms of the depressive disorders, Bowlby suggests that a perceived inability to obtain and/or maintain attachment relations becomes a crucial concern. Various processes significantly interfere with an individual's capacity to adjust to loss. Especially important is the predisposition toward feelings of helplessness (Seligman, 1975) and continuing perceptions of irretrievable loss. Predisposition to experience profound helplessness in the face of a disruption of attachment bonds may be a consequence of early learning histories. Bowlby (1980) suggests that these may be of three kinds:

(a) He is likely to have had the bitter experience of never having attained a stable and secure relationship with his parents despite having made repeated efforts to do so, including having done his utmost to fulfil their demands and perhaps also the unrealistic expectations they may have had of him. These childhood experiences result in his developing a strong bias to interpret any loss he may later suffer as yet another of his failures to make or maintain a stable affectional relationship.

(b) He may have been told repeatedly how unlovable, and/or how inadequate, and/or how incompetent he is. Were he to have had these experiences they would result in his developing a model of himself as unlovable and unwanted, and a model of attachment figures as likely to be unavailable, or rejecting, or punitive. Whenever such a person suffers adversity, therefore, so far from expecting others to be helpful he expects them to be hostile and rejecting.

(c) He is more likely than others to have experienced actual loss of a parent during childhood [. . .] with consequences to himself that, however disagreeable they might have been, he was impotent to change. Such experiences would confirm him in the belief that any effort he might make to remedy his situation would be doomed to failure [pp. 247–248].

Bowlby links these early learning experiences with the development of various predispositions for interpreting information in a negative way. In this context Bowlby pays special attention to the work of Beck and his colleagues and also to the sociological work of Brown & Harris (1978a). Since Beck's cognitive theory of depression is discussed fully later, there is no need to discuss it here. The major differences between Bowlby & Beck, however, may be noted. Unlike Beck, Bowlby stresses vulnerability in terms of (1) distorted, early parental relations; (2) potential, unresolved mourning; and (3) conflicts generated by information-processing strategies, including defense mechanisms, such as "defensive exclusion" which can operate at an unconscious level. As will be observed in Beck's work, these factors are of only minimal importance, and Beck gives no major etiological role to unconscious information processing, or mourning, in the development of depression.

Attachment Theory in Retrospect

Bowlby has done much to advance our knowledge of how attachment behaviors may either facilitate or hinder successful adaptation to the world. Undoubtedly, early disruptions of parental bonding are exceedingly stressful with various biological correlates (Reite et al., 1981). On the other hand, it appears that even gross disturbances in early attachment bonding do not automatically give rise to psychopathology (Clarke & Clarke, 1976). The presence of care-giving substitutes and the existence of rewarding peer-group relationships may do much to lower thresholds for subsequent emotional distress (Rutter, 1975, 1981). There are also other theories (e.g., Ferster, 1973, 1974) which suggest that it is the opportunity to have learned various adjustment behaviors in response to loss which may sensitize an individual to depression, rather than poor parenting per se.

Importantly, Bowlby's work points to a prepared basis for depression which revolves around the loss of important attachments and a reduction in care receiving (Henderson, 1974). Furthermore, since early relationships provide the cognitive schemata for organizing data about subsequent relationships, distortions in peer-group relations may evolve from disturbance in parent–child relationships. This provides a link between an adverse early history and the subsequent unhappiness that may surround peer-group relations (see Chapter 6). Also of significance, Bowlby points to real, not fantasy events as the basis for vulnerability. In this sense he is much closer to the behaviorists than he is to Freud or Klein.

By linking the breakdown in attachment behavior to peer-group, rather than parental attachment, we can examine various interactions between (1) behavioral ideas on depression (loss of social reinforcement and social skills); (2) cognitive data emphasizing a fall in self-esteem; and (3) psychobiological interactions which examine responses of animals in low-status positions. In Chapter 6 we look at these interactions more closely. In the present context we may note the enormously important idea of an innate and prepared basis for depression, arising from the breakdown in affectional, attachment bonding. This idea is central to the latter part of this book. As we see later, many depressive endeavors are attempts to maintain peer-group integration and social bonding. These may be exaggerated attempts to be loved and liked by significant others, respected and given social reinforcement for success, the presentation of a good image (persona). Above all they are efforts to avoid the perceived disaster of losing love, respect, and protection from significant peer-group members.

THE EGO-ANALYTIC SCHOOL

In a very different style from Freud, Klein, Jung, and Bowlby, a notable alternative to Freud's view of depression was presented by Bibring (1953). He all but abandoned energy concepts, instincts, and inherited, psychobiological response patterns. He stressed instead the importance of ego states. In his conceptualization, depression exists as one ego state with three others, which he considered to be;

1. The state of balanced narcissism (normal self-esteem).
2. The state of excited or exhilarated self-esteem, the triumphant or elated ego.
3. The state of threatened narcissism, the anxious ego.
4. The state of broken-down self-regard, the inhibited or paralyzed, the depressed ego.

This latter ego state was seen as the mechanism for depression.

In today's terms, Bibring's approach is one which emphasizes social learning and the perception of personal control; that is, the ego's ability to control the pursuit and securing of individually acquired aspirations. When these aspirations are perceived to be beyond the person's best efforts, a sense of helplessness and depression results. Thus, depression is conceived of as an ego state, that is, the ego becomes chronically aware of its inability to live up to its own internalized aspirations or standards. Bibring suggested that it was partly in the nature of these aspirations that they were unobtainable. Horney, and later Beck (1976), also placed emphasis on the individual who attempts to strive for aspirations which are absolute and in reality unobtainable. Bibring suggested three types of aspirations which the (pre)depressive may seek:

1. The wish to be worthy and loved, and to avoid inferiority and unworthiness.
2. The wish to be strong, superior, secure, and to avoid being weak and insecure.
3. The wish to be loving and good and not aggressive, hateful, or destructive.

In the latter case, Bibring suggests that the awareness of internal aggressive impulses deals a blow to the self-esteem. (As suggested before, however, the idea of aggressive impulses needs careful consideration. It is not so much that the individual does not wish to be assertive. Indeed, depressives often wish they could be more assertive. It is often the consequences of such behavior that they fear. In this regard Freud seems the more correct.) In Bibring's own words;

. . . depression is primarily not determined by a conflict between the ego on the one hand and the id, or the super-ego, or environment on the other hand, but stems primarily from a tension within the ego itself, from an inner-systemic "conflict." Thus depression can be defined as the emotional correlate of a partial or complete collapse of the self esteem of the ego, since it feels unable to live up to its aspirations (ego ideal, super-ego) while they are strongly maintained [pp. 25–26].

Becker (1979) points out that vulnerability to depression, according to this model, has a number of causes. These include: "constitutional intolerance of persistent frustration, severe and prolonged helplessness, and developmental deficiencies in skill acquisition. These deficiencies are enhanced by the ego ideals which tend to be high and rigidly adhered to by depressives [p. 324]."

Recent Developments

The past 30 years have seen many developments in ego-analytic psychology. Apart from various breakaways who have sired new theories and therapies (e.g., cognitive therapy), many have remained in the psychoanalytic household while moving further toward cultural and social theories of psychopathology. Bibring's approach to depression dawned with a new era in psychiatric thinking, especially in America. While some British analysts developed instinctual theories of pathology, some Americans moved toward more social views of psychiatric illness. This divergence may have reflected the stronger impact of Meyer's psychobiological teachings in America. In any event, once social relations and society in general became a target for investigation in psychiatry, the race was on to determine the pathological agents and their mode of transmission.

Beliefs and attitudes, incentives and goals were soon written up as the suspects and identified as possible carriers of psychological distress. The mode of transmission from parent to child, group to group, or individual to individual, was subject to speculation and research. Within this atmosphere Cohen et al. (1954) suggested that high achievement strivings, learned and acquired in response to family pressure, resulted in depression when failure was confronted later in life. Cohen et al.'s suggestions encapsulated well the idea of learned beliefs and attitudes, producing vulnerability to depression.

Recently, Arieti & Bemporad (1980a, 1980b) have presented a view of depression very much along ego-analytic lines. They suggest that vulnerability to depression can develop in response to an overdependency on a significant other, or overdependency on some goal or incentive. In the first case, great effort is invested in maintaining the relationship. The significant other is relied on to provide a positive source of self-esteem, meaning, and gratification. Threat to, or removal of, this relationship results in a depressive reaction as self-esteem falls, and there is a loss of meaning and gratification. Other individuals pursue lofty goals, which when obtained are believed to bring higher status, and all the various good things of life, whatever these may be for that person.

Arieti & Bemporad (1980a) suggest that these two predispositions exist within the personality structure. The dependency on a significant other is most noted in women with a passive, manipulative, clinging, avoidance of anger style of personality. Those who seek lofty goals as a means of securing self-esteem exhibit a more seclusive, arrogant, and often obsessive personality style; this is a more common predisposition in men.

Arieti & Bemporad also identify a chronic form of depressive predisposition. Such individuals suffer a constant feeling of depression which they are unable to ward off, either by the pursuit of goals or with a meaningful relationship. Personality characteristics of this group include hypochondriasis, harsh attitudes to self and others, and pettiness. The pursuit of pleasure is inhibited because of strong taboos instilled by family and culture. All three types share a difficulty in obtaining pleasure from spontaneous activity, have overvalued opinions of others, overvalue social approval, and overestimate their effects on other people.

As with many ego-analytic theorists who have been writing and developing concepts for some time, ideas have filtered through to various models. Notably their observations share many common features with Beck's (1976) model of depression. Arieti & Bemporad's (1980b) work is a major contribution to the psychological understanding of depression. Some of the ideas developed in Chapter 6 also have many aspects in common with their work, including the importance of learned standards as setting the pillars for self-esteem. However, such ideas were developed by a cognitive and social learning approach.

Comment

There are many individuals whose work could be included in this discussion of ego-analytic theories. Becker (1977) offers a good review of many of these, including the work of Paul Chodoff, and there is, therefore, no point in reviewing them again here. Suffice it to say that their impact has been enormous. The main feature which many share is their change in emphasis. This is seen as a movement away from consideration of instinctive processes, especially of aggressive impulses. Depression in their scheme is determined, not as unresolved conflicts from within, but as learned styles of behaving and thinking which inhibit healthy adaptation to the world. It is impossible to say why this movement away from instinct concepts has been so powerful. Possibly the greater historical distance from Darwinian and Nietzschian philosophy may be a reason. Freud could not have had such freedom, writing at the time he did. Nevertheless, the extent to which such theories ignore brain processes, especially those dictated by evolution, may prove a limitation. Bowlby, for example, succeeded in discussing the importance of instinctive behavior, not in terms of innate aggressive impulses or as libidinal energy, but as attachment behavior.

Many of the concepts developed by ego-analytic theorists turn up in different disguises in different theories. From experimental studies, Seligman (1975) refined the concept of learned helplessness. Beck (1967, 1976) also placed importance on helplessness and hopelessness, but goes further than ego-analytic theorists by suggesting that all disordered emotional reactions are cognitively mediated. The influence of the ego-analytic theorists is therefore immense and their ideas are seen at various stages throughout this book.

CONCLUDING COMMENTS

The three implications of Darwin's theory of evolution, outlined at the beginning of this chapter, are important. In regard to the psychological formulations of psychopathology, it has been psychoanalytic perspectives which have attempted to understand the role of inherited psychobiological predispositions. While some have stressed the importance of negative, destructive instincts, such as aggressive impulses (e.g., Klein, and to some degree, Freud), others, especially Bowlby, have generally emphasized a more positive side of our evolution—the need for secure attachments. The advent of the ego-analytic position played down biological aspects and emphasized the acquired, rather than inherited, predispositions. This change in emphasis probably reflects a cultural philosophical change. The mass destruction of two world wars in all their tragedy was more easily handled if we could believe that the pathology of man was of his own making and, therefore, could be changed (in theory, at least) by a change in the social fabric of life. It is certainly the case that many see the older psychoanalytic theories as overly pessimistic, and as not in keeping with Marx's claim that the economic relations of individuals shape their consciousness.

We are, I think, at a crossroads. Once again the helplessness of the atomic age, with its potential for mass destruction, has shown clearly that the last war was not the war to end all wars; that humans developed via the maximization of survival factors, rather than via rationality *per se*. So, how do we deal with inherited predispositions which, from the standpoint of our intellectualized life, may not seem very rational? The answer to this is unknown. But we are at risk, not from the individual's innate aggressiveness, but from his loyalty to groups and attachment behaviors (Dixon & Lucas, 1982).

Today, neurobiology provides a powerful influence on our thinking. We cannot escape the fact that our psychic life is governed by brain processes, and that the structure of these brain processes represents interactions between the products of evolution and acquired behavioral representations, both overt and covert. Therefore, man is far from a blank sheet. The understanding of the interactions between biological processes and events existing in the world, to which they are focused and organized around, is the source of our greatest endeavors. The truth is that psychobiological paradigms are long overdue. Jung, of course, never wavered in his adherence to an inherited, predisposing quality of man and his pathology. The archetypes were conceptualized as inherited cognitive-behavioral-emotional predispositions. Today, the separate approach of sociobiology again concerns itself with the interactions between inherited predispositions and acquired predispositions. But this has become an extremely complex area (Crook, 1980; Plotkin & Odling-Smee, 1981) and we cannot tell where such endeavors will lead.

On the whole, the more recent theoretical developments on depression have not been much concerned with sociobiological ideas. Both operant learning theorists and cognitive theorists operate with the working hypothesis that man is a blank sheet upon which the environment places its mark. In my view, this is likely to be a major weakness, since much pathology relates to subcortical, limbic system activity whose interaction with cortical systems is still under investigation.

The unconscious is also an area where recent theorists have clearly felt uncomfortable. Yet, Freud did not "discover" the unconscious. Rather, it is a concept that has been around, in one form or another, for a very long time (Ellenberger, 1970). We should not reject the importance of the unconscious simply because we disagree with one person's concept of it. As I have tried to show, modern research would suggest this to be folly indeed.

It is perfectly clear that many psychoanalytic ideas on depression turn up time and time again in different disguises in different theories. It is no longer possible to trace the source of these ideas through different perspectives, since these have long ago been obscured by the haze of history. Freud's explanation of his observations on depression went aground because his conceptualization of brain processes turned out to be mistaken. Nevertheless, rather than warranting criticism, Freud deserves our admiration, since his approach was, at least, an attempt to be psychobiological. Many subsequent efforts to refine Freudian thinking paid the price of having long forgotten Freud's psychobiological concerns, and in consequence broke free from the need to contain theorizing within an acceptable neurobiological frame of reference. Recently, major efforts have been made to reunite psychoanalysis with its neurobiological parent (e.g., Meyersburg & Post, 1979). It is to be hoped that these efforts will continue. Moreover, it is hoped that Bowlby's attachment ideas will be united with other formulations, both psychological and biological. This, however, is all for the future.

We are witnessing a time when great efforts are being made to evaluate more adequately psychoanalytic theory and therapy (e.g., Shapiro, 1980). There seems little doubt that in response to such endeavors psychoanalytic theory will change and be adapted in the light of evidence—a long overdue process. It is to be hoped that our understanding of depression will be one of the beneficiaries of this process.

3 Behavioral Theories of Depression

The behavior theories of depression are of recent origin, with most of the newer approaches making their major impact during the last decade or so. The reasons for their late arrival are complex. They reflect historical influences favoring the study of anxiety. Also, the success of the physical therapies tended to reinforce various beliefs that depression is a biological illness and not a disorder of learning. This is not to say that important efforts were not made to understand depression from a behavior perspective in the pre-1970s period, but here we shall concentrate our attention on the more recent and generally accepted approaches.

Behaviorists have sometimes suffered the same fate as those who advance organic approaches to psychiatry. That is, they are challenged with being dehumanizing scientists, whose experimentally derived paradigms have little to do with distress and meaning. This accusation is not only unfair, but reflects some ignorance of how behaviorists actually set about helping their patients. As Wachtel (1977) points out, behaviorists are no more cold, unsupporting, or less encouraging than other types of therapist. These therapist variables are not the distinguishing factors between behavior therapy and other therapies. Nevertheless, behaviorists do approach the distress of a depressed patient with a specific set of paradigms of what is necessary if the patient is to be freed from his distress.

It is sometimes said that psychoanalytic perspectives regard the behavioral symptoms of psychopathology as indicators of a deep, underlying, often unconscious, conflict. If the behaviors are changed without resolving this conflict, symptoms will change their form, but the individual will not be restored to healthy functioning. Behaviorists, on the other hand, regard behavioral symptoms either as a sample of the disturbance, or as the actual disturbance itself. They do not, it is said, look for underlying conflicts. This polarization of perspectives is unhelpful and misleading. In fact, behaviorists also regard much neurotic behavior as originating from inner conflict. These conflicts, however, are not unconscious, but relate to approach-avoidance conflicts, problems of conditioned anxiety, and perceived response-outcome contingencies. Changing behavior for the sake of it is not the intention of the behaviorist. The idea is to remove

51

approach–avoidance conflicts, reduce central nervous system arousal, and change perceptions of response-outcome contingencies. Behaviorists believe that changing a patient's behavior directly is the best way of achieving this successfully. It is suggested by some that changing behavior directly also changes various cognitive parameters, including beliefs and expectations of self-efficacy (Bandura, 1977).

Behaviorists try to understand their patients' problems in terms of specific learning histories and environmental responses or stimuli maintaining maladaptive behaviors. Their therapeutic approach attempts to provide structured opportunities for new, more adaptive learning. Most behaviorists accept that this opportunity cannot be taken if it is not conducted with an atmosphere of concern, understanding, and support.

This chapter indicates the potential gains of incorporating behavioral approaches into a multicomponent approach to depression. With this in mind, some of the behavioral models of depression are now examined in detail. We start with Ferster's model of depression, for there is much in it that nonbehaviorists may find familiar and of value when stated in behavioral terms.

FERSTER'S OPERANT MODEL

In 1973 Ferster published an important paper on depression. In this and a subsequent paper (1974), Ferster outlined the applicability of an operant model of conditioning to this disorder. Ferster's functional analysis approach has a number of strengths. First, it outlines in a clear way how investigations of ongoing behavior may provide some insights into depression. Especially important is the emission of positively reinforced behavior, passive avoidance responses, and the degree to which some depressive behaviors are under aversive control. Secondly, it offers potential areas of overlap with Bowlby's work, in that Ferster places special emphasis on the opportunity of an individual to have learned the necessary skills to adjust to life's crises (e.g., losses of reinforcement). These skills are learned in childhood as a function of exploration. Factors which inhibit learning through exploration can produce developmental arrests and behaviors that are easily extinguished. Thirdly, Ferster suggests important processes which cast light on phenomena that psychoanalytic writers have discussed, e.g., anger turned inward and fixation.

Ferster suggests that like infantile autism, depression is especially appropriate for a behavioral approach because of the poverty and missing elements of certain behaviors. It would not be wise to push the comparison too far however, since depression can be a fluctuating disorder with returns to normal functioning, whereas this is not true for autism. Moreover, depression from an operant viewpoint is an adjustment disorder, that is, there appears to be maladaptive or reduced adjustment behavior to changes in reinforcement schedules. From this point, causes rather than symptoms require detailed investigation. Ferster makes the important distinction between functional and topographical behavioral analysis. The difference arises from the effects that the behavior is emitted to produce. Two individuals may take an overdose of sleeping tablets (similar topographic behaviors) but one may intend to die, the other may have been drunk and made a mistake. Hence the "function" of the two behaviors is different. In the case of depression it is the functional analysis of behavior which has relevance. Critics of behavioral approaches often overlook this important distinction.

Ferster's approach, then, highlights the need to look very closely at the functional behaviors of the depressed person. From this, two important observations become apparent. First, the depressed person demonstrates significant passivity in the presence of aversive events. Complying with demands from significant others is a passive attempt to avoid the aversive consequences of refusal. This is especially important when the behavior requested is against the wishes of the passive person. Thus, as Ferster (1974) points out, one connotation of a passive response is that it becomes negatively reinforced (i.e., it is reinforced because it succeeds in avoiding aversive interactions with others). The second component of passivity is associated with failure to deal with aversive (social) events. In this situation Ferster has in mind a passive tendency to assume responsibility for negative events. Though Ferster does not state it as an attribution as might Beck (1976), this it clearly is. However, for Ferster it is not so much the attribution that is the problem, but the failure to tackle the problem directly and seek confirmatory or other data for passive acceptance.

The second prominent observation, in addition to passivity, is the often (though not inevitable) reduction in the frequency of positively reinforced behaviors. Activities that may have been enjoyed previously, such as socializing, sex, games, hobbies, work, etc., significantly decline. They appear to be on an extinction schedule, where there is insufficient reinforcement to maintain them in the person's repertoire. The less the behaviors are engaged in, the less opportunity there is for positive reinforcement and so the less they are engaged in. In discussing these issues, Ferster notes the importance of reinforcement schedules in maintaining behavior. He points out that continuous, predictable reinforcement schedules produce behavior that is fragile compared to variable reinforcement. In other words, behaviors that are maintained on variable reinforcement schedules show a greater resistance to extinction than those maintained on continuous reinforcement. The relevance of this distinction (a major axiom of operant laws of learning) is that, under situations where reinforcement contingencies are rapidly changed, the continuously re-inforced behavior is much more vulnerable to extinction than the variably reinforced behavior. Thus, the schedule of reinforcement that maintains a behavior will have a significant bearing on how long that behavior will be maintained in the presence of reduced or total reinforcement withdrawal. The operant approach regards depression as a maladaptive adjustment response or set of responses. Not surprisingly, the changes that require adjustment(s) are changes in the levels (schedules) of reinforcement. Thus adjustment behavior is required in the presence of significant life events which reduce reinforcement. These may include loss of a loved one, loss of a job or friends, movement away from a community, children leaving home, etc. If the individual is to adjust to these significant changes, there must be some degree of inbuilt resistance to extinction of certain behaviors and the capacity to generate new, reinforceable behavior. Unfortunately, for the depression-prone individual, there seems to be an incapacity to achieve this satisfactorily. The previous schedules of the reinforced behavior are one variable of importance. However, the capacity to adapt to the changed situation and to maintain behavior, perhaps in the face of little immediate reinforcement, is also important.

Turning to this latter problem (the ability to initiate new, potentially reinforceable behaviors), Ferster suggests that failures in adjustment behavior may be related to distorted perceptions of reinforcement contingencies. He highlights three such distortions:

1. A limited view of the world; in this situation the person may be unable to see which behaviors are appropriate for reinstating adequate levels of reinforcement. He may sulk and complain but have little insight into what behavior on his part would bring the required reinforcement.
2. A lousy view of the world; in this situation the patient may be aware of what behaviors are required but fears the aversive consequences of such behavior. In other words, his passivity is under aversive control by its potential negative-reinforcing properties.
3. An unchanging view of the world; in this situation it is not so much a lack of perception, or a fear of aversive consequences, but a lack of skills. In other words, the behavioral repertoire is not sufficiently developed or comprehensive to be able to adjust to significant changes in reinforcement. Ferster likens this view to a kind of development arrest (similar to, but not identical with, psychoanalytic concepts of fixation).

These three views of the world freeze the individual in a set of behaviors which is not positively reinforceable in an adaptive way. Compensatory behaviors—clinging, demanding, self-blame—may have some immediate reinforcement value, but their reinforcement may be highly variable, making them difficult behaviors to extinguish and blocking the development of the more adaptive behaviors necessary for the individual to make a satisfactory adjustment. Thus, Ferster views the maladaptive behaviors of the depressed individual as crucial etiological factors.

Those most prone to depression are individuals who have developed a limited response repertoire and have failed to learn to generate alternative, adaptive, reinforceable behaviors when adjustments in responding are required. In consequence, there is a limit to the amount of behavior which can be emitted for positive reinforcement, and aversive consequences to maladaptive, inappropriate responding are inevitable.

Among the behavioral parameters Ferster calls upon to help us to understand why this limited repertoire exists is the notion of stimulus discrimination learning. Discrimination learning is a complex and important field of instrumental (operant) learning. Generally, it depends on accurate, predictable responses to specific events (emitted responses). Discrimination learning is likely to be poor if reinforcement is unpredictable and is response variable. To enable a child to predict the outcomes of his own behavior (environmental responses to him), the socializing agent must be sensitive to the subtleties of the child's behavior. If the socializing agent is insensitive and responds arbitrarily to the child, the environment is rendered unpredictable. In consequence, unpredictable or insensitively applied reinforcement can block accurate discrimination learning. Most importantly, not only does the child fail to show subtle discrimination learning in interpersonal situations, but also exploratory behavior may be inhibited. If the child does not know whether he will be shouted at, smacked, ignored, or smiled at for exploring, then exploring becomes an extremely hazardous venture.

For those interested in similarities between theories, then the idea that the inhibition of exploratory behavior significantly limits the development of a behavioral repertoire has a clear overlap with some of Bowlby's ideas. Ferster would, perhaps, put less stress on the importance of mothering per se, but lay emphasis on the predictability of reinforcement, comprehensive discrimination learning, encouragement of exploration, and the development of complex response repertoires. Poor mothering may indeed fail on all accounts.

Ferster makes a major contribution to the role and analysis of anger in depression. The psychoanalytic concept of "anger turned inward" is little discussed by most of the newer behavioral models of depression, and in this regard Ferster offers a refreshing approach. He suggests that inadequate reinforcement not only interferes with discrimination learning and the acquisition of a complex response repertoire, but also produces emotional arousal which further interferes with such learning and produces considerable conflicts. In early learning, primitive or atavistic rage may be aroused in the child by inappropriate positive reinforcement, punishment, or a nonresponse from the parent. The expression of this anger may itself produce a withdrawal of positive reinforcement or punishment. In such situations the expression of anger may become associated with punishment or the withdrawal of positive reinforcement. (The reader should note that positive punishment and the withdrawal of positive reinforcement are not the same. Both in a sense are negative outcomes, but a good deal of confusion has been generated by assuming they have similar effects on behavior.)

Ferster suggests that the expression of anger may serve to reduce the flow of positive reinforcement. Since we have a response–response situation, a hallmark for operant learning (as opposed to a stimulus–response situation which is more in keeping with classical conditioning; see Mackintosh, 1974, 1978), then anger expression becomes associated with a negative outcome. If such associative learning becomes established then situations which normally produce anger may cue anger suppression. One does not have to stretch this position too far to incorporate the notion of frustration. To tolerate frustration and resultant anger is important for humans to learn. If frustrative displays are inhibited because of the threat of reinforcement withdrawal, then the individual may fail to learn to cope and work through frustration. This is because it has been conditioned to be suppressed rather than worked through. The complex of behaviors needed to deal with frustration and anger will never develop under such conditions.

In the case of the young infant, deprivation of food may produce distress and anger. If the environmental response is to remove the source of food (the Kleinian good breast), subsequent anger may become associated with a reduction in positive reinforcement. In other words, anger may come to act as a "pre-aversive" stimulus or, most important, a condition that is the associated, preceding event for the loss (withdrawal) of positive reinforcement. Anger which alienates the reinforcement-givers adds to the depressive's anger, frustration, and rage and serves to reduce further the opportunities for positively reinforced activities.

Whether or not one accepts all the tenets of Ferster's theory, it does highlight a very important set of phenomena. It points out the need to examine the antecedents of behavior and to consider behavior functionally. Moreover, the idea that the expression of anger can arouse significant approach–avoidance conflicts for some depressives is very important. It is a theme we return to many times in this book. Many depressed individuals (though not all) have considerable difficulty with anger. They may either use it inappropriately in an irritating, demanding way, or may explode (or fear they will explode) over quite trivial things. This may demonstrate the failure to resolve an approach–avoidance conflict. The conflict exists for two reasons. First, as Ferster points out, there is a fear of positive reinforcement withdrawal contingent on anger expresssion. Secondly, there is an overdependence on existent sources of reinforcement. (Psychoanalytic writers may call this high dependency needs.) The reason for the high dependency is the failure to develop an independent repertoire, which includes the ability to work through frustration, to maintain independent behavior in the face of little reward, and to seek out alternative sources of positive reinforcement, be these people or activities. (The resolution of these conflicts would normally be a consequence of early exploratory behavior.) The overdependence on external sources of reinforcement becomes manifest as a consequence of early learning failures to develop independent repertoires. The concept of high dependency, on either goals or people, is echoed in a number of theories (e.g., Arieti & Bemporad, 1980a).

Ferster's emphasis on a perceived loss of reinforcement is important from a cognitive point of view. Cognitive theories are discussed in the next chapter, but it should be noted that what cognitive theorists call "cognitive distortions" may not be distortions at all, but the natural consequence of a specific learning history. They may appear distortions in the clinic rooms but, in fact, they are logical predications of a person with a specific learning history.

LEWINSOHN'S SOCIAL REINFORCEMENT THEORY

Lewinsohn's model of depression is, like Ferster's, based on operant learning principles. The main differences between the two is Lewinsohn's emphasis on social behaviors, and the comparative absence of discussion concerning childhood vulnerability or conditioned anger suppression.

Lewinsohn et al. (1979) acknowledge the multicomponent nature of depression (including the role of cognitive, genetic, and biochemical processes) and point out that reinforcement depression relationships are but one aspect of depression. His recent research has been particularly concerned with interpersonal behavioral interactions.

In Lewinsohn's early work (1974, 1975) depression was related to a low rate of response-contingent positive reinforcement (RCPR). Lewinsohn stresses the point that it is not positive reinforcement per se that is crucial, but its response contingency. He suggested that a low rate of RCPR could arise from (1) few reinforcing events in the environment; or (2) a lack of social skills; thus the individual is unable to emit potential, reinforceable behavior.

Low rates of RCPR, it is assumed, produce states that elicit unhappiness, fatigue, and various symptoms of depression. However, there is no clear mechanism, as yet, which shows how low rates of RCPR actually produce these specific symptoms. Becker (1977) points out, for example, that many pathological groups may experience RCPR but do not necessarily have depressive disorders.

Coyne (1976a) demonstrated that conversations (on the telephone in this case) with depressives could make recipients themselves feel more depressed, hostile, and rejecting. This evidence does support a second assumption of Lewinsohn's; namely that the interpersonal behavior of the depressive alienates potential (social) sources of reinforcement. In addition, of course, such data point to a high degree of subtlety in interpersonal verbal interactions which may have evolutionary significance. Lewinsohn suggests that the interpersonal behavior of depressives is an important modulator of the type and frequency of reinforcement they will obtain from others. Maladaptive behaviors are likely to achieve partial, inconsistent reinforcement, which makes them difficult to extinguish. Clearly, such a view has much in common with Ferster's ideas.

Much of the evidence for and against Lewinsohn's theory has been well reviewed already (Becker, 1977; Blaney, 1977) and, therefore, need not be examined closely again. In general, much of the evidence is correlational, which can at best offer only weak support. It seems more advantageous, therefore, to examine more recent trends in Lewinsohn's work.

Lewinsohn et al. (1979) point out that, behaviorally, two hypotheses of depression are possible:

1. Depressives engage in fewer pleasant activities and experience greater aversiveness in regard to *all* events.
2. Reduced engagement in positive events and increased aversiveness are related to a specific subset of events. If such a subset does exist, then it has major importance.

Lewinsohn and his colleagues have attempted to investigate this question with specially designed schedules: the interpersonal events schedule (IES), the pleasant events schedule (PES), and the unpleasant events schedule (UES). By examining the correlation matrices produced by the use of these schedules with measures of dysphoria, Lewinsohn et al. are attempting to investigate the possibility of subsets of events being important in depression. Current work does suggest that it is social reinforcements that are the crucial controlling reinforcers of depressive behavior. Positive mood states seem related to feelings of being loved, socializing, being with liked people, and so on, while aversive social reinforcement such as arguments, marital discord, and being overworked are associated with lowering of mood. Negative interpersonal interactions, especially those associated with aversiveness or feelings of reduced self-worth, are associated with low mood. Lewinsohn et al. (1979) suggest that:

. . . these are the types of events bearing a critical relationship to the occurrence of depression. When the good ones (PES) occur at low rates and the negative ones (UES, IES) occur at high rates, the individual is likely to feel depressed. We also hypothesize that these are the major types of events that act as reinforcers for people; occurrence of the ones that are negatively associated with dysphoria serve to maintain our behavior, and the occurrence of events that are positively associated with dysphoria reduces our rates of behavior [p. 313].

It is important to note that Lewinsohn et al. suggest that these are the important reinforcement parameters governing depressed behavior. They do not suggest that they are the crucial etiological determinants of pathological depression. As they discuss later in the same paper, the "causes" of depression are probably multicomponent.

Youngren & Lewinsohn (1980) provide further support for the findings outlined above. They point out, however, that differences between depressed and nondepressed patients are largely at a self-report level; the former reporting a lower frequency of pleasant social and interpersonal events and a greater frequency of aversive events. Although the depressives were rated as less socially skilled, behavioral deficits are of a subtle kind and difficult to identify objectively.

In a further study Lewinsohn et al. (1980) examined the problem of perceived self-competence. Many writers on depression have noted that depressives rate themselves low on social competence. However, this study attempted to investigate whether this perception was a cognitive distortion, or a realistic appraisal, of poor social skills. Using self and observer ratings following group interactions, the data suggest that depressed patients have a fairly accurate picture of themselves; that is, they see themselves as others see them. Of course, this does not mean that these people *are* less socially skilled since, when their depression recedes, various behaviors may again become part of their repertoire. However, it does suggest that at that point in time (when depressed), perceptions of low competency were accurate perceptions since they corresponded fairly closely with how others saw them. The most interesting finding, perhaps, was that normals had illusionary self-perceptions and saw themselves more positively than others saw them. Moreover, depressives also tended to become more positively self-illusionary as they recovered. These researchers discuss their findings in terms of the "warm glow" hypothesis of Mischel et al. (1973, 1976).

The implications of these findings are many. They suggest that when ill, depressives may not only exhibit less socially skilled behavior, but may be all too painfully aware of it. Therapeutically, a sensitivity to this is needed, since overencouragement by a therapist may realistically be interpreted as nonsense. The aim is to appreciate the patients current state of behaviors and feelings and to guide him toward alternative sources of positive interpersonal reinforcement. With an eye on possible dependency, the therapist himself may, for a short time, provide reinforcement contingent on behavior change. Lewinsohn believes that the social reinforcing elements of behavior are the central elements of changes in behavior associated with depression. However, it might also be suggested that these pleasant and unpleasant events, which Lewinsohn and his colleagues highlight, have evolutionary significance. The striking feature of these behaviors is that they relate to the person's ability to remain socially integrated with the group. Reductions in these behaviors may produce pathology, if they trigger pathways in the brain which mediate social behaviors (see Chapter 6). In that psychopathology relates to changes in brain states (i.e., nobody suggests that cognitions or behaviors occur in a vacuum), then behaviors which threaten social cohesion may be programmed to produce dysphoric states (e.g., Price, 1972). In other words, the evolutionary development of brain structure (MacLean, 1977) may have influenced the capacity for changes in certain behaviors, or indeed cognitions, to trigger neurochemical processes and tip the individual into psychopathological states. If it is accepted that social integration is probably a set of activities which has evolutionary significance for humans, then disruption in these activities may well sound biological alarm bells. Individual differences and predispositions may well affect the threshold for sounding the biological alarm. The point here, however, is that the events that Lewinsohn outlines as being important in depression may be important for other reasons apart from simply reducing positive reinforcement.

While such theorizing has its place, it should be remembered that interpersonal behavior is of considerable importance for the prognosis of schizophrenia (Leff, 1978; Vaughn & Leff, 1976). Relapse rates are much higher for those schizophrenics whose environments provide aversive interactions (e.g., high expressed emotion families). In low expressed emotion families schizophrenics do much better and drugs may make only a marginal difference to relapse. Moreover, drug effects and psychophysiological responses have been shown to be responsive to aversive social interactions in schizophrenics (Tarrier et al., 1979). Thus, while Lewinsohn's work is of considerable importance, the question of specificity of some of the variables to depression requires validation. Moreover, an increase in positive social interactions has a significant impact on the interpersonal behavior of retarded psychiatric patients (Matson & Zeiss, 1979). Thus, positive social interactions are important in both schizophrenia and depression. We need to know whether there are qualitative differences in the reduction of positive (and increase in aversive) interpersonal events between schizophrenia and depressives. Such data would have a bearing on ethological and evolutionary theories of psychopathology.

LOSS OF REINFORCER EFFECTIVENESS

Costello (1972) addresses the problem of how it is that depression brings about a loss of behaviors, for which the reinforcement contingencies have not actually changed. It is not the loss of reinforcers themselves that Costello sees as important, but their inability to maintain established behaviors; they have become ineffective for the depressed person. He notes that discriminative stimuli (e.g., a loved person) may cue many forms of behavior which may well be expected to extinguish with the removal of that discriminative stimulus.

Costello considers two processes which may account for the general loss of reinforcer effectiveness of the depressive: (1) biochemical-neurophysiological change, and (2) disruption of a chain of behavior. He suggests that: ". . . the reinforcer effectiveness of all the components of the chain of behavior is contingent upon the completion of the chain at either an overt or covert level; that this is a characteristic of complex organisms particularly humans, and that it is of functional significance in evolutionary terms [p. 241]."

While there is a good case to be made for the importance of behavioral chains, or complex network of behaviors, the argument that evolutionary pressure produces a need for complexity, and when cohesiveness is lost depression results, requires validation. It is possible, however, to suggest that "certain types of behavior" do have evolutionary importance and disruption of these behaviors in a chain will have more "pathogenic effects" than other behaviors. Thus, disruptions in socially cohesive group behavior may have great power to produce a general loss of reinforcer effectiveness—primarily because much activity is now diverted to attempting to reinstate the individual's social integration. It seems to me, therefore, that Costello's model would be considerably strengthened by considering the notion of certain reinforcers being (evolutionary) more important than others. The idea of equipotentiality may be relevant here in a similar fashion to that now investigated in anxiety neurosis (Eysenck, 1979; Rachman, 1978; Seligman, 1971).

Costello considers the experimental evidence which suggests that reinforcing properties are passed backwards from an unconditioned stimulus (UCS), that is, only antecedent stimuli and not stimuli subsequent to a UCS are endowed with reinforcing properties. There is reason to be cautious of this view, however, since humans generate new goal-directed behaviors without them ever having appeared previously. In this sense forward planning does allow for the possibility that behaviors in a complex chain develop for other reasons than being antecedent UCS associations. (For an alternative view of how chains of behavior develop and collapse see incentive disengagement theory, p. 64.)

The problems for behavior theories are well observed. For example, Costello says: ". . . there is no obvious reason why an emigrant who has not maintained contact with his father loses his appetite for food, sex and things in general on hearing of the death of his father. There is no obvious reason why a man, on failing to be promoted or on reaching retirement age, may react in the same way [p. 244]."

The idea that in some manner reinforcers simply lose their effectiveness is attractive. It certainly matches with what actually appears to happen to depressives. However, Costello's arguments of how and why this comes about are less clear. There is little argument about the role of neuro-chemical change, although the interaction between neurochemical change and loss of reinforcer effectiveness is not discussed. It is possible, for example, that the loss of an important reinforcer produces neurochemical change which then interferes with reinforcement effectiveness. Moreover, any exogenous events at either an overt or covert level may produce neuro-chemical change sufficient to interfere with other behaviors, especially if these events are evolutionarily significant. There may be no need to suggest complex chains of behavior.

Generally, this model has not generated much research. It has not been developed to a degree of specificity which would allow, say, discrimination between depression and schizophrenia. At a descriptive level, loss of re-inforcer effectiveness seems sensible. However, some behaviors may actually increase (e.g., passive avoidance), which suggests that some reinforcers (avoidance of punishment) actually became more effective during depression. Moreover, the concept that secondary gain behaviors are maintained by their reinforcing (short-term) properties is difficult to fit with Costello's ideas. Nevertheless, Costello's attempt to integrate behavioral data with evolutionary and biological considerations is a brave and valuable effort.

INCENTIVE DISENGAGEMENT THEORY

In 1975 Klinger published a major review paper on depression from an incentive disengagement point of view. This work has been subsequently expanded (Klinger, 1977). Although this theory is discussed under the rubric of behavioral theories, its data base is extraordinarily wide and Klinger's work is probably better considered as providing a multicom-ponent model of depression. This, incidentally, makes reviewing and highlighting the central elements difficult. Incentive disengagement theory has not yet generated the same amount of research as Lewinsohn's or Seligman's theories. This is disappointing, because it has at least as much potential for providing testable hypotheses and generating important new insights.

Klinger (1977) maintains that humans organize many aspects of their lives (efforts, behaviors, thoughts, and so on) around the pursuit of valued incentives. While social events (being liked, having friends, obtaining support, etc.) are incentives valued by the majority, incentives are largely personally determined. The commitment to, and pursuit of, incentives give meaning to life. The major personal upheavals and life's crises center around disappointments, frustrations, and obstacles which interrupt the pursuit of incentives or render them unobtainable. When life's circumstances force us to give up, abandon, or lose our major incentives, depression can be an inevitable consequence.

Incentive disengagement theory rests on a number of central concepts. Klinger suggests that incentives or goals obtain value because they are associated with potential sources of reinforcement, or the avoidance of aversive outcomes. In other words, they are acquired. The degree of positive reinforcement and the expectancy of final obtainment are important factors in determining the value of an incentive and the degree of commitment to it. Klinger points out that, in the process of becoming committed to goals or incentives, there must be some internal process(es) that enable the individual to pursue the valued goal in its absence, or in the absence of cues signaling its presence. Thus, according to Klinger (1977), people will work for years to obtain certain things, ". . . overcoming repeated obstacles and improvising a long succession of tactics [p. 36]." In this way individuals move nearer their incentives and goals. The process by which they become set to pursue a goal is a commitment. They will remain committed to this goal until either they achieve it or, for one reason or another, it is abandoned. Klinger suggests that during the committed stage the incentive is a current concern. Current concern is a hypothetical state which refers to the process of being committed to a goal. It is present all the time even when the person is not actively engaged in pursuing his goal directly.

Commitments and current concerns have significant influences over behavioral and cognitive processes. Plans are laid, considered, carried out, and changed in the light of information which helps or hinders the approach path to the incentive. Attention to cues signaling opportunities to reach a goal is heightened. Individuals will have more than one incentive, of course, and the processes of commitment and current concern apply to an infinite variety of anticipated outcomes. Moreover, the relation between valued incentives or goals, and therefore commitments and current concerns about them, shift and change in relationship to a variety of factors (Klinger, 1977, chapter 4). Klinger suggests that as we grow older, different incentives become important as our external and internal worlds change. Extinction, habituation, and satiation are all processes which change the arrangement of valued incentives for the individual. Depression is one of the consequences of abandonment and disengagement from incentives that are still highly valued. Not all incentives have equal value. Many acquire value by their association with higher incentives, e.g., studying and forgoing pleasure promise to bring the valued rewards of respect, money, or prestige associated with some qualification. The perception of failure or a reduction in the value of the qualification may reduce behaviors associated with it (e.g., studying). Furthermore, some potentially positive reinforceable behaviors may not develop because they are associated with a high negative outcome (e.g., drinking with the lads may be associated with failure of the qualification). The aversiveness of loss of a subincentive (e.g., the opportunity for study) will depend on the perception to which this threatens the end-point incentive. Hence, behaviors and incentives share complex facilitatory and inhibitory interactions. Some behaviors may fail to develop. For example, the student who overvalues academic qualifications and spends all his time studying may become depressed when he finds he has no friends. Instead of bringing him happiness, studying has led to alienation. He may now face conflict between presenting himself as competent, worthy of respect, and developing social relationships which require the investment of time and energy, all of which might detract from his ability to "become competent."

Klinger (1977) puts the matter clearly when he suggests:

> . . . there are ways in which extinction can spread beyond the lost object. If a complicated chain of actions is required to achieve a goal, then there are likely to be many subgoals whose value depends on the ultimate goal. For instance if a child has learned to organize much of its behavior around a parent's approval, then losing the parent may make all of the actions learned to please him or her meaningless and unattractive [p. 161].

Klinger goes on to suggest that this does not explain the depressive's pervasive sense of loss. Incidentally, it does not offer any mechanism by which these forms of extinction can produce the varied and intense symptoms of a depressed person (e.g., loss of appetite, loss of sexual interest, sleep disturbance, diurnal variation, and so on). But behaviors may vanish from a repertoire for many reasons and not all the behaviors that appear to be extinguished in the depressed state need to be under the control of the same process. A number of subprocesses might be involved which, though interactive, can nevertheless be studied individually. Vulnerability to extinction of certain behaviors seems one such process. However, we still do not yet understand how certain behaviors, which were not directly related to an incentive, appear to become so when that incentive is removed. Thus a bereaved person may have enjoyed diverse activities ranging from playing weekend football to business lunches, none of which maintained the marital relationship which is broken in bereavement. Nevertheless, the person may feel no pleasure or purpose in engaging in these activities following the death of the spouse. This suggests there can be a general shift in the capacity to experience pleasure following the loss of a loved person. To help understand this more generalized process Klinger's model stresses disengagement, rather than commitment, as the key process in depression. Since commitments and current concerns exert a powerful organizing influence on behavioral, cognitive, and biological processes, the failure to attain and or maintain a valued incentive or goal can be expected to produce significant upheaval in all three systems. These upheavals, Klinger suggests, follow a predictable cycle. First, there are attempts to resecure the incentive (invigoration). When these attempts fail the incentive needs to be abandoned and the abandonment produces depression. These processes can be explained more fully.

Invigoration

Klinger suggests that the first thing that happens when incentives become more difficult to obtain, or are blocked, is an invigoration of behavior. To support this he reviews a large body of research evidence including Amsel's (1958, 1962) frustration effect experiments. It is widely known that animals will demonstrate greatly invigorated behaviors, if previously learned avoidance responses are blocked. Mandler (1975) also suggests that interruption of ongoing behavior causes significant increases in behavior and arousal. In the early stages of invigoration, it seems that the valued incentive moves up the hierarchy of incentives, that is, it becomes more important. This increased importance may have both behavioral and cognitive consequences. Cognitively, more activity is geared toward thinking about the incentive, looking for incentive cues, and so on. In the studies of infant separation, the first behaviors to be seen are intense searching behaviors. In humans, the loss of a loved one causes cognitive activity to focus very sharply on the missing person (Parkes, 1972).

The fact that the incentive becomes more important when it is threatened or removed has implications for cognitive theory. Individuals who, when depressed, appear to have high idealized views of how they should behave may be demonstrating invigoration. In other words, the ability to be a good, lovable person (say) takes on increased importance if the ability to behave in a "good" way is threatened (e.g., loss of the opportunity to be a caregiver). As the person recovers from the depression we would expect this incentive to lose some of its importance or value. This does seem to happen.

This does not invalidate Beck's (1976) concepts (see Chapter 4). Indeed, it might strengthen his theory by indicating mechanisms whereby key themes, cognitive or social incentives, become dominant in the individual's cognitive processing at certain times. The role of cognitive distortions, styles of thinking, and negative schemata is still of major value for understanding depression, but a concept of invigoration may help to explain why certain negative constructs become dominant at certain points in time. In other words, under the threat of not achieving important incentives (be this to be loved, be a good caregiver, or whatever) they become invigorated concerns.

Klinger argues that in the process of invigoration, anger and aggression are also increased. Again, there is evidence that this is so. In rats, aggressive behavior increases following frustrative nonreward. Klinger points out, however, that there are different types of aggression, including territorial, defensive, rage, and so on. These are mediated by different brain areas and we should not regard increased aggressive behavior as being relevant to all these. He proposes that it is "irritable aggression" which is increased by blocking incentives. In depression it is indeed noted that depressives often show increased irritable anger and aggression.

Aggressive behavior, produced by frustration, is affected by the dominance position of an animal. It is unusual for low dominant animals to attack high dominant animals following frustration, but the reverse is common. Such data indicate the complexity of aggressive behavior and point to alternative formulations of "anger turned inward" models of depression (see Chapter 6).

Depression

Eventually, if invigorated behavior fails to secure the incentive, the individual must give up pursuing the now unattainable incentive. The downswing into depression commences as the expectation of success in maintaining or obtaining the valued incentive falls. The actual processes involved in this downswing are complex. Generally, it is marked by an increase in hopelessness about obtaining the incentive. Klinger points to separation studies to demonstrate this aspect of the cycle. As depression ensues, behavioral output falls. But this does not mean that cognitive activity, centered on the incentive, diminishes. Rather, it may change its form. In the invigorated phase, cognitive activity may center on how to overcome the obstacles in the path to the incentive. In the disengagement (depressed) phase, cognitive activity centers on the dire consequences of having lost. Depending on the value of the incentive this cognitive activity may be painful and intense. Preoccupations and ruminations on the consequences of the loss may appear. Although behavioral activity may significantly fall (e.g., because of a collapse of a behavioral network), cognitive processes do not necessarily decline, for invigorated cognitive activity on the consequences of the loss may be present. The processes which terminate preoccupations and ruminations on these consequences require further investigation.

Klinger suggests that individuals can be at various points in various incentive disengagement cycles, and that the depression produced by final incentive disengagement may vary from mild depression to intense clinical depression. Much would seem to depend on the pursuit of alternative incentives. He also argues that there is a natural tendency to recover. (Wolpe, 1979, on the other hand, suggests that neurotic depressions are unlikely to recover naturally.) The intensity and duration of the depressive phase will vary according to a host of factors, some cognitive, some behavioral, but some biochemical. Indeed, one of the strengths of Klinger's model is that he attempts to show how various elements of the incentive disengagement cycle are biochemically mediated. Thus, the idea that some severe depressions are biochemically driven is not at all at variance with Klinger's theory.

Klinger's theory has a number of strengths. It highlights what clinicians have been aware of for a long time. Although some behaviors are lost to the depressive, there are also, paradoxically, invigorated components. These center on agitated states and painful, often constant, internal ruminations. Moreover, it is often noted that obsessional states wax and wane with depressions. The invigoration component offers some insight into this aspect of depression.

Klinger also offers some interesting ideas on mania, though these will not be discussed here. Klinger's important contribution is to focus attention on the idea that there is a cycle of events which can include both invigoration and disengagement in depression. In pathological cases, the biological mediators of this cycle may be significantly disturbed.

There is an aspect to Klinger's theory which needs special concern. He suggests that depression, be it mild or severe, is an almost inevitable result of disengaging from valued incentives. Moreover, there is a natural tendency to recover. If this is so, then we should not ask why depressed, but why so severe or long, and why no recovery? In some cases it is not getting depressed that is surprising, but the severity of the disturbance and its failure to recover. If we look at severity and failure to recover as separate processes, then we might move closer to understanding pathological depression. The factors that affect both severity and failure to recover may be psychological, biological, or both. In other words, these factors affect the individual's ability to halt the degree of decline and to recover from it.

There is a possible confusing factor in Klinger's model. This is the implicit idea that disengagement is relevant to both mild and severe depression. As pointed out later, one problem for some depressives is their *failure* to disengage. Actually, disengagement can be a normal and good coping behavior. For some depressives, however, there is a failure to disengage and seek new incentives. The cost of doing so seems just too high. Thus they are trapped in remaining committed to incentives which are unrealistic and are not obtainable. Biologically, their systems may have moved beyond the invigoration point, yet still at a cognitive-behavioral level no disengagement is made. The level of stress is, therefore, "pathological," because it cannot be resolved.

SELF-CONTROL MODEL OF DEPRESSION

Rehm (1977) has presented a model which considers depression as a problem of self-control. The development of self-control theories of psychopathology has been reviewed by Mahoney (1974) and Mahoney & Arnkoff (1978). The self-control model of depression suggests that depressives show deficits in self-monitoring, self-evaluation, and self-reinforcement.

Self-monitoring

Rehm suggests that depressives attend selectively to negative outcomes. In this regard the model fits the idea of a cognitive distortion as suggested by Beck (1967, 1976) and others. It is, however, unclear whether extinction events, or punishment events, are equally relevant in this self-monitoring deficit. The suggestion is that negative events are attended to at the expense of positive events. Additionally, depressives attend selectively to immediate, rather than delayed, reinforcement outcomes. They lose a future perspective and are trapped by immediate consequences and outcomes.

Self-evaluation

Depressives are believed to show attributional difficulties in their tendency to make inaccurate evaluations about causality. First, depressives may make external attributions for negative outcomes and see adversity as beyond their control. Secondly, depressives may make internal attributions for the cause of adversity, but perceive themselves as lacking the skills to do anything about it. Actually, the question of whether depressives suffer internal or external attributional difficulties has been one consideration that has separated the learned helplessness theory of depression (Seligman, 1975) from Beck's (1967, 1976) theory (see Blaney, 1977). More recently, this question has been further considered by the learned helplessness theory (Abramson et al., 1978). It is a complex problem which requires more research. Kleinian theorists would argue that it makes some difference as to whether adversity (badness) is seen as lying outside of self or inside of self. Clearly, the relationship between projection mechanisms and attribution mechanisms requires further thought. Rehm also suggests that depressives set high standards for self-evaluation. In this, similarities between ego-analytic and Beckian ideas are evident. It is suggested that "all or nothing" thinking significantly interferes with self-monitoring skills. Kleinians would call this a paranoid-schizoid mechanism.

Self-reinforcement

The concept of self-reinforcement is, perhaps, the most useful development to a behavioral approach of depression. Rehm suggests that lower response initiations, longer latencies, and less persistence, may be accounted for by low self-reinforcement. This is unclear, however, since attribution theory (Weiner, 1972) suggests these variables are related to attribution tendencies. There is evidence, though, that depressives self-reward less and self-punish more than normal controls. Whether or not this is a function of a self-reward per se, or that there are "greater rewards" from punishment (e.g., secondary gains, avoidance of aversive responses from others), is unclear. In general, the concept of low self-reward implies an excessive concern with external reinforcers, that is the depressed person is heavily dependent on others for reinforcement. This idea crops up in a variety of forms, for example, in ego-analytic theory (Arieti & Bemporad, 1980b), in Freud's concept of dependency, in Kleinian concepts of a projected good object, and so on. It is one of the most important elements of many theories of depression. Perhaps describing these processes as those of self-reinforcement makes them more manageable and open to investigation.

Rehm offers little insight into how or why deficient self-reinforcement processes develop. We need to ask at what period in life self-reinforcement takes over from external sources of reinforcement. Indeed, is self-reinforcement a natural process (e.g., as in babies' play) which is lost by the depressive?

More recently, Fuchs & Rehm (1977) and Rehm et al. (1979) have evaluated a behavioral program for depression based on the self-control model. Findings suggest that the self-control model does provide a useful basis for treating mild-to-moderate depression. However, it has yet to be compared with a more standardized form of treatment (e.g., drugs or cognitive therapy) and there is some question as to whether it can be regarded as a sufficient model in its own right. At a theoretical level it is rather overinclusive and draws heavily on other models. This may make it difficult to refute. It may be, however, that it offers a clear basis for behavioral assessment, i.e., the therapist can have a clear set of processes, self-monitoring, self-evaluation, and self-reward, that can be investigated precisely.

This would contribute valuably to the planning and management of individual programs. It remains to be seen whether such a format provides any major advance on other cognitive-behavioral programs. Rehm (1977) is well aware that this model requires further investigation. It is to be hoped that further investigations of covert responses in depressives will be undertaken. (See Rehm, 1981, for further discussion of the self-control model.)

WOLPE'S CONDITIONED ANXIETY MODEL OF DEPRESSION

In 1971 Wolpe presented a model of depression which suggested that depression was a consequence of conditioned anxiety. At this time he largely favored Seligman's learned helplessness model. But, recently, Wolpe (1979) has challenged the learned helplessness model on a number of grounds and now believes it to be inadequate as a model of depression. Unlike many of the behavioral models, Wolpe draws sharp dividing lines between normal, neurotic, and endogenous depression. He suggests that symptom profiles, sedation thresholds, and evoked potentials point to the existence of qualitative differences between neurotic and endogenous depression. (Some of these issues are discussed in Chapter 1.) Wolpe tends to equate endogenous with psychotic depression and this is undoubtedly suspect (see Akiskal et al., 1978). Moreover, the biological states of psychotic and neurotic depression are probably different, but whether this suggests different etiologies is questionable. Further, Wolpe's (1979) idea that "biological depressions fade and disappear as a function of remission of the relevant biological process [p. 556]," is also questionable. The author agrees with Wolpe that differentiation of biological parameters in depression is important (e.g., Maas, 1975), but whether this will provide meaningful endogenous–neurotic distinctions is an open question.

These issues apart, Wolpe's (1979) model provides many important points for consideration. Limiting his analysis to the neurotic depressions, he maintains that depressive neurosis should be regarded as a neurosis which, like other neuroses, is fueled by conditioned anxiety. He defines neurosis as a "persistent unadaptive habit acquired by learning in an anxiety-generating situation or succession of situations." Thus, rather than examining uncontrollability as in Seligman's (1975) learned helplessness model of depression, Wolpe suggests we should turn our attention to the older forms of experimentally induced anxiety which, as he correctly maintains, tend to get forgotten these days.

To cause neurotic behavior experimentally it is necessary to produce anxiety in an animal repeatedly, in a constant situation, or to induce strong emotional conflict. This can be done by presenting food in a cage which has been associated with shock. In a situation where anxiety has been conditioned there is no tendency for anxiety to reduce unless adequate counterconditioning trials are conducted. (Gray, 1971, offers a good review of these situations.) The explanations of why anxiety reduces with counterconditioning include notions of reciprocal inhibition, habituation, and extinction. Wolpe argues that animals placed in cages that have previously been associated with shock will show significant reduction (cessation) of normal positive behavior, e.g., exploration, eating, copulation, etc. It appears that it is this general inhibition of positive reinforceable behavior that Wolpe equates with depression. However, these behaviors are under stimulus control and removal from the cage will (depending on other factors) reinstate positive behavioral responses. Thus, the question of stimulus specificity is important here, since depressives often show a general inhibition of positively reinforceable behavior which is not stimulus (situation) specific. Nevertheless, Wolpe's observation of the relationship between conditioned anxiety and cessation of positive reinforceable behaviors is an important one. Indeed, although Ferster's model does not explicitly state anxiety as an intervening process in the reduction of positively emitted behavior of the depressive, there is no reason why this could not be adapted to do so. What Wolpe is pointing out here is the emotional and behavioral consequences of strong approach–avoidance conflicts. One is inclined to agree with Wolpe that it need not be controllability per se which causes problems for the depressive, but, rather, that certain behaviors become entangled in these types of conflict.

Wolpe (1979) offers a neat subclassification of neurotic depression along the lines of differently acquired conditioned anxiety responses. He suggests four subtypes of depression:

1. Depression as a consequence of severe and prolonged anxiety that is directly conditioned.
2. Depression as a consequence of anxiety based on erroneous self-devaluative cognitions.
3. Depression as a consequence of anxiety based on an inability to control interpersonal behavior.
4. Depression as a consequence of severe or prolonged responses to bereavement.

Wolpe suggests that in the absence of counterconditioning of these habits of responding, they will not dissipate over time. He suggests that this explains why neurotic depressions are relatively enduring and contrasts it with the dissipation effect (Miller & Weiss, 1969) often noted in learned helplessness experiments.

Wolpe outlines various therapeutic strategies based on a counterconditioning model. Because Wolpe stresses the role of conditioned anxiety the approach is primarily one of classical conditioning (i.e., stimulus-response conditioning). If this model was integrated with some of Ferster's ideas (surprisingly Ferster is not mentioned in Wolpe's [1979] paper), then this could lay the foundations of a more comprehensive behavioral model. In addition to the evidence Wolpe examines in support of his approach, there is other clinical evidence which has some bearing on this model. For example, Kendell (1974) found that a high percentage of anxiety states go on to be diagnosed as depressive states at some subsequent period (see Chapter 1). Gilbert (1980) found that recovered depressives continue to show elevated anxiety scores as measured by pencil and paper tests. Clinically, depressives are often highly anxious individuals, especially along one or more of the four dimensions outlined by Wolpe. Depression in anxiety states appears to be less common. Moreover, anxiety difficulties do sometimes become manifest as depressive disturbances worsen or recede; for example, agoraphobia and obsessional symptoms sometimes intensify as an individual becomes depressed. These clinical data point to an important interaction between depressive and anxiety conditions, and Wolpe's analysis goes some way in helping us to understand why this might be. It also highlights the dangers of attempting to package symptoms into neatly labeled disorders. Cognitive attempts to delineate illness boundaries, according to cognitive appraisal content (Beck, 1976), must thus be problematic. As Wolpe's paper suggests, we will have to be prepared to see that there is a considerable overlap with many disorders.

More recently, Wolpe (1981a) has outlined important concepts on how various fears can be acquired, either by direct autonomic conditioning, or via new cognitive associations to the feared stimulus. The idea that some depressions are autonomically conditioned responses does require urgent consideration and this is touched on in later chapters. Wolpe (1981b) claims that pure exposure to strong anxiety-arousing stimuli for any length of time, without an interposing competitive anxiety response, is completely ineffective. This area is complex since some behaviorists now question the need for relaxation in the treatment of anxiety. Although it is a crucial question, we cannot examine it here. Only careful trials of pure exposure versus exposure with competitive anxiety responses can decide the issue. The role of relaxation in therapies for depression is yet to be investigated.

In regard to depression, Wolpe's model is the only model that clearly outlines a classical conditioning model for this disorder. Although Gray's (1971) reworking of Eysenck's model offers a possible foundation for a classical conditioning theory of depression, as far as I am aware this has not been developed. The main concern regarding Wolpe's model is that it may place too much importance on anxiety as the conditioning substrate for depression.

It is possible that biological responses which more directly parallel those of depression are conditionable. Moreover, it is possible that individual differences in the physiological reactivity to (say) early separation may provide one dimension through which subsequent negative events (e.g., losses) act as conditioned events. The conditionability of the cues associated with loss will depend upon the biological sensitivity of the individual to separation. It is possible that there are high and low separation responders, in much the same way as there are reactive and nonreactive rats. These ideas require refinement and cannot be taken further here. A link between Bowlby's work and Wolpe's would be fascinating!

CONCLUDING COMMENTS

The behavioral theories of depression are young indeed, compared with other formulations, e.g., psychoanalytic. They have, in their short history, provided fascinating insights and testable hypotheses. In general terms, there is one area which will need careful consideration—the question of equipotentiality. The study of anxiety has shown that different classes of stimuli are more easily fear-conditioned than others. Thus, various conditioned stimuli (CS) differ in their propensity to acquire fear-arousing properties from an association with an unconditioned stimulus (UCS) (See Eysenck, 1979, for a good review of these issues.) In the study of anxiety, early conditioning theories failed in their ability to adequately explain the acquisition of anxiety conditions and their resistance to extinction (Rachman, 1978).

It is quite possible that this problem, in one form or another, is going to emerge in our study of depression. The issue is complex, however, because, unlike anxiety, the behavioral theories of depression are not formulated within a classical conditioning model, but more generally are formulated as operant processes. Lewinsohn's work has already demonstrated the possibility that there are specific subclasses of events (e.g., interpersonal aversive events) which are related to depression. These considerations throw up a number of areas for thought.

First, we need to ask how far our investigations of depression can be guided by our anxiety-based models of neurosis. Consider, for example, Eysenck's (1979) definition of neurotic behavior. He suggested that: "We may provisionally define neurotic behaviour as maladaptive behaviour, accompanied by strong, irrelevant and persistent emotions, occurring in full awareness of the maladaptive and irrational nature of the behaviour in question [p. 155]."

While such a definition may be true for the compulsive hand-washer or socially anxious patient, I am unsure whether depression can be regarded in this way. Indeed, many depressives, far from being aware of the irrational aspects of their behavior, are marked by the fact that their negative ideas and behaviors appear utterly rational and correct. Suicide by some may be seen as a perfectly logical response, if only the patient has the courage to carry it out. Indeed, the so-called loss of rational evaluation is one area which cognitive theorists have spent much effort discussing.

Secondly, the relationship between anxiety and depression is unclear. What, for example, should be the status of anxiety states that arise in conjunction with a change in mood and recede as the mood component is treated? This seems an especially difficult question when the treatment is specifically antidepressant (e.g., ECT or antidepressant drugs). Moreover, should we make a distinction between depression with anxiety and agitated depression? To what extent are agitated states and anxiety states similar and/or different?

Thirdly, as mentioned before, the role of inherited predispositions, as they loosely apply to some concept of instincts, is problematic. Interestingly, Eysenck (1979) points out that Watson's triumph over McDougall during the 1920s resulted in psychologists ignoring the role of instincts. For this reason the problem of equipotentiality in the study of anxiety states has only recently become apparent. But if behaviorists are to take seriously the possibility that inherited predispositions may play some role in the acquisition of depression, then what are the important behavioral predispositions that we should investigate? If they are related to the importance of attachments, interpersonal behaviors, and so on, then Bowlby's work must be included. At present, few, if any, behaviorists have attended systematically to Bowlby's work. Chapter 6 looks at this question again and examines how Bowlby's work can be considered from a cognitive-behavioral perspective.

Fourthly, the relationship between classical and operant conditioning in theoretical models of depression is obscure. Apart from Wolpe's model, there is no behavioral model which outlines classical conditioning strategies for the acquisition and extinction of dysphoric responses to specific events. Solomon's (1980) work (see Chapter 5) provides a possibility for understanding depression within a classically conditioning paradigm, and Ramsay's (1979) work with pathological grief is a good example of the use of treatment based on a classical conditioning perspective. Wolpe's model suffers from being too dependent on anxiety. Yet there does not seem to be any logical reason why the counterconditioning of dysphoric responses could not be tackled directly. The question is whether relaxation or some other affect, e.g., anger, should be used as the competitive affective response. Seligman (1975) mentions the possibility that induced anger can break up helplessness, and psychoanalytic writers have long stressed the importance of the expression of anger. Unfortunately, some depressives are pretty hostile anyway and such responses do not necessarily carry specific antidepressant effects. At the present time it is not certain which affect will provide a useful counterconditioning response. Wolpe may be correct for those cases where anxiety is clearly a major problem. However, it is unclear whether all cases of depression, including the milder endogenous types, do respond to the counterconditioning of anxiety. At the present time, we desperately need more systematic investigation. In Chapter 6 it is suggested that abandonment and loss of peer-group bonding, together with low status and the biological changes associated with these states, may provide various avenues for investigating possible biological, conditioning substrates of depression.

Although we have concentrated on theory, one or two points on therapy seem useful at this juncture. These revolve around the issue of direct exposure. One of the important principles of behaviorism is the firm belief that there is a need to modify the actual anxiety state by direct exposure. Although behaviorists argue they are seeking to change behavior directly, this is only useful in that it makes the aversive affective state associated with certain behaviors available for modification. In the treatment of anxiety there is always an effort to bring on line the target aversive affect by directly engaging the behavior associated with it. Whether we do this by gradual exposure or flooding, the pursuit is the same: to produce changes in the central nervous system so that engagement of specific behaviors does not produce catastrophic arousal. This is a fundamental difference between the so-called talking therapies and behavior therapy.

This question is raised here because while using cognitive therapy patients may say, "Well, I understand the principles very well, but when I'm depressed it does not seem to work." What seems to happen here is a problem of state-dependent learning (Reus et al., 1979a). The importance of a behavioral approach is that learning takes place *in the anxiety state* or in states which approximate to it. They allow for the direct desensitization of the aversive state. In other words, new learning is associated directly with the aversive anxiety state. This is not necessarily the case with talking therapies. In cognitive therapy patients can analyze their problems, as it were, cold, that is, disassociated from the aversive affective state for which they are seeking help. Yet most therapists are well aware that patients who are not "emotionally involved" in the therapy do less well.

It is probably unpopular to suggest that many of the so-called emotional expression groups which seem to thrive on the expression of emotion are actually engaging in desensitization procedures. Unfortunately, stripped of the scientific framework of behaviorism, such attempts do not systematically attempt desensitization, but rather believe in some processes of catharsis. (Indeed, the relationship between catharsis and desensitization is an interesting one requiring research.) However, for such procedures it may be arbitrary whether the person gets better or worse, since it is known that under some situations the aversive affective response to a CS can actually be increased. Continually expressing anger or anxiety may simply rehearse it, not reduce it. When it comes to depression, therefore, I think we have to give much more thought to classical conditioning ideas. We have to consider state-dependent learning problems (Reus et al., 1979a), and ways of helping patients more directly to modify affect and not just behavior or cognitions. I know this is not a popular view these days. Cognitive theorists will say that if patients cannot use the techniques of therapy then it is because they do not really believe in it. Well, there is no way you can force a patient to believe in a technique.

Actually, of course, most cognitive therapists are aware of this problem and have their patients engage in those behaviors which cause most difficulty. For example, a colleague who went on a RET course had to dress up and fool around in her group, since her "fear" was being seen as foolish. But really such procedures are much more than cognitive restructuring. They are a form of desensitization. They involve invoking the feared affect and then modifying it directly.

In spite of these thoughts for the future, it is clear that behavioral formulations have moved us forward in important ways. Ferster's ideas on approach–avoidance conflicts and the presence of passive compliance give important insights into the conflicts of the depressive. Lewinsohn's work on subclasses of events, especially social events, probably has something to tell us about evolutionary processes and depression. Klinger's incentive theories point out how depression can be part of a circle of changes which include invigoration. Wolpe's classical conditioning model has much promise, both theoretically and therapeutically. Thus, we can see that behavioral approaches to the study of depression promise to bear great fruits in the future. It is to be hoped that we do not get too bogged down in the dogma and competition between theories to be able to pick these fruits.

4 Cognitive Theories of Depression

Cognitive theories of psychopathology have proliferated at an enormous rate in the past 15 years (Mahoney, 1974; Mahoney & Arnkoff, 1978; Marzillier, 1980). In some cases they represent extensions of behavior theory to covert processes. In others, they are developments of ego-analytic theory. This union has not always been a happy one and much debate revolves around the interpretation of experimental results.

It is the case, however, that throughout history, ideas, beliefs, and attitudes have been regarded as sources of distress (Ellenberger, 1970; Zilboorg & Henry, 1941). Albert Ellis, one of the founders of the cognitive approach, tells us how the Greek philosopher, Epictetus, over 2000 years ago, argued that it is the view we take of things, and not things in themselves, which disturbs us. Kant believed that mental illness resulted when private sense and common sense drifted too far apart. Charot believed that certain dissociated ideas could cause symptoms of hysteria. Jung (1963, 1964) argued that complexes, which are integrated sets of ideas, attitudes, and emotions, often caused mental distress. He also suggested that unconscious disturbance represented a conflict between unconscious predispositions and maladaptive conscious attitudes. Furthermore, as Weiner (1972) indicates, many of Freud's theories pay particular attention to memories and fantasies and in that respect are cognitive.

The major axiom of the cognitive theories is that cognitive processes (e.g., schemata) translate external events into meaningful internal representations (Beck, 1976; Kelly, 1955; Lazarus, 1966; Raimy, 1975). It is these "internal representations", and not the events themselves, which are the pathogenic agents. Thus, learning contributes to pathology not because of a direct relationship with behavior, but via the development of maladaptive internal mechanisms for the organization, storage, and retrieval of information. In this chapter we examine depression from this perspective, beginning our examination with the most important cognitive theory, that of Beck.

BECK'S COGNITIVE THEORY OF DEPRESSION

Psychiatry has tended to regard mental life as capable of considerable dissection. As Zilboorg & Henry (1941) point out, psychiatry's view of depression was no exception:

> What formal psychiatry chose to consider as emotions were not emotions at all but verbal and muscular manifestations. Emotions were considered a separate functional department of man's body structure; they were considered subject independently to abnormal variations and were therefore thought to cause "affective psychoses"—disturbances of the so called "affective field" or of the "emotional level," which could be considered apart from other faculties such as thinking and imagination. Such a departmentalization of the human personality made it easy to give one's methods of psychological investigation the appearance of scientific work. Each part could be studied separately and "objectively," that is to say, only from the standpoint of what it looks like from the outside and not how it works from the inside [p. 496].

Clearly, such a departmentalization of emotion obscures the complexity and diversity of emotional experience, and tends to play down the importance of the interaction between thinking, imagination, behavior, and biology. Moreover, by viewing emotionality (at least in its pathological forms) as an autonomous system, those theories that emphasize the role of biological dysfunction in depressive disturbance have tended to pay little attention to the role of behavior and cognition in the etiology of the disturbance. This consideration offers a good starting point for examining Beck's work. Beck (1974b) points out that there are those who believe that for normal subjects the conceptualization and appraisal of events determine the affective state, but in psychopathology the affective state is believed to determine cognitive content. This complete reversal of cause and effect, between normal and abnormal emotion, is, in Beck's view, erroneous and constitutes a major source of confusion. In Beck's model of depression the difference between abnormal and normal emotional states:

> ... lies in the degree of correspondence between the conceptualization and the veridical stimulus configuration. In psychopathological states perseverative faulty conceptualization leads to excessive or inappropriate affective disturbance.
>
> The typical conceptualizations leading to specific affects appear to be the same in both "normal" and "abnormal" responses. In abnormal conditions, however, conceptualizations are determined to a greater extent by internal processes which distort the stimulus situation [pp. 128–129].

The concept that the theme of the appraisal is the same for both normal
and pathological mood states is a crucial element of Beck's theory and leads
directly to two basic assumptions: (1) that normal and abnormal states exist
on a continuum and are determined by the same processes; and (2) that the
factors (conceptualizations) which determine normal emotion also
determine abnormal emotion. For abnormal emotion, however, the congruence between the external event and its cognitive appraisal (meaning and
implications) is low and the affective disturbance is a consequence of this low
congruence.
  These two assumptions need careful consideration. In regard to the first
assumption, it is possible that discontinuities are manifest in abnormal
emotional states but are not observable in the cognitive domain; that is, they
may be present in biological or behavioral response systems only. In this
sense we can hear again Zilboorg & Henry's warning that an overconcern
with how things appear from the outside may lead us to derive unwarranted
conclusions about how things work inside. In regard to the second assumption, sociological models of depression (Brown & Harris, 1978a) have some
grounds for argument. These researchers have shown that depression is not
so much a problem of cognitive incongruence (or distortion) but is related to
real-life events.
  Beck (1963, 1967, 1970, 1974a, 1974b, 1976) has published many accounts
of the cognitive model of depression. The model is primarily relevant to the
unipolar, nonpsychotic depressions, at least as regards its current
therapeutic implications (Beck et al., 1979). Recently, Beck also notes that
biological factors may be important in some depressions. However, Beck
suggests that the general content of the depressive appraisal system is much
the same throughout the spectrum of the depressive disorders, and cognitive
distortions are ubiquitous among persons suffering from depression.
  The major theme of the depressed person's cognitive appraisal system
centers on the appraisal of loss. Beck suggests that loss is "the clue" to
understanding depression. He proposes that a lowering of mood occurs when
individuals appraise or evaluate that a reduction in their domain has taken
place. Moreover, the attribute or object that is perceived as being lost must
have had some positive value. For the depressed person the appraisal of loss
pervades evaluations concerning the self, the world, and the future. As a
result depressives perceive their world as full of obstacles; they see themselves as losers, having experienced some significant loss(es) in their personal domain, and lacking the necessary skills and opportunities to make up
the perceived deficits and inadequacies; they see the future as unchanging
and empty and that they are doomed to be this way for ever. The light has
gone out on life. These powerful negative attitudes all contain significant loss
implications. Together, the negative view of the self, the world, and the
future are referred to as the "negative cognitive triad."

Hence Beck suggests (1) that the content of idiosyncratic systems c appraisal determine affective state, and (2) that in depressed individual there is a pervasive appraisal of loss which significantly influences evalu ations of the self, the world, and the future. Beck's theory also outlines th processes which bring the negative cognitive triad into being and maintai its prominence, distorting information processing. There are a number c influences involved in these processes which will, for ease of exposition, b referred to as learned attitudes and styles of thinking.

In the category of styles of thinking, automatic thoughts and cognitiv distortions are the main explanatory variables. Automatic thoughts ar conceptualized as habitual styles of thinking which relate to ongoing plans activities, and events. The depressed person may be hardly aware of hi automatic thoughts or the negative conclusions arising from them, bu experiences significant changes in mood. In interpersonal situations thes thoughts may relate to how a person thinks others perceive him; that is whether he is liked or disliked, what the consequences are, and so on Especially important is the information the individual attends to, to mak these judgments. Beck's (1976) description of how he became aware of th powerful effects of automatic thoughts is illuminating. He describes tha during an analysis with a patient who was relating sexual material he note an increase in her anxiety. At first he thought this anxiety was related to th material being presented. Later, however, Beck discovered that whil talking to him, this patient also had a series of self-evaluative thought about how she thought Beck regarded her. The more she thought Beck di not like her and wanted to terminate therapy with her, the more anxious sh became. Thus, Beck reasoned that her anxiety in therapy was not related t the sexual material itself, but to her automatic negative thoughts abou how the interaction between Beck and herself was going.

Now classical analysts may ask why did these thoughts appear at thi time. They may suggest a connection between forbidden sexual ideas, fea of rejection, and separation anxiety. A transference approach may hav offered an interpretation along those lines, pointing out, perhaps, that fea that the therapist would reject the patient was producing anxiety. It is c some importance, I suspect, that this approach might have interpreted thi patient's negative-thinking content, which points to possible similarities i the effectiveness of different therapies. The cognitive approach would nc focus on unconscious fears of separation, but more directly on modifyin the automatic thoughts. Separation anxiety as a cause of depression is littl considered by Beck.

Cognitive therapy provides training procedures which allow patients t re-evaluate faulty premises by attending to and monitoring thoughts an ideas of which they might not otherwise have been aware. These importar aspects of therapy cannot be taken further here, but clearly the procedura differences between Beck's cognitive therapy and other approaches demand the attention of research. It may be that many types of therapy are changing affect-cognitive interactions, but only time will tell which procedures are the most effective for which types of patient. At this point in time the cognitive approach is most useful because of its clear guidelines for therapy and its testability. This includes testability in the actual therapy situation; that is patients are encouraged to test out their beliefs.

By focusing on automatic thoughts therapists are able to pinpoint a variety of errors (cognitive distortions) in the depressed person's appraisal processes. Beck et al. (1979) suggest that depressed people tend to make at least six types of error, which produce highly negative conclusions. These include:

1. Arbitrary inference—drawing a negative conclusion in the absence of supporting data.
2. Selective abstraction—focusing on a detail out of context, often at the expense of more salient information.
3. Overgeneralization—drawing conclusions over a wide variety of things on the basis of single events.
4. Magnification and minimization—making errors in evaluating the importance and implications of events.
5. Personalization—relating external (often negative) events to the self when there is no connection for doing so.
6. Absolutistic, dichotomous thinking—thinking in polar opposites (black and white). Something is all good, or totally bad and a disaster.

Thus, as Beck et al. (1979) describe:

As is apparent, depressed persons are prone to structure their experiences in relatively primitive ways. They tend to make global judgments regarding events that impinge on their lives. The meanings that flood their consciousness are likely to be negative and extreme. In contrast to this primitive type of thinking, more mature thinking automatically integrates life situations into many dimensions or qualities (instead of a single category), in quantitative rather than qualitative terms and according to relative rather than absolutistic standards. In primitive thinking the complexity, variability and diversity of human experiences and behavior are reduced into a few crude categories [pp. 14–15].

They suggest an analog between the primitive thinking of the depressive and the childlike styles of thinking outlined by Piaget. This is an important comparison because it raises a number of questions. First, to what degree have depressives learned adult (mature) styles of thinking? Beck himself is unclear on this. Sometimes he seems to suggest that depressives have, by nature, a tendency toward primitive thinking. At other times primitive thinking only emerges as the person begins to become depressed. It would be untenable to suggest that all depressives (when well) have a tendency toward primitive thinking, though this may be true for a subgroup (e.g., those with personality difficulties). Some depressives make very good adjustments when their illness is treated, and there is no evidence, as yet, to suggest that they are any more primitive in thinking when well than non-depressives. Moreover, if this style of thinking were present all the time, would the individual ever be free of depression? Why do some depressions not appear until comparatively later in life? If Beck is correct in his primitive thinking argument, then we must be observing a fluctuating picture. The second question, then, is what triggers this style of thinking? Is it incidents which invoke dormant evaluative schematas, biological shifts associated with mood change, or real events in the world?

Beck places his money on (1) the invoking of dormant schemata, and (2) learned attitudes which predispose to primitive styles of thinking. Beck suggests that various internal constructions of the world are learned in childhood. Later experiences may displace these learned constructions (or schemata) so that more adaptive ones are normally used, but the early constructions remain, ready to become dominant again when situations similar to those existing at their initial developmental period are present. Beck (1967) argues thus:

> The vulnerability of the depression prone person is attributable to the con-
> stellation of enduring negative attitudes about himself, about the world and
> about his future. Even though these attitudes (or concepts) may not be promi-
> nent or even discernible at a given time, they persist in a latent state like an
> explosive charge ready to be detonated by an appropriate set of conditions.
> Once activated, these concepts dominate the person's thinking and lead to
> typical depressive symptomatology [p. 277].

Thus, Beck's theory of predisposition suggests that the negative cognitive triad already exists in the depression-prone adult, but in a latent state. The development of this triad, the place of origin, can be found in the early learning history of the individual. Beck (1974a) comments:

> In the course of his development, the depression-prone person may become
> sensitized by certain unfavorable types of life situations such as the loss of a
> parent or chronic rejection by his peers. Other unfavorable conditions of a
> more insidious nature may similarly produce vulnerability to depression.
> These traumatic experiences predispose the individual to overreact to anal-
> ogous conditions later in life. He has a tendency to make extreme, absolute
> judgments when such situations occur [p. 7].

Beck (1967) also argues that the depression-prone individual attaches negative attitudes to certain attributes, such as "It's terrible to be stupid," or "It's disgusting to be weak." The tendency to label the self as having these "bad attributes" again appears to occur in the early learning history of the individual. Beck (1967) believes that failure may be labeled as evidence of being inept or inadequate. For example:

> ... a child who gets the notion that he is inept, as a result of either a failure or of being called inept by someone else, may interpret subsequent experiences according to this notion. Each time thereafter that he encounters difficulties in manual tasks he may have a tendency to judge himself as inept. Each negative judgment tends to reinforce the negative concept or self-image. Thus a cycle is set up: each negative judgment fortifies the negative self-image which in turn facilitates a negative interpretation of subsequent experiences which further consolidates the negative self-concept. Unless this negative image is extinguished, it becomes structuralized, i.e., it becomes a permanent formation in the cognitive organization. Once a concept is structuralized, it remains permanently with the individual, even though it may be dormant; it becomes a cognitive structure, or schema [pp. 275–276].

Thus, Beck's model of depression suggests that the depression-prone individual, early on in life, develops particular negative cognitive schemata relating to the world, the self, and the future. Although these negative schemata may not be discernible at any given time, they are easily invoked by life events which are similar to those that were responsible for their formation. Thus, for example, the individual who has been labeled as inept or inadequate by others in failing at a certain task will tend to respond to failure with this concept (of being inadequate or inept) when he confronts failure in the future. The result of this is the activation of the negative view of the self. As this view dominates the individual's cognitive processes, he will interpret all failures, trivial or otherwise, as evidence that he is inadequate. This shift toward a negative appraisal of other events outside the invoking situation is a cognitive distortion which results from the activation of the (previously dormant) negative view of the self. The cognitive distortion, however, confirms the correctness of the invoked negative schema and leads to a further increase in its dominance in cognitive processing. The more dominant the negative cognitive schema becomes, the more cognitive distortions occur and the greater the disturbance of affect and depth of depression.

It is not only experiences concerned with learning negative attributes about the self which predispose to depression, but in addition powerful life events in childhood can also sensitize cognitive processes to act in a pathological way under stress. For example, parental death may sensitize the individual to thoughts of irretrievable loss when separations occur later in life. However, the sensitizing influence of life events needs much more work in cognitive theory (see, for example, Brown & Harris, 1978a). It is clear that only a minority of persons who experience these early events do become vulnerable to depression.

Beck often equates learned attitudes with the notion of schemata. These are important explanatory concepts in cognitive theory. Beck regards schemata as organizing systems which structure inputs into meaningful events. The three elements of the negative cognitive triad are examples of schemata. However, though many writers have incorporated such ideas into their work, schemata remain hypothetical constructs which, as Marzillier (1980) suggests, require much more careful evaluation and description. It is in fact debatable whether the notion of a schema is particularly useful. Not all depressives are negative about all aspects of themselves. Indeed, in many areas of their lives they may see themselves as functioning well and it is only in (for them) the pursuit of important goals that they perceive themselves in a negative light. Moreover, as Neisser (1967; 1976) points out, some decisions must be made about what to attend to in the environment and what to expect. The strategies and organization of attention allocation and decision making are not well understood. Thus, although the notion of schemata may be a helpful shorthand for considering what may be many highly complex cognitive processes, it should be remembered that they are probably crude oversimplifications of complex cognitive processes.

In important ways, Beck's model of depression uses ego-analytic ideas. For example, Beck (1976) discusses the importance of the "shoulds" and "oughts." I "should" be a perfect lover/parent/teacher/student/spouse. I "should" find a solution to all my problems, etc. Here we can see clear similarities with Bibring's (1953) ideas of rigidly held, unrealistic aspirations. However, are these learned styles of thinking, schemata or attitudes? Are they present when the depressed person is well? Are they part of the negative cognitive triad or do they contribute to it? Or even, do these shoulds and oughts actually produce the triad when the oughts and shoulds cannot be met? All these questions are for further research to decide. At this point theory is not enough.

In summary, Beck's model of depression suggests that predisposition is laid early in life. Sensitizing experiences which produce negative views of the self, world, and future become dormant cognitive schemata. Under certain types of stress these schemata become invoked again as organizing cognitive systems and produce a variety of distortions in sampling (attending to) information and deriving conclusions from that information. Cognitive errors and distortions confirm these negative schemata and lead to a vicious circle. In this situation the negative schemata produce cognitive distortions and the cognitive distortions produce greater dominance of the negative schemata which, in turn, produce still greater distortions and so on. The style of thinking becomes more primitive and the probability that accurate conceptualizations of external events can be made is reduced.

Comment

The cognitive approach to the emotional disorders provides a very useful model. There is little doubt that cognitive variables exert significant influences on emotion (Ellis & Whiteley, 1979; Hollon & Beck, 1979; Lazarus, 1966; Lazarus & Averill, 1972). What is less clear is the degree to which cognition is the main determining factor in the causation of pathological depression. Hence, there are a number of areas which are problematic for this approach. In view of the clear importance of the cognitive approach, these need to be outlined:

1. Zajonc (1980) has suggested that stimulus events can be appraised by emotional systems and cognitive systems relatively independently. He suggests affective judgments are precognitive, automatic, holistic, and irrevocable, and to a considerable degree occur independently of cognitive processes. These suggestions seriously challenge the cognitive axiom that abnormal emotions are "nothing but" the products of specific, cognitive conceptualizations. This area is controversial, but potentially embarrassing to cognitive theory. (See Rachman, 1981, for a discussion of these issues.)

2. The role of unconscious processes is not easily handled by Beck's (1976) theory. Shevrin & Dickman (1980) suggest that unconscious processes may operate with rules that are different to those of conscious ones, and conscious awareness may occur at a relatively late stage in information processing (see also Dixon & Henley, 1980; Nisbitt & Wilson, 1977). The extent to which latent cognitive schemata, and some automatic thoughts, operate at levels below awareness is not clear from Beck's theory. But they are certainly processes which are not always in the forefront of consciousness. Ellis (1977c), on the other hand, does not rule out the role of the unconscious as does Beck (1976). Ellis (1977c), suggests individuals may be unaware of the ideas and attitudes which predispose to distress, but this does not mean they are deeply hidden or repressed. The relationship between unconscious activity and lack of awareness was noted by Jung in discussion of the shadow archetype (see Ellenberger, 1970). Hence, for Ellis the unconscious may simply mean lack of awareness. But unawareness is not what Shevrin & Dickman refer to as unconscious processes.

3. Some of the cognitive variables held responsible for depression are not specific to depression. Anorexia nervosa, alcoholism, personality disorder, and some schizophrenias are often associated with low self-esteem and a negative view of the world. Hopelessness occurs across diagnostic subtypes (Melges & Bowlby, 1969) and is more highly correlated with

suicidal intent than depression per se (Minkoff et al., 1973; Wetzel, 1976). In a similar vein, the use of the Beck Depression Inventory (Beck et al., 1961) for comparing depressives with nondepressives (Loeb et al., 1964) is suspect, since many psychiatric patients score highly on this scale. The extent to which an appraisal of "loss" is specific to the negative cognitive triad of depression is unknown. Hence, as Blaney (1977) suggests, the cognitive theory of depression may be too open and flexible, lacking sufficient specificity to make it refutable. Cognitive theory may also be guilty of a tautology, by defining depression in cognitive terms. Furthermore, the theory may shade over real and important differences between subgroups. For example, guilt (personal attribution for negative outcomes) may be more marked for endogenous depressives than for neurotic or reactive depressives, even though the quantifiable "level" of depression may appear relatively similar.

4. There is some doubt as to the importance of work using students as subjects, and mood induction procedures in nondepressives. While such investigations point up important cognitive-mood interactions, they may show little more than the fact that cognitive appraisal is "one of" the variables which influence affect. There is no evidence, as yet, to suggest that it is the only variable or, indeed, the most important in the depressive disorders. Recently, this doubt has been voiced by others (e.g., Coyne, 1982).

Very few, if any, of the studies using unhappy students have controlled for personality or background levels of stress, although this is more of a criticism of the learned helplessness model of depression. Since real-life events are related to depression (Brown & Harris, 1978a) and recovery from some neurotic disorders (Tennant et al., 1981a), factors external to the person may be just as important in the etiology of depression as factors internal to the person. This suggests that it is person–environment interactions which are crucial determinants. In some depressions, cognitive bias and distortion may be gross and across the board. In other cases, cognitive distortion of the real world may be relatively minor. This suggests that cognitive distortion may be dimensionally represented and not equally relevant for all cases. Whether or not the degree of cognitive distortion correlates with severity, or type of disorder, is unknown.

These problems apart, there is growing evidence that cognitive therapy is very effective with unipolar, nonpsychotic depressives (Blackburn et al., 1981; Kovacs et al., 1981; Rush et al., 1977), but therapies based on other models are also effective (Weissman, 1979). Moreover, Beck's cognitive therapy is an eclectic therapy which uses many behavioral techniques (Beck et al., 1978, 1979), and its effectiveness may be strengthened when used in combination with drugs (Beck et al., 1979; Blackburn et al., 1981). Indeed, evidence suggests that drugs and psychotherapy are not competitive (Rounsaville et al., 1981) and are more effective in combination than when either is used alone (Di Mascio et al., 1979). The strength of the cognitive model lies more in its semistructured therapy approach than in its theoretical rationale. This does not imply that the theory is incorrect, but at present it is incomplete. Recently, some efforts have been made to expand the theory and practice of cognitive therapy with psychoanalytic formulations (Ryle, 1982). Very importantly for the classification debates, endogenous symptoms do not rule out the use of cognitive therapy (Blackburn et al., 1981). The cognitive approach may also help us to understand grief-related depressions (Horowitz et al., 1980a). All in all the cognitive approach constitutes a major advance in our understanding of depression and its treatment, in spite of certain limitations in the theory.

LEARNED HELPLESSNESS

The learned helplessness theory of depression generated a considerable amount of research during the 1970s. It contains many elements which make such models appealing to research psychologists. For example, it was derived from careful laboratory experimentation and seemed to offer a good animal model of depression. Most of all, it was clearly stated and presented avenues for research by which the various axioms of the model could be tested. Its clear predictions and testability did much to insure its popularity. Some of the biological research it has stimulated has proved very illuminating and there is little doubt that, from this point of view, learned helplessness has been a highly useful model. However, as to it offering an adequate theory of depression, there remains some dispute.

The antecedents of the experimental data on helplessness stretch back some 35 years. In 1948 Mowrer and Viek discovered that if rats were pretreated with inescapable shock they demonstrated subsequent deficits in escape-avoidance learning. Some 20 years later Seligman and his colleagues (Overmier & Seligman, 1967; Seligman & Maier, 1967) studied the effects of inescapable shock on escape-avoidance learning in dogs. In this procedure dogs were placed in a Pavlovian harness and inescapable shocks contingent on a conditioned stimulus (CS) were presented. The original idea was to study the incubation of fear produced by inescapable shock. When the dogs were released from the harness and allowed to learn an appropriate escape response, a large majority (though not all) of these animals demonstrated considerable difficulty in learning how to avoid the shock. Instead of actively attempting to avoid the shock, following the presentation of the CS, many of the pretreated dogs passively accepted the shock in a clear state of distress. Seligman found that this passivity was very difficult to extinguish. This apparently unexpected finding led Seligman to postulate that rather than "no learning" in the inescapable situation, these animals actually learned that their responses were ineffective in controlling the shock. Subsequent research (Seligman et al., 1971; Seligman, 1974, 1975) points to this being a very reproducible finding in a variety of species.

The idea that learning about the uncontrollability of trauma could have powerful effects on subsequent behavior led Seligman to suggest that there may be a parallel between such learning and depressive states. Seligman (1975) reasoned that:

> When a traumatic event first occurs, it causes a heightened state of emotionality that can loosely be called fear. This state continues until one of two things happen; if the subject learns that he can control the trauma, fear is reduced and may disappear altogether; or if the subject finally learns he cannot control the trauma, fear will decrease and be replaced by depression [pp. 53–54].

Thus, the central axiom of the learned helplessness theory is controllability. Although the above extract suggests that anxiety is replaced by depression when a trauma is perceived as uncontrollable, this "replacement" idea does not appear to be crucial to the learned helplessness theory. Rather it is controllability over reinforcers in general that relate to depression. In this way Seligman attempts to provide a solution to the so-called success depressions.

While Seligman has popularized the helplessness view and has pointed up many parallels between learned helplessness states and depressive states (Seligman, 1975, especially p. 106), there are, of course, many other theorists who place special emphasis on perceptions of helplessness (Beck, 1976; Bibring, 1953; Lazarus, 1966; Melges & Bowlby, 1969, to name but a few). Nevertheless, it is probably fair to suggest that much of the subsequent research on learned helplessness and depression was largely stimulated by Seligman's ideas.

During the 1970s much human experimental work was published examining: (1) the degree of generalization of the disruptive influence on subsequent behavior (e.g., problem solving) following experience with uncontrollable trauma or unsolvable problems; (2) the similarities between experimentally induced learning disruption and the deficits in learning observable in depressed individuals; (3) the depressant effect following experience with uncontrollable situations. Most of these studies have been well reviewed by others (e.g., Blaney, 1977; Costello, 1978) and will not be reviewed again here. In general the findings suggest that the disruption in learning produced by uncontrollable events does, to a degree, generalize to other learning situations; that there are similarities on persistence measures and expectation of success in skilled situations between pre-treated (with uncontrollable events) individuals and depressed students; and that experience with uncontrollable events can have a dysphoric impact (Gatchel et al., 1975; Hiroto & Seligman, 1975; Klein et al., 1976; Klein & Seligman, 1976; Miller & Seligman, 1973, 1975). Blaney (1977) suggests, however, that much of the above data is open to alternative explanations. For example, manipulations of self-esteem often have a contaminating effect in some of these experiments. Moreover, Forrest & Hokanson (1975) demonstrate that for some forms of learning (e.g., self-punitive responding following assertive behavior from others), depressives actually show superior learning, while Thornton & Jacobs (1971) failed to observe significant differences between a control and an inescapable shock-treated group.

Klinger (1975, 1977) suggests that it is not loss of control but the disengagement from certain incentives which is the crucial variable in depression. Often, people who become depressed have not experienced chronic uncontrollable trauma (though this does not deny the role of uncontrollable life events for some depressions). Individuals may be coping adequately with their lives, but lose a sense of meaningfulness or enjoyment. They can still obtain these incentives if they wish—they are controllable—but they no longer have the value they once did. Thus, meaningfulness (incentive value) is an important factor in some depressions. More recently, the *Journal of Abnormal Psychology* (February 1978) dedicated a special edition to the learned helplessness model. In this edition arguments for and against Seligman's theory were put forward. Depue & Monroe (1978a) suggest that the parallels drawn between learned helplessness and depression make it appear more in keeping with endogenous rather than reactive depression. Costello (1978) critically examined a number of papers relevant to the learned helplessness model of depression and points up possible, alternative explanations. Moreover, whether one believes in the dimensional or categorical approach to depressive illness, there is dispute over the value of using students as experimental subjects for a theory of pathological states.

In addition to the possible contaminating influences of self-esteem manipulations which were apparent in some of the learned helplessness experimental data, it was noted that the learned helplessness theory and Beck's cognitive theory made opposite predictions about self-attributions. It will be recalled that in Beck's theory, depressives are seen to blame themselves (internal attribution) for negative outcomes (personalization). In Seligman's theory, however, negative outcomes are themselves seen as uncontrollable (external attribution). Despite Klein's (1974) claim that neurotic depressives actually blame others, and Harrow et al.'s (1966) finding that many depressives blame their illness, Seligman has reformulated his model to agree with Beck's theory. As a result Abramson et al. (1978) reformulated the learned helplessness theory within the framework of attribution theory. By so doing, Seligman has introduced important, new dimensions into his theory, making depression more cognitively determined. To be able to appreciate the importance of this development it is useful to break off this discussion of learned helplessness and briefly examine some of the important propositions of attribution theory. This is useful since cognitive theories of depression place importance on attributional processes (see Kovacs, 1980).

ATTRIBUTION THEORY

Attribution theory rests on the philosophical positions of Hume and Kant, who asserted that causes cannot be observed, but are constructed by the perceiver to render the environment more meaningful. In this sense they are psychologically determined. Attribution theorists have addressed themselves to the question of how causes are attributed to different events. The general events most studied by attribution theorists have been success and failure in achievement-related tasks (Weiner, 1972).

Weiner and his colleagues (Weiner, 1972, 1974; Weiner et al., 1972) have argued that causal perceptions require two dimensions of explanation. One of these dimensions comes from the social learning theory of Rotter (Rotter, 1966; Rotter et al., 1962). This dimension is the locus of control, or internal–external dimension. According to this theory, causality is attributed either to internal factors (self) or external factors (the world). Those that adhere to the locus of control dimension of causality argue that expectancy and the persistence of behavior depend on whether the individual perceives an event as being internally controlled (by self) or externally controlled (by others or the world). Perceptions of internal control produce high persistence; perceptions of external control produce low persistence.

Attribution theory, on the other hand, argues that it is a stable–unstable dimension that best explains expectancy change and behavioral persistence. If the individual perceives the cause of success or failure as due to stable factors, then the same outcome can be expected in the future, and persistence is determined accordingly. If the person perceives the causes of success or failure as due to unstable factors, then persistence may be high in the case of failure (tries harder, effort attribution), or low in the face of success (e.g., slot machine, luck attribution). The stable factors most investigated by attribution theorists have been ability and task difficulty. The unstable factors are effort and luck. The interaction between these two dimensions of perceived causality is shown in *Fig.* 4.1 (Weiner, 1972; Weiner et al., 1972).

	Internal	External
Stable	Ability (a)	Task difficulty (b)
Unstable	Effort (d)	Luck (c)

FIG. 4.1 Interaction between internal–external and stable–unstable dimensions of perceived causality.

These two dimensions have often been confounded in research. As Weiner (1972) points out: "In experiments conducted by the Rotter research group, ability and luck instructions are varied between experimental conditions. Thus, the effects of internal, stable attributions are compared with the consequences of external, unstable attributions. The two dimensions of causality are confounded [p. 397]."

The predictions of the two theories are different. With regard to depression it is the prediction of an attribution in quadrant (a) (internal–stable) in response to failure that is important. According to social learning theory, the perception that the event is internally controlled should generate high persistence. Attribution theory, however, would argue that since failure is attributed to a stable factor, the same outcome (failure) can be expected in the future, thus persistence is low. Although these issues are not straightforward, there is some evidence that the stable–unstable dimension is a better predictor of behavior persistence and expectancy change (Dweck, 1975; Weiner, 1972; Weiner et al., 1976).

Caution should be exercised in the consideration that these two dimensions are independent. For example, effort probably depends on the perception that the individual does have the basic ability, but needs to try harder. If the individual perceives that he does not have any ability, then there is really not much point in trying. Indeed to what extent is effort simply a measure of behavioral persistence? Similarly, for luck and task difficulty; luck attributions are more likely if the task is first perceived as being either unpredictable or difficult. Outcomes of tasks judged to be predictable and simple probably do not lend themselves to luck attributions. The interactions of these various attributions require further research. Such possible interactions between attributions would seem to carry significant implications for research using the Rotter (1966) internal–external scale. For example, an internal attribution of low ability may produce a high external score (I cannot control my environment because I

do not have the ability). These factors complicate interpretations of research using the internal–external scale (see Lefcourt, 1976).

Attribution Theory in Depression

Research into attribution processes, inspired by Seligman's (1975) theory,
has demonstrated that attributions are important variables, influencing
mood changes and performance decrements (Douglas & Anisman, 1975;
Dweck, 1975; Klein et al., 1976; Roth & Kubal, 1975; Tennen & Eller,
1977).

Weiner et al. (1978, 1979) provide evidence that different attributions, in
success and failure situations, can produce different affective reactions.
Weiner et al. (1978) presented students with a brief story that offered a
cause for a success or a failure, and asked them to rate the expected affective reaction. Most relevant to depression were the affective reactions given
to failure, according to different attributions. Weiner et al. (1978) found
that the most dominant affective reactions given to a lack of ability attribution for failure were incompetence and inadequacy. Stable effort (as opposed to unstable effort) seemed closely related to depression with the
affective reactions of hopeless, depressed, and disheartened. Similar negative affects were associated with internal attributions to personality factors
in the failure conditions. It may be that trying and failing, because of a
perceived personal deficit, are more depressing than not even bothering in
the first place.

In general, evidence suggests that depression is associated with internal
and not external attributions as the original learned helplessness model
predicted. Consequently, Abramson et al. (1978) have offered a reformulated model of depression. This model stresses three dimensions of
attributions: universal–personal, stable–unstable, and internal–external.
Abramson et al. suggest that when individuals find they are unable to
control desired outcomes, they seek causes for this state of affairs. The
severity and chronicity of depression are in part the result of the perceived
cause for not being able to control desired outcomes. Internal, personal,
stable attributions will lead the individual to believe that the failure to
control an outcome is due to deficits within himself and that (because of a
stability attribution) the same state of affairs will remain in the future. In
this way the chosen dimension of attribution will lead to both a fall in
self-esteem and a hopeless view of the future.

This reformulated model is thus a two-stage model. First, individuals
must become aware of a response-outcome incongruency; depression will
then result if the individual blames himself for his helplessness and sees the
situation as unchangeable (stable). It is suggested that depressed
individuals make more global, stable, internal attributions.

Seligman et al. (1979) demonstrated that depressed college students do tend to attribute negative outcomes to more internal, stable, and global causes than nondepressed students. Garber & Hollen (1980) further demonstrated that the attributions of depressed college students relate to personally relevant variables rather than universal variables. In other words, depressed students tend to see themselves as less able to control outcomes, but do not view the outcomes themselves as uncontrollable. This is important for, in the original learned helplessness theory (Seligman, 1975), it was the perceived uncontrollability of events themselves that produced depression. Now, however (though this view accounted for the animal data), it is abandoned in favor of personal attributions, which animals do not have. Garber & Hollon suggest that their data support both Abramson et al.'s reformulation model and Bandura's (1977) distinction of personal efficacy expectations and outcome expectations.

Comment on the Learned Helplessness Model

The learned helplessness theory has opened new territories for exploration, including biochemical ones (see Chapter 5). Because, we assume, animals do not make internal attributions for a lack of control, it is not entirely clear whether internal constraints on coping produce the same biological disturbances as external constraints.

As it stands, the learned helplessness model pays little regard to attitudes, e.g., "I should be hard working," "I must be loved," etc. As with Beck's model, the role of anger in depression is also not discussed, yet for some theories (e.g., psychoanalytic) anger is a central component of certain depressions. Other difficulties exist concerning the role of real-life events and the role of social support systems in inhibiting or invoking a depressive episode. The question of pre-episode vulnerability is not discussed. It is also unclear whether the internal attributions of the depressive are associated with mood change or actually cause it. Hence, there is dispute over whether the cognitive aspects of the learned helplessness model provide a systematic theory in their own right, or whether they are one aspect of a more comprehensive model (e.g., Beck, 1976; Kovacs, 1980). There seems to have been very little in the way of practical therapy, flowing from the model, in spite of the mass of theoretical and experimental papers.

There is an area of theory and research which might help with some of these problems; this is achievement theory. Achievement theory suggests that attributional style may be learned in response to achievement needs. As we shall see in the following section, individuals who aspire to high standards as a means of obtaining social approval also tend to self-blame for failure. These data allow an important link to be made between attitudes and attributions. Although children may learn to blame self for failure in response to being labeled as having bad attributes for failure, this learning may also take place in response to rigid efforts to obtain social approval and reinforcement. Self-blame protects the agents of reinforcement from criticism and reduces the chances of rejection.

ACHIEVEMENT AND FAILURE

Although attributions may vary with mood state, it is also the case that attributions can reflect underlying motivation and attitudinal predispositions. Weiner (1972) summarizes some of the work on achievement motivation and points out that:

Individuals differing in level of achievement needs differ in their dispositions to allocate causation to these (task difficulty, luck, effort, ability) factors. Persons high in achievement needs ascribe success to high ability and high effort, and ascribe failure to lack of effort. Persons low in achievement needs, on the other hand, relatively attribute success to external factors and failure to a lack of ability. These causal dispositions, in turn, mediate between achievement tasks and the final achievement-related responses of approach behaviour, intensity of performance, persistence of action, and risk preference [p. 417].

In general, the low-need achiever is believed to have a stronger motivation to avoid the aversive consequences of failure than to approach the positive consequences of success. Although considerable confusion exists over the actual measurement of achievement motivation (Birney et al., 1969; Peck & Whitlow, 1975; Weiner, 1972; Weinstein, 1969), this perspective, nevertheless, has significant implications. It suggests that individuals will make different attributions for failure depending upon their motivation to approach success or avoid failure. Although it might be assumed that the latter individual is fearful of failure, we need to move beyond this possibility and ask why failure is feared.

McClelland et al. (1953) furnish some insight into this question. They suggest a distinction between need achievers and value achievers. The high-need achiever is the individual whose behavior is determined by internal standards. Such individuals prefer moderate risks and are relatively independent of social or authoritarian influences. Value achievers, on the other hand, overtly avow to high standards, but these may be unrelated to actual performance and are significantly influenced and guided by social approval and expectations of social approval. McClelland et al. speculated that value achievers develop in response to: "... authoritarian pressure from parents to be ambitious and the resultant motive which has originated in external sources shows itself as a fear of being unsuccessful [p. 419]."

This points up possible links between high (ideal) standard setting—value achievement motivation—and consequences for styles of attribution in failure situations. Clearly, each of these is an enormously complex issue. Nevertheless, the fact should be underlined that much of the anxiety of the value achiever is related to a rigid view of the contingency of success and social reinforcement. No success results in no love or affection from others (in Jung's terms, the individual is persona dominated). This undoubtedly is learned in childhood, though various influences (peer-group relationships) may be expected to dilute its rigidity. Nevertheless, a tendency to regard success as necessary to maintain social reinforcement can significantly influence cognitive and behavior systems. As Birney et al. (1969) point out, fear of failure, be it a personality trait or situation specific, will tend to increase arousal and attentiveness to failure cues. Before failure actually occurs, individuals who fear it, but see it coming, can engage in a variety of behaviours that will reduce its impact. They may withdraw, cheat, increase their effort, and because it is the loss of social reinforcement that is feared, they may self-demean, seeking sympathy for failure rather than rejection. The implications of each coping strategy will be different. Depressives, for example, may not be able to cheat because of internal (moral) restraints which would act to lower self-esteem in a cheating situation. Fearing failure, but without an internal system that rules out cheating, may allow individuals to engage in all sorts of behaviors to stop their perceived failures, personal or otherwise, being found out—we may note such behaviors in the behavior disorders.

While we must be aware of oversimplification, it does seem that fear of failure, related to a withdrawal of social reinforcement, may have much to do with psychopathology. For example, Sadd et al. (1978) factor-analyzed objective measures of fear of failure and fear of success. They found that a factor related to fear of failure (self-depreciation and insecurity—relating to failure to live up to internal standards, unassertiveness, and self-consciousness) was significantly correlated with a number of psychological symptoms. These included feeling low in energy, feelings of guilt and worthlessness, difficulty in making decisions, trouble concentrating, plus a number of others.

In relation to fear of failure and psychopathology, Gilbert (1980) found an anxious patient group and a depressed patient group to have significantly higher fear of failure scores than a normal control group. In a subsequent experiment Gilbert (1980) sampled a normal population (n = 119) with the success–failure inventory (McReynolds & Guevara, 1967). The lowest 16 consenting scorers (high fear of failure) and the highest 18 consenting scorers (low fear of failure) were compared on a number of measures. The extremes of the distribution were compared because, as McReynolds & Guevara point out, this scale measures relative dispositions rather than absolute states. The experiment included an investigation of a number o psychophysiological variables which will not be reported here. However on pencil and paper measures a number of differences were observed; thes are briefly presented in *Table* 4.1. (There was no significant difference i age or sex distribution of the groups.)

TABLE 4.1
Difference between High and Low Fear of Failure Motivated Subjects

Measures	Low Fear of Failure	High Fear of Failure	P
Beck Depression	0.7	6	P>0.00
Inventory	(1.16)	(5.9)	
(Beck et al., 1961)			
General Anxiety	2.83	7.25	P>0.00
(Sarason, 1972)	(1.72)	(4.17)	
Locus of Control	7.61	11.56	P>0.05
(Rotter, 1966)	(4.2)	(4.6)	
Negative Thinking	29.67	45.37	P>0.00
(Weintraub et al., 1974)	(5.9)	(14.15)	

The relationships between attribution processes, achievement motiv ation, and behavior and affect are interactive and complex. Many theorist have examined different aspects of these relationships. For example, high achievement striving of the (pre)depressive is noted by ego-analysts (Ariet & Bemporad, 1980a; Becker, 1960, 1974; Cohen et al., 1954; deCharms e al., 1955). Bibring (1953) and Beck (1976) outline how depressives adop unrealistic standards (shoulds, oughts, musts). As discussed, such striving noted for the value achiever, is associated with the tendency to make inter nal, personal attributions for failure. Such attributions are associated with depression (Abramson et al., 1978; Beck, 1974a). Moreover, as Katkin e al. (1966) found, depressives are often conformist in their behavior. The suggest that social conformity has secondary reinforcing properties since i has been previously associated with security and acceptance.

Taken together, the foregoing suggests that the (pre)depressive has a systematized set of rules (beliefs) which conveys information regarding the requirements for stable relationships with others. In general terms, these rules say "be successful or risk rejection." As it is fear of rejection that is a stake, others cannot be blamed for failure, because that also risks rejection. It also follows that because so much activity (covert and overt) is concerned with success "in order to secure stable attachments," such individuals are likely to be highly sensitive and dependent on external sources of comfort, security, and reassurance.

To explain why fear of failure can activate biological disturbance re quires recognition of the fact that attachment behavior is an evolved predisposition. As such, it is concerned with survival. Hence, threats to an individual's perceived capacity to secure positive reinforcement from others (love, care, comfort) can, in complex ways (see Chapter 6), be interpreted by the brain as a threat to survival. In Jungian terms, because so much of the psyche is dominated by persona function, threat to the persona is devastating, because the other aspects of the psyche are underdeveloped. In behavioral terms, threat to the capacity to secure positive reinforcement is devastating, because of a lack of alternative adjustment behaviors.

This sad state of affairs, most theorists believe, arises from the early learning history. Most probably, there has been a tendency to reinforce a child's results and not his efforts. As a consequence, an individual may know what behaviors are necessary to secure love and comfort, but not how to appropriately set about securing them. If parents reinforce effort they will, in the process, reinforce many component skills, for example breaking problems down, coping with frustrations and failing, working at long- and short-term solutions. Without such reinforcement, it may be a matter of luck whether these skills are learned. Not surprisingly, therefore, that psychiatric patients have poor coping skills (D'Zurilla & Goldfried, 1971) and poor self-efficacy expectations (Bandura, 1977).

SELF-ESTEEM AND DEPRESSION

Self-esteem remains a central concern for most theories of depression (Beck, 1976; Bibring, 1953; Brown & Harris, 1978a; Freud, 1917; Raimy, 1975). Becker (1979) offers an excellent review of the many theories that regard low self-esteem as a central vulnerability factor in depression.

In general terms, self-esteem develops according to an interaction between a child and significant others. Experiences that consistently lead the child to think badly of himself or to be labeled by others as having bad attributes lay the foundations for the development of negative self-schemata. Holt (1969) points out this aspect well:

> Note the danger of using a child's concept of himself to get him to do good work. We say, "You are the kind of sensible, smart, good, etc. etc. boy or girl who can easily do this problem if you try." But if the work fails, so does the concept. If he can't do the problem, no matter how hard he tries, then, clearly, he is not sensible, smart, or good.
>
> If children worry so much about failure, might it not be because they rate success too highly and depend on it too much [p. 55].

Holt goes on to suggest that most strategies that children use in school are self-protective, to avoid embarrassment, disapproval, and loss of status.

Gibby & Gibby (1967) found that induced failure in children resulted in a lowering of the self-estimate and an expectation that others (teachers and parents) would think less highly of them. It is a sad reflection of our society that, increasingly, children are driven to suicide by the stresses of having to succeed, perceptions of failure, and a consequent loss of self-worth.

Self-esteem also depends on the capacity to acknowledge strengths, regardless of success. This requires an awareness of competencies beyond immediate outcomes to specific events. It depends on having had the opportunity to become aware and develop such capacities. Maternal overprotection may be one process which inhibits this learning (Blatt et al., 1979; Parker & Lipscombe, 1981). Overprotective parents are less able to tolerate independent or aggressive behavior, are insensitive to the child's needs, and are overly intrusive. As Coopersmith (1967) found, high self-esteem children (10–12-year-olds) tend to have high self-esteem parents, who are capable of showing warmth and acceptance with the capacity to help their children set clear limits to their behavior. Low self-esteem parents, however, are more likely to have low self-esteem children.

The concept of self-esteem remains a multifaceted issue. Jung believed in a spiritual process, where the self emerges from the resolution of archetypal activity and conflicts. In this sense, "the self" may have little direct relationship to "self-esteem" which is more of an ego–persona relationship. Ellis (1977a) has pointed out that self-esteem and self-acceptance are different. Self-esteem depends more on social approval, whereas self-acceptance lives comparatively independently of such approval. Crook (1980), in his excellent book on the evolution of human consciousness, proposes that self-esteem is an evolved capacity for the organization of information about self in relation to others. As an evolved capacity it is related to perceptions of social status in dominance–submissive interactions. The notion that the self-concept is totally based on learning is further disputed by Kagan (1982). He has shown that biological maturity plays a significant role. This also points to an inherited predisposition to acquire information about self in relation to others.

In the depressive context, self-esteem cannot be divorced from the individual's perception of self in relationship to others. This makes it an essentially social interactive mechanism. A perception of low self-esteem always conveys a perception of the individual's relative standing in relationship to significant others. It is this aspect which links self-esteem so closely to the depressive experience. It also allows for individuals to have high self-esteem when things are going well, but to experience catastrophic falls in self-esteem when they do not. A self-esteem based on the success of the persona alone is vulnerable indeed!

CONCLUDING COMMENTS

The strength of the cognitive theory lies in its semistructured approach to therapy. It has developed important techniques for: (1) the monitoring of automatic thoughts; (2) problem solving; and (3) the development of skills for generating alternative perceptions of difficulties. In regard to the therapy, the approach has been a landmark.

As to the theory, however, a number of issues remain controversial. First, to what extent are cognitive schemata and distortions associated with depression and to what extent are they causal? Lewinsohn et al. (1981) studied a community population of 998 over one year. Three hypotheses were investigated: (1) depressive cognitions are antecedent to depression; (2) depressive cognitions are a consequence of depression; (3) recovery from depression leaves residual negative cognitions. In general, their evidence suggests that it is impossible to detect a depressive style, prior to becoming depressed, but negative cognitions certainly accompany depression. Although not necessarily related to etiology, depressive cognitions may make recovery more difficult. For example, negative cognitions may inhibit the abandonment of unrealistic incentives (Klinger, 1977), which in turn inhibits the possibility of recovery and maintains the individual in a high state of unresolvable stress. Thus, negative cognitions may play different roles in etiology and recovery. This issue is complex, for it may be that new learning takes place in the actual depressed state. In other words, if, when depressed, an individual finds himself abandoned or rejected by others, this experience itself may produce considerable self-doubts about his capacity to maintain relationships. Hence, events taking place during the course of a depression may be of some importance to recovery, especially if a depression lingers on in a mild chronic form.

Secondly, some of the psychoanalytic concepts of depression are not examined by cognitive theory, especially the role of the unconscious and the role of anger. Separation anxiety, and anxiety in general, do not find much attention. Ryle (1982) has introduced some psychoanalytic ideas within a cognitive, information-processing framework (see also Erdelyi & Goldberg, 1979).

Thirdly, cognitive theory may pay too much attention to the internal world of the individual at the expense of an environmental contribution. Recent evidence suggests that up to one-third of neurotic disorders respond to changes in the environment (Tennant et al., 1981a). The social aspects of depression as they relate to attachment needs and possible difficulties in mourning, and the lack of adequate care giving early in life (Bowlby, 1980), could be examined more fully by cognitive theory.

Fourthly, the suggestion that the themes of the depressive appraisal system are similar across subtypes may hide real differences between subtypes. For example, Shaw et al. (1979) examined the factor structure of the Beck Depression Inventory (BDI) from depressed heroin addicts. They found that the structure from depressed addicts was similar to that from nonaddicted, depressed patients. These data suggest that the BDI, as a measuring instrument, may hide real differences between patient groups.

In my efforts to use cognitive therapy, I have found the technique of some help with a few depressed schizophrenics, especially those with a tendency toward high self-blame and negative thinking. Although these patients were not "cured," they suggested that they obtained some relief in alleviating their tendency toward high, internally generated arousal. It is of some interest that "the voices" heard outside of themselves said much the same thing as the negative internal dialog of the depressive, e.g., "You're no good," "You're useless," "You should be punished." It is unknown why the schizophrenic (or more correctly the schizoaffective patient) should hear the voices outside while the true depressive carries on the dialog inside. At this stage insufficient work has been done to know how effective cognitive techniques may be with these patients. This issue is raised to highlight the fact that the therapy may be a much stronger element to the approach than the theory.

It is because of the importance of the therapeutic approach and framework of the cognitive model, that I have attempted to offer psycho-biological suggestions which may strengthen the theory behind the therapy. This issue is examined in Chapter 6. The central elements of this approach rest on the proposal that the cognitive factors outlined in this chapter act as amplifiers for various psychobiological response patterns. In their amplified state, cognitive and biological changes feed each other.

Taken as a whole, the cognitive theory is at its strongest when it is seen as a model that points up the internal rules individuals use to predict outcomes and plan behavior in an interpersonal world. Basically, the rules that are manifest in the depressive suggest a personal failure to do what is necessary to be entitled to, and secure, the social reinforcements of love, care, and comfort from other members of the species.

5

Psycho-neurochemical
Approaches

Freud believed that, eventually, the physiochemical correlates of psychological processes would be described. Although he was hindered in his efforts by the lack of knowledge in the neurosciences, such a claim cannot be made today. Indeed, if anything there is too much information, and we are constantly amazed by the complexity of brain processes. Consequently, psychobiology has faced major difficulties. Beliefs regarding reductionism, disease entities, mind–body dualism, and even spiritual questions, have lurked behind the arguments on psychobiology. Nevertheless, efforts are being made to accept Freud's general challenge, to develop models of pathology which can give due regard to both the psychology of man and the biological basis of suffering (Akiskal & McKinney, 1973b, 1975). That this is a difficult endeavor is echoed in Schwartz's (1978) claim that, today, psychobiology is something of a revolutionary approach.

The great challenge for psychology and psychiatry lies in the development of a scientific approach that can mark clearly the bridges of psychological–biological interactions. To answer the question: How can nonphysical events, which neither injure directly, nor infect, cause such havoc in the central nervous system?—mind–body dualism and disease entity issues are put on one side. This is not to deny their importance, but to suggest that they overcomplicate what is already a complex area.

Depression is especially relevant to psychobiology, for it is clear that many depressions are not independent of psychogenic factors, and yet some of the biological dysfunctions of the disorder are well recorded. The approach to the biological concomitants of depression taken here is determined by behavioral biology. It is suggested that the biological changes that occur in depression are one set of factors in a complex matrix of factors. Moreover, the interdependence of the structure of the matrix makes selection of one group of factors as etiological agents arbitrary. In other words, it is not particularly helpful, at a macro-level, to view the causes of depression as due only to cognitive changes, or only to biological changes. Rather, these factors are locked together in complex relationships, and it is the change of the whole person, determined by the relationship of factors within the person, which provides the most useful conceptualization of depression. In this way we are led to a view that depression constitutes a change in "brain state," and that this change in brain state is determined by the cognitive-behavioral-biological relationships of that individual.

Before considering further the idea of "the depressed brain state," attention is given to some of the biological changes associated with depression. This is too large a task to be in any way comprehensive and, therefore, the biology of depression is discussed only in so far as it furnishes the materials by which we can begin to build psychobiological bridges.

NEUROCHEMICAL ASPECTS OF DEPRESSION

The biological concomitants of depression are exceedingly complex, and the brief discussion which follows is only sufficient to allow a reasonable linking of biological and psychological data. Present-day neuroscience is expanding at a tremendous rate and many of the issues touched on are very complex. The reader who is interested in, but not familiar with, either the basic processes of neurotransmitter synthesis, release, and control, or the neurochemistry of receptor changes, may wish to consult Iversen's (1979) excellent paper on neurochemistry before commencing this section. Iversen & Iversen (1975) and Cotman & McGaugh (1980) also provide excellent texts on neuroscience issues. For those interested in the complexity of biological changes associated with depression, Maas et al. (1980) provide a good review, which is well referenced. Anisman & Lapierre (1981) also provide a good review of biological changes associated with depression. In this chapter a very brief review of some of the neurochemical changes associated with depression is presented.

During the late 1950s and early 1960s there was a gradual accumulation of evidence which suggested a link between mood disorder (mania and depression) and the availability of the catecholamines, noradrenaline (NA) (norepinephrine [NE] in the USA), dopamine (DA), and the indole-amine 5-hydroxytryptamine (5-HT) in the central nervous system. (NA, DA, and 5-HT are known collectively as the monoamines.) The evidence was largely indirect and rested on observations from the use of the drugs reserpine and iproniazid. There are a number of excellent reviews of the monoamine theories of depression (Anisman & Lapierre, 1981; Baldessarini, 1975; Bunney & Davis, 1965; Coppen, 1967; Iversen & Iversen, 1975; Schildkraut, 1965, 1975).

Reserpine, used in the treatment of hypertension, was reported to produce a disorder resembling endogenous depression in 10–15% of patients so treated. Reserpine depletes the brain of NA, DA, and 5-HT. Conversely, iproniazid, used in the treatment of tuberculosis, was reported to have mood-elevating properties. This drug increases the availability of NA, DA, and 5-HT in the central nervous system. The original catecholamine hypothesis of depression thus postulated that depression was associated with central catecholamine depletion and mania with central catecholamine elevation. Prange et al. (1974) suggested that a reduction in 5-HT may be common to both depression and mania, with the catecholamines determining the type of mood disorder.

Development of, and animal work with, the antidepressant drugs both reflected and helped to develop this basic hypothesis. The two major groups of antidepressant drugs, the monoamine-oxidase inhibitors (MAOIs) and the tricyclic compounds, both change catecholamine and indole-amine synaptic mechanisms (Coppen, 1967; Iversen & Iversen, 1975). Theoretically, however, a rise in the storage level of these amines, as produced by MAOI treatment, does not necessarily imply that, in response to nerve activity, more transmitter is automatically released, though this remains a plausible explanation (Iversen & Iversen, 1975).

With the development of histochemical fluorescence, adapted for use in the central nervous system by Dahlström & Fuxe (1964), it became possible to map monoaminergic pathways in the brain. A major observation from the use of this technique showed that the "reward areas" (Olds & Milner, 1954), especially in the region of the lateral hypothalamus, coincided with the major bulk of noradrenaline tracts. The "reward areas" received their name from the finding that direct electrical stimulation of various parts of the limbic system and extrapyramidal system was found to be innately rewarding (Milner, 1971; Olds & Milner, 1954), the best results being obtained from the medial forebrain bundle (MFB). In contrast to these areas is the periventricular system. This appears to be the anatomical substrate of punishment, for which 5-HT and acetylcholine (ACh) may play a significant role.

Over the past 20 years, research has demonstrated that the functional integrity of the reward system depends on appropriate noradrenergic and possibly dopaminergic activity. A number of reviews of this work already exist and need not be further discussed here (Crow, 1973; Lipton, 1972; Stein, 1968, 1972; Synder, 1975).

The 5-HT hypothesis of depression has had a varied history (Eccleston, 1981). Burns & Mendels (1979) and Anisman & Lapierre (1981) offer good reviews of the possible role of this neurotransmitter in depression. It seems quite likely that some depressions may be better understood as 5-HT-mediated disorders (Maas, 1975). Unfortunately, the role of 5-HT in the area of psychobiology that will be examined shortly (changes in coping behavior) is far less clear than it is for changes in the NA, DA, and ACh. Consequently, it is necessary to note the probable importance of 5-HT in at least some depressions, while at the same time recognizing that its role in adaptive coping is, as yet, less clearly worked out. Mandell (1979) points out that 5-HT has been implicated in many behavioral and physiological changes associated with depression, including temperature and appetite regulation, aggression, sleep, and others. His paper provides an interesting synthesis of much of the biological concomitants of depression and he places some importance on 5-HT mediation of mood change.

The Acetylcholine Hypothesis of Depression

The monoamines have enjoyed a monopoly of the research conducted on neurotransmitter changes in depression. However, Janowsky et al. (1972) also proposed a role for ACh. They postulated that under normal circumstances an equilibrium is maintained between the activity of ACh systems and noradrenergic systems. In depression there is a disruption in this equilibrium in favor of cholinergic dominance, while in mania the disruption shifts to a noradrenergic dominance. This hypothesis derives some support from experimental evidence which has demonstrated an antagonistic relationship between NA and ACh in certain brain areas (Glisson et al., 1972, 1974; Karczman, 1975). Indeed, some neurochemical research has attempted to map antagonistic interactions between neurotransmitter systems in some brain areas (e.g., Perez De La Mora & Fuxe, 1977). Much of this work has been reviewed elsewhere (Karczman, 1975, 1976; Roth & Bunney, 1976). There are a growing number of studies which provide evidence for the view that neurotransmitter activity depends on a complex process of interaction, and that different areas of the brain function according to the outcome of these complex interactions (e.g., Antelman & Caggiula, 1977; Eccleston, 1981; Harrison-Read, 1981). Such data add theoretical feasibility to Janowsky et al.'s (1972) view of depression, and to various ideas that the substrates of depression are best understood by consideration of neurotransmitter interactions.

Clinically, Janowsky et al. (1973) demonstrated that manic symptoms could be alleviated by the use of drugs (e.g., physostigmine) whose main mode of action is to facilitate ACh activity. With regard to depression, Gershon & Shaw (1961) reported an increased incidence of depression in patients who had been poisoned by organophosphate cholinesterase inhibitor insecticides. Further evidence of the role of ACh in depression comes from observations that many of the anti-parkinsonian agents, which are used for their atropinelike effects, have mood-elevating properties (Janowsky et al., 1972; Loudon, 1977). In the same vein, it is also interesting to note an observation by Hollister et al. (1964), who used atropine as a placebo control in a comparison study of amitriptyline and imipramine. They reported that although each drug was superior to the control treatment in some respect, most differences were small and inconsistent. In a later study Hollister et al. (1966) found that, in a group of depressed patients, a period of treatment with atropine as a preliminary screening procedure resulted in the loss of half the potential sample. Clearly the use of atropine as a placebo can be criticized (see Becker, 1974). For Janowsky et al.'s hypothesis, these observations, together with the use of atropine in depression, add some additional support to their theory.

Recent evidence from various sources also points to the possible importance of ACh in depression:

1. Carroll et al. (1978) investigated the role of ACh in dexamethasone suppression. Using normal subjects they found evidence supporting the view that hyperfunction of a muscarinic, cholinergic system may play an important role in the early escape from dexamethasone noted for endogenously depressed subjects (Carroll et al., 1981).

2. McCarley (1982) suggested that REM sleep and some depressive phenomena may be mediated by the same neurobiological control mechanisms. He proposes a reciprocal interactional model between ACh and the monoamines NA and 5-HT. He suggests that increases in ACh promote both REM sleep and some depressive phenomena. Increases in the monoamines in the brain stem suppress REM sleep and depression. This model has been shown to have some validity (Sitaram et al., 1982). Furthermore, these data may be used as a test for cholinergic hypersensitivity in depression-prone subjects.

3. Although it has been reported that physostigmine does not produce mood change (Davis et al., 1976), recent evidence from a different experimental design suggests that under some conditions mood changes are produced with this drug (Risch et al., 1981).

At present the ACh hypersensitivity hypothesis of depression remains to be proved, although there is growing evidence to support it. Many interesting questions arise from the hypothesis. For example, clinical impression suggests that on recovery from depression, and in anxious depressed states, dreams may increase. Is it possible that increased REM density, mediated by ACh, is a physiological process to compensate for behavioral retardation? In other words, retarded depressives may show increase in REM density and latency. This question is important in view of the suggestion put forward later, that ACh mediates the inhibition of coping behavior and may be related to retarded (noncoping) behavior following inescapable shock. Finally, the question arises as to the wisdom of producing specific antidepressant drugs (e.g., those that work on the 5-HT system alone). Drugs without anticholinergic properties may be weaker for some patients, although there is as yet no evidence to support this view.

LIMITATIONS OF NEUROCHEMICAL THEORIES OF DEPRESSION

While the advent of antidepressant drugs has constituted a major advance in the treatment of depression, neurochemical theories of depression are significantly limited as explanations of depression in their own right. In the first instance, human subjects receiving biogenic amine-depleting drugs have not shown any significant tendency to develop true depressive disorders. Mendels & Frazer (1974) have presented a good review of both animal and human studies involving reserpine (which depletes the brain of NA, DA, and 5-HT), alpha-methyl-para-tyrosine (which depletes the brain of NA and DA but not 5-HT), and parachlorophenylalanine (which depletes the brain of 5-HT but not NA or DA). They concluded that there was little evidence to support the claim that biogenic amine depletion is a primary causal event in depression. They did, however, propose that depletion of the biogenic amines at specific sites in the brain may act as a secondary factor in depression, a view also taken by Akiskal & McKinney (1975). Some work has shown that complete destruction of NA pathways in newborn rats, by subcutaneous injection of 6-hydroxydopamine, produces no significant behavioral deficits (as measured on two-way active avoidance, activity, reactivity, and discrimination learning) in adult life, compared to normal controls (Isaacson et al., 1977). The implications of such findings for a theory of depression are, however, unclear.

The evidence that changes in ACh activity are a primary causal event in depression is also uncertain. Davis et al. (1976) examined affective and cognitive changes in a group of normal subjects given an intravenous administration of physostigmine. They reported that there was no significant difference in effect between this group and a saline control group. However, two physostigmine subjects did report depressed mood: a woman with a past history of premenstrual depression and a man who admitted to marijuana use. Physostigmine does produce side effects, sometimes referred to as the physostigmine syndrome, which include lethargy, loss of energy, and irritability, all of which are commonly observed in depression. However, the issue of whether ACh does have a direct effect on mood remains controversial (Davis et al., 1976; Risch et al., 1981; B. Weiss et al., 1976). As Mendels & Frazer point out, although drug-induced alterations in neurotransmitter systems can produce symptoms which resemble those of depression, true depressions following exposure to such drugs are rare. The more the consequent symptoms resemble true depression, the more likely is the individual to have a history of psychiatric disturbance. This suggests either a genetic vulnerability (most likely for bipolar patients and some unipolars) or a process of biological sensitization (see later sections). Interestingly, Hartmann & Keller-Teschke (1979) found that induced dopamine-β-hydroxylase inhibition in normal subjects produced a variety of changes in a psychopathological direction. Such studies indicate the complexity of neurochemical interactions, and intersubject response variability to the same neurochemical stressor.

It is also important to be aware that Maas (1979) has reviewed evidence that would support either a "too little" or a "too much" neurotransmitter hypothesis of the affective disorders. He makes clear that there is evidence for both positions, and suggests that it is the stability and integrated functioning of neurotransmitter systems that might offer the best neurochemical clue to understanding depression.

Some of these considerations (especially those relating to drug effects on nondepressed subjects) argue strongly in favor of there being some other significant factors, apart from changes in internal neurochemistry, which need to be present in the etiology of depression. These other factors may actually play some role in inducing neurochemical changes. As Schildkraut (1965) was aware some time ago, it is in the psychological functioning of the individual that these "other factors" may exist:

> Such hypothetical changes in catecholamine metabolism may be concept-ualised to be part of the pathophysiology of depression, although not necessarily of primary aetiological significance. Since the importance of psychological factors in the aetiology of at least some depressions is well established, investigations of the possible effects of psychological factors on catecholamine metabolism seems a most promising area for future research [p. 517].

In fact, the investigation of such psychological–biochemical interactions as may exist in depression has proved extremely difficult, especially in the human subject. Moreover, such an interactive approach has not been helped by classification difficulties relating to disease versus nondisease issues, and hence to conceptualizations of whether one type of depression is biological (psychosis) while others are regarded as nonbiological (neurosis) (see Chapter 1). Nevertheless, it is this area of investigation that presents the greatest challenge for psychiatry, and promises to offer important insights into depression.

Neurochemical Changes as Secondary Events

At a rather crude level the research on the biochemical correlates of depression seems to present the psychologist with a number of biological events that need to be explained. These include changes in monoamine metabolism, and possibly a change in ACh metabolism such that ACh activity increases. Essentially, we need to ask whether there is any evidence that these are secondary events. Although these neurochemical changes (monoamine and ACh) may appear as separate events because of the way neurotransmitter systems seem organized in the central nervous system, that is, in terms of mutual antagonism and interaction, they may share common etiologies. In other words, if it is shown that certain psychological events increase ACh activity, then it is possible that the same events may also produce changes in monoaminergic activity. Indeed, research examining manipulations of effective coping behavior on ACh activity and monoamine activity strongly supports the idea that differences in coping behavior may underlie both these neurochemical changes that take place in depression.

It is important to examine some of this research because it provides one possible link through which maladaptive coping behavior (and hence the various factors discussed in previous chapters) exerts a disturbing influence on internal neurochemistry.

The idea that neurochemical and other biological changes may be secondary events to psychogenic processes is not new. As mentioned earlier, Schildkraut was aware of this possibility during the early days of the monoamine hypothesis. It has also been known for some time that stress in animals can produce significant neurochemical changes. But "stress" has not been a specific enough concept to allow precise predictions of what neurochemical changes can be expected in response to what events. Separation stress, as investigated in infant monkeys, does appear to produce a variety of neurochemical changes similar to those associated with depression (McKinney, 1977). In addition, separation stress is physiologically very disruptive (Reite et al., 1981).

The emphasis of recent work, however, has not been on stress itself, but on the response(s) to it. There is a growing body of literature which demonstrates that coping with stressful events alters neurochemical pathways in a radically different manner to not coping with such events. Thus coping behavior and the controllability of stress have been shown to be critical factors determining stress → neurochemical change outcomes. There are various conceptual models for considering these data. Ursin (1980), in an activation theory, proposed that two types of activation can occur with stress. First, there is phasic activation which is short-lived with a specific profile-response pattern. This may be followed by longer-lasting tonic activation, which is more severe and biologically disruptive. The degree and severity of tonic activation depend critically on the effective coping responses of the individual. Failure to cope leads to a great propensity toward tonic activation.

Most of the neurochemical data which have accumulated on the consequences of coping or not coping with stress have arisen from animal experimentation. These data seem especially appropriate to consider because many of the neurochemical responses of a failure to cope (adaptively respond) parallel some of those associated with depression. Such work provides one possible bridge by which coping behavior (which may be cognitively mediated in the human subject) can produce neurochemical disruption. Over the next few sections some of this work is examined in more detail. As active avoidance is the most commonly manipulated coping response investigated, we start with a consideration of the interactions between ACh and active avoidance coping behavior, and look later at monoamine coping behavior interactions.

ACETYLCHOLINE ACTIVITY AND THE HIPPOCAMPUS

The role of ACh in active avoidance learning is of interest to psychologists for two main reasons. First, neurochemically the septum and hippocampal areas appear to be a focal point of the limbic ACh system (Lewis & Shute, 1967). Moreover, in the hippocampus itself, ACh appears to be the activating or excitatory neurotransmitter. NA terminals are also present (though more diffused) in the hippocampus and appear to inhibit hippocampal activity (Storm-Mathisen & Fonnum, 1972). However, there are a variety of neurotransmitter systems operative in the hippocampal system, including 5-HT and endorphin. Although the relationship between NA and ACh seems particularly interesting, other interactions are also likely to be of great importance.

Research has shown that drugs which block ACh activity (e.g., atropine) produce similar behavioral deficits to lesions to the septum and hippocampal areas (Carlton, 1969; Hington & Aprison, 1976).

The second reason why the role of ACh in active avoidance learning is of interest to psychologists is that, behaviorally, the septum and hippocampus appear to be important brain areas regulating inhibitory behavior. Lesions to these areas result in an animal which is deficient in the acquisition of passive avoidance, but facilitated in the acquisition of active avoidance. Deficits in extinction are also noted. In general, destruction of parts of these areas can produce animals who have difficulty withholding or inhibiting certain behavioral responses (Altman et al., 1973; Carlton, 1969; Gray, 1971, 1981; Milner, 1971). Gray (1971) has referred to these areas of the brain as the septo-hippocampal stop mechanism. He suggests this system is responsible for bringing punished behavior and unrewarded behavior to a halt. Altman et al. (1973) argue that: ". . . the hippocampus may be thought of as the focal point of a septal and a limbic loop exercising facilitatory influence on a central nervous braking system [p. 578]." These authors argue that the concept of braking, rather than inhibition, is a better term to describe hippocampal function, because the term "inhibition" implies an inactivated state, where as the term "braking" implies an unabated state of arousal which does not produce any effective behavior as long as the powerful brakes (controlled by the hippocampus) are applied. Drug studies (Carlton, 1969; Hington & Aprison, 1976) have shown the importance of ACh in the operation of this hippocampal braking system. Moreover, rats that have been bred to have high levels of brain ACh have been found to be significantly more inhibited in their behavior, and show deficits in the acquisition of active avoidance learning compared to controls (Buxton et al., 1976). Such results show that animals with high levels of brain ACh have a greater tendency to inhibit or "brake" certain behavioral responses. Such data incline to the view that ACh may be of some importance in the execution of certain types of coping behavior.

In view of these data, it can be speculatively argued that psychological events which produce an aroused, but inhibited, animal may activate the hippocampal braking system, which is mediated by an increase in ACh activity. If such a view is valid, it leads to the question of which psychological events produce an aroused but behaviorally inhibited animal. It is in the area of active avoidance learning that some of these psychological factors may be found.

The Hippocampus, Acetylcholine Activity, and Coping Behavior

The experimental manipulation which most commonly results in an aroused but inhibited animal is active avoidance learning. The reason for this lies very much in the demand characteristics of the experiment. Carlton (1969) explains why:

> Consider the kind of experiment in which the experimenter arranges things so that the animal can avoid shock. But it is a rare rat that knows how to avoid when the experiment starts; accordingly we may find substantial shock in-duced suppression of behavior, suppression of that very behavior that we want the animal to emit. From the rat's point of view, there is no way to cope with shock until the appropriate means of coping is learned. And the suppression consequent to the lack of coping behavior may preclude learn-ing how to cope. Accordingly, we expect many animals to fail to learn in many kinds of avoidance situations, as in fact they do. Those situations in which poor learning (or coping) occurs are those that reduce the chance of the animal's "catching on" to the programme contingency [pp. 308–309].

Carlton argues that the suppression (or inhibition) of behavior is due to some inhibitory hippocampal mechanism which "switches in" in the pres-ence of a traumatic event. However, coping behavior (active avoidance learning) can be facilitated by giving the animal ACh-blocking drugs, sug-gesting that it is acetylcholine which is responsible for behavioral inhibi-tion. The proposition that follows from this is that situations which expose an animal to an aversive event, but with reduced means of coping, should result in an aroused, but inhibited animal, that is, an animal deficient in learning and executing the required avoidance response. This inhibition of behavior may in part be mediated by an increase in ACh activity in the septo-hippocampal braking system. Preventing an animal from acquiring adaptive coping behavior when exposed to a stressful event should increase the probability of activating inhibitory centers (the septo-hippocampal system), resulting in an aroused but passive animal.

More recently, the role of the cholinergic system in active avoidance learning and coping behavior has been systematically investigated (for good reviews of this work see Anisman, 1978; Anisman et al., in press; Bignami & Michalek, 1978). As might be expected, the role of ACh in coping behavior is extremely complex and seems to exert a different influence from that of aminergic depletion (Anisman et al., in press). For example, ACh may have more to do with long(er)-term changes in coping behavior than short-term changes. If this is true, then this would produce a fascinating link-up with the idea that some depressives are cholinergically hypersensitive. It may imply that some depressives are biologically disadvantaged for dealing with stress over long periods of time. Hence chronic, long-lasting stress (e.g., marital conflict, high ego ideals, etc.) may be more disruptive than short-lived, acute stress. This may explain why some depressives can "rise" to a crisis, but get bogged down in coping with more chronic difficulties.

In most biological theories of depression changes in monoamine activity have been the main focus of interest. Consequently, the monoamines have also been prominent in research investigating neurochemical changes induced by coping behavior manipulations. The link between depression and induced neurochemical (monoaminergic) change arises from the original learned helplessness experiments and subsequent hypothesis on depression advanced by Seligman (1974, 1975). It is therefore useful to re-examine this hypothesis, and to see some of the neurochemical investigations that have been stimulated by the learned helplessness theory. As discussed in Chapter 4, Seligman has moved his theory along a more cognitive road. However, there are reasons why this is less than satisfactory. The development of the learned helplessness theory has already been discussed. It will be recalled that following inescapable trauma, animals show considerable deficits in subsequent avoidance learning. As we have seen, Seligman favors a learning explanation. Other researchers, stimulated by these observations, have suggested neurochemical explanations for such learning deficits. A crucial link between the data discussed in this chapter and earlier psychological chapters is the finding that a failure to cope with certain traumata opens up the possibility for the manifestation of a significantly disturbed neurochemical response system. Moreover, the observed neurochemical consequences of not coping are similar to those associated with depression.

It is reasonable to suggest, therefore, that as in the case of Carlton's rats the absence of an effective coping repertoire can result in an aroused bu behaviorally inhibited subject. The longer this noncoping state continues the greater are the chances of significant biological dysfunction occurring In this way we can see the importance of interactions of many psychogenic factors (outlined in earlier chapters) with neurochemical events. As al ready shown, many theorists place special emphasis on a lack of coping skills in the depressed patient, these having arisen from environmental constraints on learning various coping responses (e.g., to anger, frustra tion, loss of love, and so on; Ferster, 1974) and/or from specific styles of cognitively appraising personal coping effectiveness (Bandura, 1977; Beck 1967, 1976).

Let us therefore examine further the possible consequences of having no effective coping behavior for certain traumata.

THE ROLE OF NORADRENALINE IN COPING BEHAVIOR

One group of workers who have not accepted Seligman's learning explan ation of learned helplessness is Weiss and his colleagues in New York J. Weiss et al. (1976) reviewed a series of 12 experiments conducted by them over a number of years. What these experiments purport to show is that the phenomenon of learned helplessness may be mediated by physi ological and neurochemical changes.

In the original learned helplessness experiments, Overmier & Seligman (1967) reported that the learning deficits, resulting from exposure to in escapable shock, dissipated over 48 hours or so. Miller & Weiss (1969 argued that this dissipation effect is not at all common in most learning situations. Such an effect suggests that physiological variables mediate learned helplessness. J. Weiss et al. (1976) proposed the model shown in *Fig.* 5.1 to explain the development of learned helplessness.

This model explains that the failure to learn adaptive coping behavio following exposure to inescapable shock is due to biochemical disruption which impedes certain adaptive responses. In an early experiment, J. Weiss et al. (1970) found that animals who received inescapable shock had lowe levels of brain NA than animals who received exactly the same shocks while performing an avoidance escape response. A number of subsequent studie (J. Weiss et al., 1976) demonstrated this to be a consistent result and these researchers went on to investigate the neurochemical mechanisms that might underlie such changes. They also demonstrated that the administra

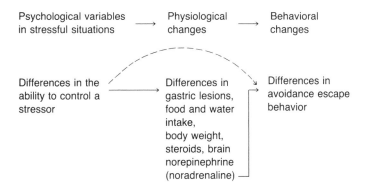

FIG. 5.1   The development of learned helplessness.

tion of an MAOI (pargyline) can protect against the development of learned helplessness. The hypothesis proposed by Weiss and his colleagues was that brain NA is important for the execution of certain motor activities. Stress, beyond the coping ability of the animal, produces central changes in catecholamine metabolism, notably NA depletion. This depletion in central NA produces a deficiency in the ability of the animal to perform the required motor responses necessary for active avoidance. It was suggested that the failure to respond appropriately to escapable shock, following pretreatment with inescapable shock, was due to a motor-activation deficit mediated by changes in NA.

Whether the motor-activation deficit hypothesis as proposed by Weiss et al. is accepted as an explanation of learned helplessness is something of a secondary issue here. The point is that Weiss and his colleagues demonstrated that severely limiting an animal's ability to cope with stress results in substantial metabolic changes.

Thus, manipulations of active avoidance learning procedures seem to produce two types of data:

1. A reduced ability to cope with stress can result in the animal inhibiting its behavior. This inhibition of behavior may reflect the activation of a hippocampal braking system which is significantly influenced by the neurochemical, ACh. ACh-blocking drugs will facilitate the acquisition of adaptive coping behavior. For example, Seligman (1975) reports a study in which atropine, injected directly into the septum of cats, dissipated learning deficits produced by inescapable shock.
2. A reduced ability to cope with stress results in a disruption in catecholamine metabolism. Such disruption may produce an animal unable to perform the necessary motor responses required for adaptive responding.

This fascinating work has been extensively extended by Anisman and his colleagues (Anisman, 1978; Anisman & Sklar, 1979; Anisman & Zacharko, 1982; Anisman et al., 1980a, 1980b; see also J. Weiss et al., 1979). Interest has focused on synthesis–utilization rates in specific brain areas. There is some evidence to suggest that in uncontrollable stress situations, utilization outruns synthesis, producing monoamine depletion. The processes are complex and may involve a number of mechanisms in the rate limiting steps of catecholamine production (e.g., changes in tyrosine hydroxylase, MAO, presynaptic receptor mechanisms, and so on).

Anisman and his colleagues have shown that various drugs which deplete monoamine stores can produce behavioral coping deficits similar to those associated with inescapable shock. Moreover, MAOIs tend to protect against the development of behavioral deficits associated with inescapable trauma.

Anisman (1978) has provided an excellent summary of the neurochemical changes associated with stress, and for conciseness and clarity this is reproduced in full. The following observations have been noted:

1. Moderate levels of stress tend not to affect the endogenous level of NE and 5-HT. Given that stress does result in faster disappearance of labeled NE and 5-HT, and since stress after enzyme inhibition results in greater reduction of NE and 5-HT, it is probable that stress increases both synthesis and release of NE and 5-HT.
2. Besides increased synthesis of amines, partial inhibition of MAO occurs, thereby preserving NE and 5-HT. The net effect of the increased synthesis of amines together with the MAO inhibition is that the demands of the organism are met. Indeed, with relatively mild stress, an initial increase of NE and 5-HT levels may be observed.
3. With intense stress, a decline in endogenous levels of NE and 5-HT is seen. Presumably, synthesis does not keep up with utilization. The effectiveness of NE released apparently is also reduced by increased reuptake of NE under these conditions.
4. With mild stress, DA, ACh, and 5-HT are unaffected. As the stress severity increases, ACh levels rise. While DA has been reported to decrease, the effect of stress on DA is considerably less pronounced than on NE neurons. The differential effects of stress on DA and 5-HT relative to NE might indicate that the former two systems have superior regulatory systems, thereby maintaining balance between synthesis and utilization of the neurochemical. [...]
5. Under conditions of stress, activity of anterior pituitary hormones increases, as do levels of plasma corticosterone.
6. Under conditions in which control over the stress is possible, whether this is considered in terms of actual escape/avoidance responding or coping by fighting, NE levels are not found to decline. Moreover, the source of degradation is also varied away from the side of COMT and toward MAO. Additional

reports also indicate that with controllable stress neither ACh nor cortico-sterone levels are affected.

7. The effect of stress on neurochemical activity varies as a function of the excitability of the organism and may vary as a function of the strain involved.

8. After repeated exposure to the stress, neurochemical adaptation may occur, i.e., NE and corticosterone levels, which might otherwise vary, remain constant after exposure to stress over a series of sessions.

9. Stimuli associated with stress may come to elicit neurochemical changes [pp. 159–160].

As Anisman makes clear, the coping responses to stress, that is, its controllability, is a crucial factor for determining neurochemical change. The observation is so consistent that its importance cannot be over-emphasized. Moreover, the reader is able to note that many of the psycho-logical processes discussed in earlier chapters may serve the function of reducing the coping ability of the individual. In such a situation neuro-chemical changes are possible. In this way we can see how psychogenic factors may actually produce a biological vulnerability.

Although the relationship between synthesis and utilization of the monoamines under stress conditions is complex, Anisman's summary of stress–neurochemical interactions raises some important points. It seems that under mild stress conditions, changes occur which allow demands to be met. It is possible that the perception of a viable coping option may be one condition which limits the intensity of stressful events (Lazarus, 1966). We might also consider these data in Klinger's (1975, 1977) terms and regard the neurochemical substrates of mild stress as providing the neurochemical basis for invigoration. If demands can still not be met, then disengagement may switch in as utilization begins to outrun synthesis. Unfortunately, for the depression-prone individual, during invigoration some incentives may have become so important that they cannot be aban-doned. For example, specific cognitive schemata relating to low self-esteem may make it exceedingly difficult for the individual to perceive any opportunities for developing new behaviors. A poverty of adjustment responses may have a similar effect. In relation to social aspects, the individual may be unable to perceive any hope of obtaining new rela-tionships, thus he clings to maladaptive relationships in maladaptive ways. But as Klinger (1977) observes, depression may well be a normal and natural process. Most of us at various times have to give up things of importance, be they aspirations or relationships. Disappointment and redirection are part of life.

The problem for depressives is that they often harbor deep desires to continue as before, and remain wedded to unrealistic pursuits and goals. Those goals then become almost magical; if only they can be obtained everything would be fine. The linking concept is that depressives may "maintain themselves" in high states of distress for which no coping behavior is viable. This pushes them further and further into a disturbed biological state. Recovery may only begin when the individual begins to truly mourn the lost goal or incentive and fully disengage.

The factors that may affect this capacity to mourn have been outlined by Bowlby (1980). Hence Bowlby's description of predisposition can be seen to produce biological vulnerability to the extent that it blocks the individual's adaptive capacity to engage and disengage from specific incentives (e.g., suitable attachment relationships). The point at which biological coping mechanisms begin to break down may lead to an intensification of the disturbance, heightening further the depressive's fears of abandonment and isolation.

ASPECTS OF BEHAVIORAL BIOLOGY

The previous sections were concerned with the idea that some of the neurochemical changes associated with depression could be secondary consequences to a failure in coping. Generally it is found that the controllability of a stress significantly influences the form and direction of a variety of neurochemical events. This work has major implications for a psychobiological approach to depression because it helps to trace psychological–biological interactions. However, such work should be seen in the context of a guiding light which focuses our thinking on such interactions, but should not be expected to provide a watertight theoretical model of depression.

In the discussion of classification problems of the affective disorders (see Chapter 1), the point was made that etiology, symptom presentation, and failure to recover may each have a separate set of factors upon which these phenomena depend. Let us therefore assume that lack of control over stress may be one etiological factor of depression. (This does not mean that lack of control is the most relevant etiological factor in depression, only that we will assume it to be a major one in order to develop a particular line of thinking.) If this assumption is allowed, then the important points to grasp are that: (1) the neurochemical consequences of a failure to cope with stress are varied; (2) similarities between the hypothalamic dysfunctions of depression and those following inescapable shock are noted; (3) inescapable shock produces changes in other NA pathways apart from hypothalamic ones. Following on from (3), we could ask whether some of the changes associated with inescapable shock, in pathways other than hypothalamic ones, are of any interest for a psychobiological theory of depression.

In order to answer this question we need to make a slight detour into behavioral biology. The reason for this will become clear as we proceed. The data of J. Weiss et al. (1979) show that, in addition to hypothalamic, hippocampal, and cortical NA changes, disruption of NA transmission in the brain stem is very marked following inescapable shock. As we will see, dysfunction of NA transmission in this brain area may turn out to be very relevant to factors relating to a failure of recovery from depression. It may also account for some variations in symptom presentation. In view of this hypothesis it is of interest to focus on the important NA pathway in the brainstem known as the dorsal bundle. (The dorsal bundle is one of three NA pathways in the brain; see Kostowski, 1980.)

The behavioral consequences of a disruption in the dorsal bundle have been well reviewed by Mason & Iversen (1979). Lesions to the dorsal bundle, with the neurotoxin 6-hydroxydopamine, produce significant deficits in an animal's ability to extinguish nonrewarded behavior. In their review, Mason & Iversen examine a number of possible theories to explain this finding. The theory which they suggest has most to offer to account for the behavioral data, may also provide some interesting insights for depression. Let us examine this theory step by step.

Mason & Iversen suggest that the learning theory best supported by the dorsal bundle lesion data is that of Sutherland & Mackintosh. Now these learning theorists have suggested that most learning is subject to the mechanisms of attention. For most learning to occur, the animal must learn (1) what cues in the environment are relevant, that is, which cues (stimuli) share an association with outcome; and (2) what behaviors to attach to them. Generally, the theory proposes that an animal has a matrix of stimulus analyzers (e.g., for color, size, shape, and so on), and learning occurs as one of these analyzers comes to provide predictable information about the experimental contingency. The complexities favoring such a theory of learning cannot be taken further here. However, the hypothesis that attentional mechanisms play an essential role in learning, and these mechanisms in turn may be dependent on the functional integrity of the NA dorsal bundle system, would seem to have clear implications for a theory of depression.

Mason & Iversen's review suggests the possibility that the resistance to extinction, following lesions of the NA dorsal bundle, may be due to an inability of the animal to switch analyzers. In other words, the animal is incapable of performing the necessary shifts and switches of attention to facilitate adaptive learning. Congruently, there appears to be an inability to filter out irrelevant information, because animals with such lesions have been shown to be easily distracted by various irrelevant cues in learning situations. By the same token, these data imply that the dorsal bundle may play an important role in orientating the animal to relevant stimuli—a necessary operation for learning.

The link between such data and depression may not seem clear. However, changes in brainstem NA (which includes the dorsal bundle) are pronounced following inescapable, but not escapable shock (J. Weiss et al., 1979). The possibility exists that the dorsal bundle noradrenergic pathway is very much influenced by the controllability of a stress. If these data offer a psychobiological link with depression, then we would expect depressives to show significant difficulty in attending to relevant cues for adaptive learning. Weingartner et al. (1981) have examined information-coding deficits in depressed patients. They found that depressed patients tended to use weak and incomplete encoding strategies. These strategies made information less easy to remember and thus (presumably) would place the depressed patient at a disadvantage when it comes to encoding information necessary for new learning. Although Weingartner et al. were interested in memory function in depressives, the possibility exists that in depression there may be some attentional deficit. This involves an inability to structure information in a way which enables ongoing data to be incorporated into new repertoires. Clearly, the ability to switch analyzers must depend on adequate processing so that the subject is able to use information acquired from previous trails. Thus, Weingartner et al.'s data are consistent with the possibility that depressives have attentional (and encoding) deficits, which make them unable to adequately process new information. These deficits may be partially mediated by dorsal bundle NA changes. Moreover, Weingartner et al. note that drug treatments which are believed to affect noradrenergic pathways have a restorative effect on encoding deficits in depressives. Add to this the clinical finding that some depressives are highly distractable (often by their own inner thoughts and feelings), and the link between dorsal bundle NA deficits and depression becomes fascinating. Thus, the depressed person may literally get stuck, cognitively and behaviorally, in a response set which is maladaptive, for he is unable to initiate the necessary cognitive-behavioral operations to get him out of his plight.

Such theorizing should not blind us to the fact that this is only one small part of the story. Changes in NA activity may, or may not, be highly localized in depression. In any case, neurochemical changes following inescapable shock occur in a variety of brain areas including the hippocampus, hypothalamus, and cortex (Anisman & Lapierre, 1981; Weiss et al., 1979). Moreover, hippocampal lesions also produce behavioral deficits on extinction tasks. If, however, we leave aside etiological considerations, and consider instead failure to recover, then perhaps the above data may furnish a clue as to how this distressing state gets "locked into" the individual's response system. Dorsal bundle noradrenergic changes may be one system which renders the individual unable to orientate (encode) environmental data adaptively. Other changes (e.g., in the medial forebrain bundle) may combine to produce a dysphoric state which is impervious to change.

Reversal of the functional deficit in NA transmission in the dorsal bundle (e.g., via drugs or, indeed, direct behavioral intervention) may unblock the attentional and encoding deficits, allowing more adaptive learning and response initiation to proceed, by facilitating more adaptive attention to relevant stimuli.

SEPARATION–ABANDONMENT

The evidence reviewed in this chapter so far suggests that a failure to control severe stress, which goes on over time or is repeated, is behaviorally and biologically very disruptive. Armed with this observation we need to consider what sorts of psychological event occur in the "natural environment"—events which are both stressful over time and uncontrollable. It is obviously the case that repeated electric shocks are not the cause of depression as it commonly presents. The natural psychological events capable of fulfilling these criteria are limited and point to an evolved dimension of functioning. The most obvious candidate which occurs naturally is separation–abandonment. In view of the biological disruption produced by uncontrollable traumata, separation stress may fit the requirement of being a naturally occurring uncontrollable trauma. There are a number of reasons to support this view:

1. Separation stress continues over time, i.e., it is stressful over the period the separation is operative and, dependent on the context (e.g., availability of alternative attachment objects), there is no escape from it.
2. It is physiologically (Reite et al., 1981) and neurochemically (McKinney, 1977) very disruptive.
3. In parallel with electric shock-induced uncontrollable stress, coping attempts following separation seem to have at least two components: invigoration–disengagement (Klinger, 1977), or protest–despair (Bowlby, 1980).

Indeed, the separation–abandonment model of depression has a long history (for a review see Mineka & Suomi, 1978). The separation model, however, has been criticized. For example, in his review of animal separation experiments, Colotla (1979) points out that various peer-group, social, and other behavioral disturbances are noted for isolates but, he suggests, "all in all, severe and prolonged clinical depression has not been a prominent characteristic result of Harlow's rearing experiments ... [p. 232]." Furthermore, various authors have questioned the adequacy of a separation model of depression, pointing out that even gross social deprivations do not automatically produce severe psychopathology (Clarke & Clarke,

1976), and that many factors (e.g., peer-group attachment opportunities) mediate between the experience of separation and subsequent pathology (Rutter, 1981).

In spite of these reservations, there are good grounds for regarding the dimension of separation–abandonment as being extremely important for understanding depression. These arise from an examination of patients' belief systems and major cognitive premises (see Chapter 6), and various animal experiments. Many of the symptoms produced in isolates mimic those of depression, including withdrawal, appetite change, sleep change, and various disturbed behaviors, e.g., rocking, hand clinging, etc. Klinger (1977) suggests that the first behaviors, following separation, are invigoration e.g., searching, agitation, distress calling. These are followed by disengagement behaviors—withdrawal, passivity, and disturbance in self-stimulatory behavior. Others describe these two components as protest–despair (Bowlby, 1980).

There have been a number of issues which have been examined by separation experiments: first, the degree to which severe separation–stress reactions are limited to mother–infant separations; secondly, the degree to which vulnerability to subsequent loss is subject to previous experiences, and the timing of these experiences.

In regard to the first issue, there is no doubt that infants separated from their mothers during the first year of life demonstrate considerable disturbance. (For some qualifications to this view see McKinney, 1977). It is also the case, however, that semiadult animals, with no previous history of separation, demonstrate depressivelike reactions to separation from peer-group and family members (Mineka & Suomi, 1978; Suomi et al., 1975). Hence, there is growing evidence that peer-group separation for adult social animals is also disruptive, and that the type of disruption is not limited to mother–infant separation. In regard to the issue of vulnerability, there is preliminary evidence that vulnerability to loss can be laid down by losses occurring in adult life. Rasmussen & Reite (1982) studied loss reactions in a female who, they suggest, had been sensitized to loss because of the death of her infant and a miscarriage of a subsequent infant. These researchers were able to demonstrate that depressivelike symptoms, following her miscarriage, responded to amitriptyline. Suomi et al. (1978) have also shown that disruptive behavior, produced by separation, could be reduced with imipramine. Rasmussen & Reite (1982) demonstrated further that depressivelike symptoms could be invoked when this female was separated from her closest companion in the group. Thus, adult–adult separation, involving a close relationship and in the presence of a vulnerability, can induce depressivelike symptoms. Rasmussen & Reite also highlight another extremely important point to their case. They suggest that:

Another characteristic shared by R30 and other depression-prone adult females is their low rank in their social groups. Social stresses on subordinate female monkeys in social groups may disrupt their reproductive system by means of heightened cortisol and prolactin levels [...]. It is possible that social stress and the attendant endocrinological changes may sensitize low-ranking individuals by lowering their threshold to a variety of other stressors. On a more cognitive level, subordinate animals may be especially vulnerable to depression because of their relative powerlessness in a social setting [...]. Of course, it is equally plausible that lower social rank may itself be a result of previous depressive-type reactions [p. 680].

The role of social rank and its relationship to separation–abandonment is of some significance. This is because, in addition to animal work, depressed individuals express very negative appraisals in regard to their social rank. They often see themselves as useless, bottom of the pile, lacking in social skills, and so on. It is also interesting to note that, as Rasmussen & Reite indicate, low ranks are limited in social opportunities. Most especially, rank is a very powerful inhibitor of aggression. These aspects are examined more fully in Chapter 6.

In spite of various difficulties to the interpretation of results, it is fair to suggest that separation stress is likely to be a naturally occurring psychological event which mimics uncontrollable stress (although this need not imply they are functionally equivalent). It should be added, however, that abandonment of social animals by their group is not only unpleasant, but is also related to survival. Hence, abandoned animals outside captivity often die. In the natural world, abandonment is a survival-related stress of the most crucial order. It is difficult to find any other, naturally occurring psychological stress which is so crucially important to social animals. To offer a thought for the next chapter, we can suggest that patients may find it difficult to disengage from certain incentives if, in doing so, they court the possibility of total abandonment (as they perceive it) by others. In these circumstances the brain may be "aware" that the chances of survival are low! As a consequence, the brain may activate various brain-state changes which have evolved as psychobiological response patterns to abandonment.

At the present time, the neurochemical changes associated with separation stress have not been investigated to the same degree as neurochemical changes associated with uncontrollable shock. This is partly because the rat is not so sensitive to separation as are the higher primates. Nevertheless, it is quite feasible that in so far as separation stress is uncontrollable, many of the neurochemical changes noted for uncontrollable shock are likely to be present for separation stress. Hence, all of the preceding analysis, in terms of having analyzers which have predictive value, holds for both uncontrollable shock and separation stress.

SENSITIZATION–CONDITIONING

So far it has been shown that uncontrollable stress is highly disruptive. Furthermore, we have seen that separation–abandonment sets in motion various changes which mimic both depression and the effects of uncontrollable trauma. Unlike uncontrollable shock, however, separation stress is even more uncontrollable in that it is present constantly, 24 hours per day, until some adaptation is made or the animal dies.

There is growing interest in the idea that depressive responses (both biological and behavioral) can be conditioned. For example, Mason & Iversen's (1979) review of dorsal bundle function may suggest that having analyzers which work, that is, point toward a coping response, significantly influences neurochemical change in response to stress. These researchers point to the finding that normally a loud auditory stimulus will inhibit most hippocampal cells. This response is antagonized by drugs affecting NA transmission. However, if such a stimulus is paired with food reward, the presentation of the stimulus actually has an excitatory effect on hippocampal cells. Here is a clear example where learning about a stimulus (i.e., whether it is a danger or a predictor of food) has a significant impact on neurochemical activity. The conditioning implications are clear.

It is not unreasonable to propose, therefore, that the neurochemical consequences of a stimulus event can be determined by its previous associations. It is already known that considerable conditioning of biological response patterns does take place in stress situations, especially those of the endocrine system (Brady, 1975). A recent review of the conditioning of physiological responses has been provided by Eikelboom & Stewart (1982). Such data open up the possibility that the ease by which some individuals seem to experience significant biological disruption, in response to stress, is the product of some sensitization or conditioning process. This possibility is further advanced by Anisman & Sklar's (1979) study, which found that the neurochemical depletions produced by inescapable shock are conditionable or, at least, open to a process of sensitization. Animals exposed to inescapable shock and allowed to recover (biologically) show a more rapid rate of depletion than controls, following a reintroduction of inescapable shock, or cues associated with it.

The possibility that a biological vulnerability to depression results from a process of learning is important. A notable and fascinating attempt at highlighting biological–psychological interactive processes in the development of vulnerability has been advanced by Meyersburg & Post (1979). They suggest that at critical stages in development, various stressors can occur which interfere with the healthy development of various (especially limbic) brain areas. Consequently, later in life, these central nervous system vulnerabilities can act in a way which is similar to a process of kindling in epilepsy. In other words, they act as destabilizers within the biological system, and exert a devastating impact on biological functioning when ignited by stressors later in life. Especially important is the notion that such vulnerability can be formed before adequate cognitive development for appraisal of stress has occurred. As a result, cognitive mediation of the pathological stress response is enormously difficult, since it was primed into the system without any sophisticated cognitive coding.

This notion is of some interest, since early Freudian and Kleinian views of vulnerability were criticized because they paid attention to essentially cognitive (fantasy) data, which many believed were totally outside the capabilities of the young infant. Meyersberg & Post, however, bypass the need for cognitive rationalization and point directly to the acquisition of a biological vulnerability. In this scheme of things cognitive appraisal is a *post hoc* process imposed on perceptions of high internal distress states.

The idea of a biological vulnerability to depression, which is the product of learning, may be advanced with a Pavlovian conditioning approach. Although classical conditioning theory is now highly complex (e.g., Pearce & Hall, 1980), there is evidence that at least some conditioned, biological responses can be understood with a Pavlovian model (Eikelboom & Stewart, 1982). One theory derived from Pavlov, which may have particular relevance for depression, has been advanced by Solomon (1980).

Solomon has offered a fascinating theory of how aversive motivational states can be conditioned. He suggests that for each motivational state there develops, in contrast to it, an opponent state. This opponent state becomes manifest when the CS or UCS controlling the first state is withdrawn. Solomon labels the first state an "A state" and the contrast, opponent state, as a "B state." In a simple experiment, Solomon provided a UCS (food) to sleeping babies who were not actually hungry. Allowing them to suck for one minute, and then withdrawing the UCS, resulted in crying and brief distress before the babies went back to sleep. Solomon suggested that the crying resulted from the development of an opponent motivational B state which built up during UCS presentation. This state was not manifest while the positive A state of feeding existed, but became so when feeding was terminated. Other experiments have demonstrated that the B state is conditionable and can be prolonged and intensified. In separation experiments the negative motivational state (characterized by distress calling and searching) could be prolonged and intensified by repeated separations.

The implications of Solomon's work are quite far reaching. They suggest that the intensity of distress states may be a conditioned phenomenon. It is possible to propose, therefore, that individuals with particular histories may find themselves experiencing prolonged, aversive motivational states in certain situations, especially those of rejection or loss. Moreover, these aversive states may actually be conditioned states. Solomon's work also suggests that it may not be the adversity of a stress per se that prolongs and intensifies the negative contrast states, but rather the repeated presentations and withdrawal of positive events. As he suggests, too much pleasure can have a physiological cost because there is always an aversive state which develops in contrast to the positive state. He points out that the physiological cost of too much pleasure is often overlooked by stress researchers.

It seems perfectly feasible that Solomon's classical conditioning paradigm has great potential for understanding the damaging effects of maternal overprotection. It suggests that overprotection may bear critically on the physiological dynamics of coping with rejection and frustration. In the first place, overprotection may place considerable limits on the capacity of the child to learn adaptive coping behavior. This is because the child is never allowed to be in control of its own distress and therefore learn (itself) adequate coping responses. From a classical conditioning point of view, this is quite serious for it may carry with it the possibility that negative B states are reinforced time and time again. To take Solomon's example a step further, we can envisage a situation where the transient distress of an infant continually prompts responding from the mother and in this way fails to allow negative emotional states to extinguish. However, the dynamics of exactly what distress to attend to are not easy to pinpoint. The work of Aniswworth and her colleagues has shown quite clearly that responsive mothers have babies who cry significantly less at one year, than unresponsive mothers. It seems likely, therefore, that the relationship between the distress signal(s) from the child and the mother's behavior is critically important, as well as competent judgments about what is and is not real distress. Since these arguments are speculative it would be unwise to carry them too far at this stage. Suffice it to say that Solomon's work may carry important implications for such considerations.

The idea that animals and humans learn specific biological patterns of responding to certain events is not very new. Indeed, this is the basis of all classical conditioning work, even before Pavlov. It is therefore rather remarkable that, outside of Wolpe's work, there is no clear classical conditioning theory of depression. Since Wolpe's work focuses on anxiety as the conditioning substrate, it may fail for those depressions in which anxiety is not a major component.

The more one considers this difficulty, the more strange it seems. It is probably due to the overwhelming importance that conditioning theorists have placed on anxiety. It is also true to say, however, that classical conditioning theory has not yet caught up with neurobiology. It would seem that the essentially electrical concepts of inhibition, excitation, and transmarginal (protective) inhibition, have not been entirely successful in considering complex processes, for example of experimental neurosis (Gray, 1979). The actual functioning of neurons operates under complex laws of neurochemistry. Neurons may be excited or inhibited by various processes within the cell itself, for example, changes in monoamine oxidase, synthesis, membrane and uptake mechanisms, receptor mechanisms, and so on. Thus, the processes of inhibition and excitation are themselves complex. We may need to be more aware of this problem in the future, if we are to develop classical conditioning ideas of neurochemical mechanisms. For example, changes in protein synthesis occur in response to learning. Siegle (1979) has shown that morphine tolerance (a clear neurochemical process) is very much amenable to conditioning. Electrical models of brain function (e.g., of inhibition and excitation) may prove insufficient for understanding these complex learning processes.

This difficulty apart, it does seem that neurochemical mechanisms are amenable to processes of sensitization (Anisman & Sklar, 1979). We can speculate, therefore, that the pathogenic outcome of a failure to cope arises from two processes, one operant, one classical. The classically conditioned sensitivity results from the sensitization of various neurotransmitter systems to specific stresses. Thus, specific stressors may more readily ignite hyper- or hypoactivity in certain brain pathways for certain individuals. For some, this sensitivity may exist as an increase in monamine oxidase, but for others it may exist in a sensitivity in the actual production/synthesis of certain neurotransmitters, or even as a change in receptor sensitivity. In the final analysis such distinctions would be important.

Suppose we assume that the actual sensitized pathways are noradrenergic, then it might be that conditioned or sensitized changes in these pathways ignite a sequence of events which includes hypothalamic dysfunction, and changes in other noradrenergic pathways, for example, in hippocampal and dorsal bundle pathways. This would predispose the individual to suffer (in the presence of the specific stressor or cues associated with them) symptoms relating to hypothalamic dysfunction, for example, sleep and appetite disturbance, together with hippocampal and dorsal bundle malfunction. These latter disturbances may manifest as difficulties in initiating coping behavior, in attending to relevant stimuli, in extinguishing maladaptive behavior, and so on. Moreover, these latter dysfunctions, especially in the dorsal bundle, may operate against reality testing and thus "lock in" the depressed state. As coping efforts fail, further distortions in these pathways may ensue.

Operant processes may further sensitize the individual. A learning history that has been barren of opportunities to learn to cope with specific stressors will require the individual to start to learn how to cope in the actual depressed condition. For reasons outlined, relating to various neurochemical changes, such learning is likely to be very difficult indeed at this time. The relative contributions of classical and operant conditioning vulnerabilities require further thought. It is most likely that, for different individuals, the exact balance of the acquired vulnerability (e.g., classical versus operant) will be different. Thus, for some individuals the vulnerability exists primarily at a neurochemical level. The presentation of certain stressors (or CSs) causes significant biological disruption. For other individuals, the vulnerability exists at a cognitive-behavioral level, which produces significant biological disturbance when the individual is faced with an evaluated stress with which he cannot cope. The interplay between these two processes requires further thought, but they point to one potential source of variance between depressed subgroups.

There are, of course, many ways in which we can consider the biological and structural basis of depressive vulnerability. For example, predispositions may manifest in asymmetrical disturbances in brain function (e.g., Mandell, 1979, 1980; Tucker, 1981). Kapp & Gallagher (1979) suggest that the recall of painful memories is mediated by an opiate system in the amygdala. Thus, interactions between NA and opiate systems may produce distortions in the recall of negative information and thus set up a negative (cognitive) feedback loop. Opiate changes in depression may explain changes in pain thresholds for some depressives. The possible interactions, then, are numerous and we should never lose sight of this fact. Moreover, there are many neurotransmitters in the brain, and many yet to be discovered, any of which may ultimately prove more important than NA, DA, 5-HT, or ACh.

For these reasons, we should consider the psychobiology of depression as a change in brain state. The exact mapping of the neurobiological interactions will be provided by neurobiologists. However, it is clear that neurochemical changes do not, of themselves, produce pathological depression (Mendels & Frazer, 1974), nor do cognitive changes, of themselves, produce pathological depression. It is the complex psychobiological interactions which predispose, ignite the disorder, produce symptoms, and impede or aid recovery. As we begin to understand these interactions, we will, perhaps, make more sense of the immense heterogeneity of the depressive disorders.

CONCLUDING COMMENTS

This chapter is unavoidably patchy and selective. The vast amount of data that is relevant to the issues discussed constitutes a book, or a number of books, in its own right. It is, however, worth summarizing a number of points to bring these data into sharp focus:

1. There is growing evidence that various neurochemical disturbances may be involved in depression. At the present time NA and 5-HT, and possibly DA and ACh, seem likely candidates.

2. Central depletion of these neurotransmitters may be a secondary change to psychological or other neurochemical changes. Although direct-acting depleting agents can produce symptoms resembling some of those observed in depression, true depressions are not at all as common as would be expected if the etiological mechanisms of this disorder were solely neurochemically mediated.

3. If the neurochemical changes are secondary, then we need to ask secondary to what? One promising line of research has been the demonstration that coping failure produces a number of neurochemical changes, which appear similar to those believed to be involved in depression.

4. The changes associated with inescapable shock are observable in a number of systems and brain areas. Hypothalamic changes for both uncontrollable stress and depression are clearly noted. In addition, there may be some value in examining other, possible similarities between uncontrollable stress and depression, and in considering hippocampal and dorsal bundle mechanisms. Disturbances in these areas may limit the biological capacity of the individual to get out of his distressing condition, by reducing the initiation of effective coping behavior. Moreover, it was suggested that perhaps the dorsal bundle may function in depression as a "lock-in" mechanism, which distorts attention. Under such a scheme the individual loses his power to attend adaptively and respond to new information, both of which are necessary for learning to cope and reverse a disturbed biological system. Either drugs or psychotherapies, which act directly on this attentional disturbance, may be very effective in producing changes in a coping direction.

5. There seems no logical reason to assume that depressogenic biological changes are not subject to classical conditioning. Some possibilities for such a theory have been examined, without being able to advance very far. It is, indeed, surprising that no such theory as yet exists. Although operant theories have much to offer, psychobiological concepts of vulnerability may benefit greatly from further research on such a model. In any event, the idea that biological vulnerability can only be inherited is overly limiting. My own view is that classical conditioning models of psychopathology, including depression, may go some way to providing part of a basis for understanding etiology.

The uncontrollable stress model has been, and will continue to be, enormously useful for investigating neurochemical consequences of stress and coping failure, and the relation of these consequences to pathology. However, as a model of depression it has a number of important limitations, some of which are now considered. First, one difficulty for the inescapable shock-depression model is the fact that antidepressant drugs take at least 10–21 days to be therapeutic. Yet behavioral changes in animals, as tested in the laboratory, appear effective within hours. More over, L-dopa is not a noted antidepressant and yet it does appear to have a restorative effect on behavioral deficits produced by inescapable shock The role of L-dopa is controversial, since some bipolar depressives may show a tendency toward hypomania under L-dopa challenge (Henry et al. 1976). There is some evidence that the monoamine precursors may affec cognitive-behavioral variables (Henry et al., 1973), and tricyclic drugs may produce cognitive change as a forerunner to mood change (Glass et al. 1981). These data may suggest that depressed mood, and the behaviora changes associated with it, are mediated by subtly different neurochemica substrates (for a further discussion see Chapter 7). Indeed, it is already known that monoamine-depleting drugs do not significantly affect mood except in a small percentage of people (Mendels & Frazer, 1974). Thus, we should beware of the equation, uncontrollable stress = depression.

Secondly, description and experience of mood are highly complex Linguistically, we can discriminate between sadness, misery, unhappiness depression, and so on. These internal subjective feelings may be qualita tively different. Starkman et al.'s (1981) observations of mood change ir patients with Cushing's disease is particularly interesting in this regard They investigated a number of depressionlike symptoms in this illness Increases in irritability and anger were frequent and often an early symp tom. In regard to mood change, however, they argue that some patients experienced a spontaneous onset of crying and depressed mood in the absence of any preceding thought or event: "Depressed mood is experi enced not simply as demoralization common to patients with medical ill ness, but also as an episodic sadness and crying often occurring in the absence of depressing thought content [p. 13]."

In some depressed patients it is possible to observe excessive unhap piness and sadness, and in others there appears to be more anxiety. Whether or not the appearance of subtle, qualitative differences in the subjective experience of mood is a real phenomenon is unknown, but it is an area requiring further research. Most certainly, mood change associated with negative ideation (e.g., I'm a failure, the future is hopeless) should not be equated with mood change that reflects a sadder and less despairing quality which is without negative ideation. Moreover, in some depressions changes in the quality of mood may be seen. Some patients move from depressed mood to a greater flattening of mood. The difference between extremely depressed feelings and a flatness of affect is often regarded as a change in severity, but sometimes patients experience these two states as qualitatively different. Once again, more research is needed to investigate whether such differences are qualitative or quantitative in nature.

Thirdly, it is clear that the dog, rat, or mouse may be frightened by what will happen to it, but it is less likely to be frightened by what "it" intends to do. Thus, animal data do not provide a model for investigating distortions in coping which are generated by the person. In other words, animal data may not provide a model whereby cognitive factors, such as self-efficacy, perceptions of the future, or anxieties generated by the person's own perceived (in)capacity for action, can be investigated neurochemically. Yet, we know that for humans powerful inhibitors of coping behavior are not determined by the uncontrollability of the stress itself, but by internal (cognitive) perceptions of what can be done about it.

Fourthly, related to (3) is the complex issue of the causes of helplessness. Depressed people often actually "know" what behaviors will produce what outcomes (i.e., outcome expectations are not distorted). The trouble is that such behaviors are too emotionally costly. Depressives find themselves helpless in certain stress situations, not because the stress is uncontrollable, but because they find themselves in a powerful approach–avoidance conflict.

I suggest, therefore, that we should discriminate two forms of helplessness. The first is helplessness related to genuine perceptions of uncontrollability. In this situation we would expect the person to disengage and give up. As Klinger (1975, 1977) observes, this disengagement may well be associated with a lowering of mood. The second form of helplessness is more complex. This relates to stress which sets up powerful approach–avoidance conflicts, where the emotional cost of moving in either direction is perceived as unbearable. This form of helplessness is related more closely to a Pavlovian model of experimental neurosis. The behavioral states associated with experimental neurosis are disorganization, heightened arousal, and behavioral inhibition.

At the present time, the animal data examined in this chapter focus on helplessness induced by uncontrollable stress and not approach–avoidance conflict-induced helplessness. It may be that approach–avoidance helplessness is at least as important for understanding depression as uncontrollable stress-produced helplessness. This is because, as we see in the next chapter, although in some cases a complete breakdown in coping, resulting from a genuine loss of control, is evident, in other cases patients are coping to some degree. The problem for these latter cases is that their coping efforts are maladaptive and either increase their distress or, at least, fail to reduce it.

It is also unknown whether helplessness produced by uncontrollable stress and helplessness produced by approach–avoidance conflict are biologically equivalent. It may be that helplessness states, regardless of their origin, will produce the neurochemical disruptions already outlined. It is also unknown whether approach–avoidance conflicts produced in animals, by pairing aversive events with previous positive events (e.g., Wolpe, 1979), can be considered as being similar to the approach–avoidance conflict of the depressed patient (e.g., Ferster, 1974).

Finally, the extent to which depression has a final common pathway is still under discussion. Real differences in NA-mediated and 5-HT-mediated (and even ACh-mediated) depressions may indicate important sources of variance which are not easily handled by the uncontrollable stress model. Indeed, the efficacy of different drugs for different types of depression is well known (e.g., Stern et al., 1980). Drugs appear to affect symptoms rather than people (Raskin & Crook, 1976). Thus, the biological changes associated with different depressions may not be equivalent. A good deal of confusion has been generated by this assumption.

None of these comments detracts from the enormous insights gained from uncontrollable stress research. That uncontrollable stress is biologically unhealthy is clear. It has an adverse affect on tumor growth (Sklar & Anisman, 1981), and in the human subject has been linked with various psychological symptoms (Mills, 1976). The neurochemical similarities between uncontrollable stress and depression are fascinating but, as discussed in the next chapter, uncontrollable stress is probably only part of the story.

These problems apart, I think we can make some general statements regarding the biological basis of depression. First, there is conclusive evidence that pathological depression is associated with biological change. The biological disruptions of depression are one set of factors which determine its intensity and symptom profile. Secondly, it is likely that differences in the disturbed biological profiles are evident across subgroups. But this does not necessarily point to differences in causes or triggering events. Rather, different central nervous systems may respond to stress in different ways. Thirdly, these differences in central nervous system response patterns across different individuals most probably reflect genetic–learning interactions. Fourthly, uncontrollable stress offers one model which outlines how environmental events (stressors) are converted into pathological agents and produce monoaminergic depletions. Fifthly, and most important, depression constitutes a change in the cognitive-behavioral-biological response system(s). In this sense we can regard depression as a change in brain state. This change in brain state is associated with changes in how individuals attend and interpret information, how they adapt to their environments (e.g., seek out new sources of positive reinforcement), how they exist in the world (e.g., how long or how often they sleep), and how they feel (e.g., sad, tired, and so on).

We have some way to go before we have an adequate psychobiological model of depression. There are hints and clues, and a good deal of spade work has been done. In the next chapter, we develop this line of thinking further, but try to point out how current cognitive, behavioral, and biological data can be integrated to make sense of the complex interactions which occur in depression. For this we will need to pay particular attention to the evolutionary and social relevance of depression.

6

Psychoevolutionary Aspects of Stress, Coping, and the Environment

The brain is an evolved system and as such its structure and function are determined by mechanisms which have been important in the process of evolution. It follows that human capabilities are not limitless, but are bound by the structure and function of brain as it has evolved for survival. Furthermore, since the evolutionary process operates for animals as it does for humans, we can usefully study animals in order to derive certain insights into various brain–behavior patterns which occur under various conditions. But in important ways evolution has made humans unique, and it is this uniqueness which adds special dimensions to the study of the psycho-pathology of humans in contrast to that of animals.

Bronowski (1977) makes the point clearly when he suggests that if we were not unique as a species, rats would be discussing Skinner and ducks would be debating Lorenz. For psychologists, one of the functions which contribute to the uniqueness of the human is the plasticity of functioning of the human brain. This allows, amongst other things, the enormous potential for modification and amplification of various predispositions. In psychobiological terms these capacities, for amplification and modification of innate predispositions, form the psychological dimension of inquiry. Consequently, it may be argued that much psychopathology arises from maladaptive amplification and modification operating on innate predis-positions. In this sense amplification and modification can be understood in various ways, for example, from the perspective of behavior theory, cogni-tive theory, and analytic theory. Sociological data also contribute greatly to an understanding of how environments can amplify and modify innate predispositions.

In Chapter 5 the nature of the innate mechanisms of depression is discussed with reference to (1) the (un)controllability of stress, and (2) the social-attachment status of an animal (separation–abandonment). The psychobiological response patterns to these events have two distinct components, which are innately determined and are reproducible in a variety of species. These two components are described variously as activa-tion–helplessness, invigoration–disengagement, or protest–despair. It has been suggested that the second component—helplessness, disengagement, or despair—may closely resemble clinical depression. Furthermore, these components are often marked by biological and physiological retardation, supporting Lader's (1975) view that "the basic pathological mechanism of depression is biological retardation." It follows, therefore, that depression is not an arbitrary set of maladaptive responses, but to a large degree is dependent upon the activation of an evolved (innately determined) psychobiological response pattern.

From this viewpoint it is reasonable to suppose that genetic factors will affect the threshold of activation of the depressive response pattern. The psychological approach should not be exclusive of such data, but point to those psychological factors which act to amplify and modify the depressive response pattern. Hence, psychological amplification refers to those cognitive-behavioral factors which distort stimulus inputs along dimensions of loss of control and abandonment. This approach allows for a significant linking of psychological and sociobiological approaches.

A considerable amount of work has been conducted on the relationship between social behavior and depression (e.g., Lewinsohn et al., 1979) and the importance of the attachment status of adults (Bowlby, 1980). This chapter shows how cognitive factors may amplify and, hence, invoke depressive (innately determined) psychobiological response patterns, by exaggerating the degree to which individuals perceive themselves as open to abandonment from important others. The framework for this approach is taken from Lazarus (1966), who draws a distinction between (1) primary appraisal (the evaluation of an event) and (2) secondary appraisal (the evaluation of possible coping options) and reappraisal. In addition, consideration is given to the environmental factors which are associated with depression. Hence, this chapter is divided into three major sections: stress evaluation, coping, and the environment. But, first, consideration is given to the terms "primary appraisal" and "secondary appraisal."

Primary appraisal is concerned with the evaluation of the meaningfulness of an event. Lazarus & Launier (1978) suggest that there are various dimensions for such evaluations. Events can be appraised as (1) irrelevant; (2) benign–positive; or (3) stressful. Stressful appraisals can be of three types: (1) harm–loss; (2) threat; and (3) challenge. These are not mutually exclusive, since events can (say) be appraised as threatening and challenging. Harm–loss evaluations imply a perception that some damage has been done to self- or social-esteem, future goals, and incentives. It is this dimension (harm–loss) that is the most crucial for understanding depression, especially an evaluation of a loss of important attachments, and a loss of various opportunities for (and control over) group integration and participation in socially reinforcing activities.

Secondary appraisal deals with an evaluation of available coping resources and options. This appraisal will depend upon a host of external factors (e.g., social support) and internal factors, such as perceived skills, abilities, attributions, and so on. Thus, the response repertoire of the individual and his ability to obtain outside support will dramatically influence this appraisal. Lazarus and his colleagues (Folkman et al., 1979; Lazarus, 1966; Lazarus & Averill, 1972; Lazarus & Launier, 1978) point out that stress (primary appraisal) which is perceived as beyond coping is likely to be more "stressful" than if a viable response option seems available. Thus, the interplay (reappraisal) between primary and secondary appraisal determines the overall emotional reaction to stress. The distinction of these two appraisal systems is useful for a psychobiological approach to depression. Individuals who are prone to make negative primary appraisals will find themselves in high states of arousal, for which some coping response is required. If coping options are significantly limited because of cognitive constraints (e.g., beliefs that nothing will work), poor coping skills, or impoverished environments, then such individuals may become biologically vulnerable in a similar way to the rat who is shocked with no coping response.

This analog helps to trace the interactions between high stress, low coping, and neurochemical change. In such a scheme the usefulness of the animal data, discussed in the last chapter, is clear. The suggestion is that amplification and modification of innate, depressive predispositions occur in response to (these) two types of appraisal. Moreover, the content of these appraisals, in the depressive, centers on issues concerned with loss of attachments, abandonment, and socially interactive opportunities. Hence special attention is given to the content of depressive appraisals.

In this chapter, primary and secondary appraisal are discussed in an essentially cognitive way. However, behaviorists would point out that primary appraisal may reflect classical conditioning processes, while secondary appraisal reflects operant conditioning processes. In other words, neutral events elicit (biological) stress reactions, because of previous associations with aversive UCSs. Operant learning provides the response repertoire for dealing with conditioned stress reactions. Wolpe's (1981b) recent ideas on the conditioning of cognitive associations to the feared stimulus may provide one explanation of how cognitive events come to elicit unpleasant autonomic reactions.

The UCSs relevant to depression are not so easily identified as they are for anxiety. However, there are a number of clues. The first is related to the loss of attachments and perceived position in the social hierarchy. The second relates to the consequences of these evaluations (e.g., increasing dependency needs, low self-esteem, etc.).

It is not the aim of this chapter to provide a conditioning model of depression, but rather to provide a psychobiological discussion. Nevertheless, there is reason to highlight possible conditioning processes as part of the complex of psychobiological interactions that takes place in depression. It is emphasized that this chapter does not constitute a review of the social theories of depression, but simply tries to relate the cognitive dimension of the depressive experience with psychobiological formulations, based on evolved mechanisms.

STRESS EVALUATION

Primary Appraisal

Primary appraisal concerns the evaluation of the meaningfulness of an event. In depression the processes which govern such appraisal require careful consideration. Beck's (1976) model of depression describes how depression-prone individuals interpret specific events in ways which lead to exaggerated perceptions of loss from the personal domain. We could suggest, therefore, that depressives show a tendency toward self-generating states of stress (harm–loss) arousal. These states are the products of specific negative primary appraisals. The predisposition for such appraisals resides in the establishment and subsequent invocation of various negative cognitive schemata, which structure the meaningfulness of events. As these schemata become dominant, organizing structures, there is a shift toward distorted stress (harm–loss) appraisals. The termination of this self-generated aversive state is dependent on either direct modification of the processing schemata and/or successful coping. By emphasizing concepts of cognitive distortion, Beck's model indirectly highlights the importance of the "self"-generated component of stress arousal. In Beck's model, depression is not primarily a natural consequence of environmental events, but is the product of particular processes of cognitive evaluation that are individual to the person.

In different formats other writers provide insight into the reasons why depression-prone individuals are subject to high, internal states of self-generated arousal. These include ideas, such as self-concepts, which rely heavily on external reinforcement, with disturbances in self-monitoring and self-evaluative processes (Rehm, 1977), a narrow pursuit of unrealistic ego ideals (Bibring, 1953), approach–avoidance conflicts (Ferster, 1974), and conditioned anxiety (Wolpe, 1979), to name but a few. These data suggest that in an ambiguous world, various cues (discriminative stimuli) may come to trigger stress arousal. In cognitive theory, ambiguous cues are interpreted as threatening because of distortions in information processing. Behavior theory, on the other hand, may suggest that such cues trigger arousal according to the laws of discriminative learning. As Beck (1976) points out, behavior theory does not require cognitive mediation for the acquisition of emotional responses. These ideas should not be seen as mutually exclusive. There seems little doubt that cognitive processes do modify threat appraisal and subsequent emotional reactions. On the other hand, it would be untenable to suggest that various stimuli can only trigger arousal via a cognitive route. Animal data would not support such a view. Enough has been said to suggest that some of the gross, cognitive processes which appear in consciousness may hide more than they reveal. The interplay between emotional (biological) and cognitive processes, below the level of awareness, may point to depressive-type vulnerabilities not yet clearly outlined. In other words, part of the mood content of negative primary appraisals may be a manifestation of biological responses which occurred very early in the stimulus-processing chain. Such interactions would play a significant role in the final form and intensity of the emotional response.

Within a biological paradigm, it is possible that events which are threatening to survival or events that are evaluated along some evolutionary (survival)-relevant dimension will have greater biologically disruptive potential than events which are not so interpreted. If such a view has validity, then it may be possible to observe dominant schemata which are indeed survival related in depressed individuals.

Major and Minor Premises.   Beck (1976) suggests that specific cognitive evaluations may be examples of an underlying generalized attitude(s). For example, an appraisal that one individual may not like the patient, may relate to a major premise that no one loves the patient, or that the patient is unlovable.

Beck's ideas are fascinating, but there is some doubt whether they have been taken to their logical conclusion. If we take the major premise as "being an unlovable person," it could reasonably be suggested that such an evaluation has certain survival properties. In the context of the depressive experience unlovable people are limited in their capacity for social integration. Generally, depressives view unlovableness in themselves as indicating that they will remain on the periphery of social integration and, in extreme cases, be abandoned and rejected by everyone. It is my suggestion that, in most cases, major premises are not simply generalized attitudes, but actually focus on some evolutionarily relevant dimension, for example the (perceived) capacity for social integration and the avoidance of abandonment. Such a view provides interesting links between cognitive theory and Bowlby's work. Moreover, it opens up an avenue whereby specific major premises can be seen as having significant, biologically disruptive potential. This can be made clear with two examples.

Some time ago I was asked to treat a very depressed, obsessional, suicidal man. This was not his first episode and though chemotherapy had been of some benefit, he continued to be very depressed. While helping him to use the daily record of dysfunctional thoughts (Beck et al., 1979), he made the following comments. He said that one of the things that really worried him at work was not being able to assimilate information quickly enough. (He was an insurance planning executive.) He said he hated having to ask questions because he felt his colleagues would think him stupid and a dunce. For him, that would be awful and he would feel very inferior, in spite of the fact that, actually, he knew he could do the job well, and was highly thought of. As all this was as Beck describes, it would have been possible to work on these themes as they were. However, without prompting the patient continued to probe these themes more deeply. He said feeling "awful" was like being at school, struggling to understand mathematics. Somewhat bemused I asked him to help me to understand this connection further. He then explained that the mathematics teacher had also been the football coach. If you were good at football, the teacher tended to look more favorably on you and provide extra help with mathematics. This preferential treatment was well known among the boys. Unfortunately, this fellow had been bad at both football and mathematics and the teacher had shown little interest in him. In spite of his wish to do well in mathematics, he felt he could not receive help, and was regarded as an inferior by his teacher. He concluded by saying he felt a lot of his life was like that; always struggling to keep up. "If you don't," he said, "people will abandon you, nobody will care and you'll be left to cope as best you can." He saw much in his early life to support such a view.

. Over a period of time it became clear that this theme of abandonment was very strong. Moreover, he suggested that feeling inferior was not that bothersome in itself, but the feeling of being left behind, rejected, and generally existing on the periphery of the social group was very upsetting. It was the thought of social isolation which was "awful." As we progressed through therapy, it became clear that many of his "shoulds" and "oughts" were aimed, above all else, at trying to maintain himself well integrated with his social group. These oughts included being sociable, competent at work, maintaining a happy family, liking people, and so on. Above all, they were aimed at maintaining a position within the social fabric of life and avoiding being left behind and abandoned. As he later said, "keeping up" was almost a matter of life and death for him. When he believed he could not, or was not, keeping up, his overwhelming feeling was one of impending isolation, abandonment, and aloneness.

All this is perfectly handled by cognitive theory, except for one aspect. The major premises in this case seemed to be related to the survival themes of avoidance of low status, isolation, and abandonment. My view is that if survival themes are at stake, then the influence of this form of construing on biological response systems could be profound.

Investigations with other patients have indicated to me that if you chase the major premises, more often than not they focus on survival themes. Such themes usually refer to the degree of social integration that the subject can enjoy. High social integration may be taken as having evolutionary advantage, since social animals abandoned by their group do not survive. Often, major premises focus on themes such as isolation, abandonment, being alienated, an outcast, not like other people, rejected, bottom of the pile, and so on. Many of the strategies used by depressives are efforts to stop these events from actually happening.

A depressed anorexic girl provided additional evidence of the importance of survival themes in stress evaluations. I presented her with the daily record of dysfunctional thoughts and helped her work through the event–emotion–automatic thought sequence described by Beck et al. (1979). However, I did not stop when a dysfunctional thought was identified, but asked the patient what was her logical thought following on from the one she had given, that is, what implications did she herself draw from such a thought. In this way a series of premises were plotted, down to the major premise. Two examples of this approach are given in *Figs.* 6.1 and 6.2.

From the situation shown in *Fig.* 6.1 it was clear that the patient believed that only if she was not angry would she be cared for and not abandoned, or left alone. Therapy progressed when work began on her "fear" of abandonment.

In another example, the patient had gone to town with a friend. While out, they had parted, but eventually met again half an hour later. In the meantime, however, the patient had become tense and miserable. Later, in therapy, she worked through her thoughts (*Fig.* 6.2).

Situation	Emotion	Automatic Thoughts
S. bosses me about at work	Angry Depressed	1. If I'm angry with S. other people will think I'm horrid
		↓
		(Therapist asks what would happen then.)
		↓
		2. People won't like me or want to be with me.
		↓
		(Therapist again asks what would happen then.)
		↓
		3. I'll eventually be alone and nobody will care 'cos I'm so horrid.
		(Patient very upset by discussion of this premise.)

FIG. 6.1

Situation	Emotion	Automatic Thoughts
Friend goes off in the town	Miserable	1. She's left me on purpose to go off on her own.
	Nothing to live for	2. I don't blame her 'cos I must be a pretty boring person.
		3. I've got no friends now; she won't like me any more.
		4. I'm going to end up with no one. No one will be my friend. I'll be all alone.

FIG. 6.2

There are, of course, many therapeutic points that could be discussed here, not least the large number of cognitive errors involved in her series of evaluations. My own view is that it is the last premise that is a major problem, and indeed the fear of abandonment, as a dominant structure, could well have given rise to the others. Interestingly, the patient later said that she herself did not really believe the first two premises until she felt miserable, and then they seemed quite true to her. Moreover, until she worked through her thoughts in therapy, she was relatively unaware of the fear of being left alone.

A number of interpretations are possible. My preference is for the view that finding herself alone in the town activated the major premise, "I am (will be) all alone." This produced a direct emotional (biological) change which affected the evaluation of the actual event. Her affect deteriorated further as she sought reasons for the possibility of being abandoned, and came up with the view that she was a boring person. I do not think there is any major controversy here between the foregoing and Beck's theory. The only point to stress is how the major premise was related to an evolutionary, survival theme and, therefore, (in theory) carried the capacity for being directly, biologically (emotionally) disruptive.

Cognitive therapists provide further evidence for the hypothesis put forward here, that the major premises of the depressive are clustered around survival–abandonment themes. Kovacs (1980) points out how a 30-year-old depressive had construed her need for others. The patient believed that her survival depended on others; she believed: "I need others to survive." Kovacs suggested that this premise had arisen from the schematization of early life events. These were outlined as: "If I misbehave, mom and dad don't talk to me and send me to my room → maybe they'll leave me there alone → I'll die.'' Kovacs goes on to suggest that: "The original premise 'I need mom and dad for me not to die' was reformulated by the adult as 'I need others to survive (literally).' This cognitive template would be reactivated by a variety of external conditions which the patient construed as 'I am being left' [p. 137].''

Kovacs' example provides important insights into the development of negative cognitive schemata. We need to go one step further, though, and highlight the survival aspects of this patient's evaluations. Although this construction may "appear" illogical, from an evolutionary point of view it clearly is not. Young animals and even adults may not survive if they are abandoned or rejected by the group. Social animals, especially those that are low in the social hierarchy or who are injured and who cannot integrate with their group, are often abandoned and die.

As suggested at the beginning of the chapter, there is an innate psycho-biological response pattern which is activated under conditions of perceived abandonment. It is reasonable to suppose that as social integration has become more important for survival, there must be brain pathways which mediate these behaviors. Cues which signal abandonment and rejection, regardless of whether they are illogical or irrational evaluations, may ignite disturbances in brain function because, in evolutionary terms, failure to integrate with the group reduces the chances of survival.

These clues may provide some insight into the known association between hopelessness and suicide. De Catanzaro (1980) has given a biological account of suicide. However, suicide is a very complex behavior which is related to various motivations and causes (Stengel, 1971). The importance of perceived integration within one's relevant social group is, in various complex ways, important to such considerations. It is, however, unwise to discuss suicide at this point, since it is primarily a coping behavior, rather than a stress evaluation. The main point to be emphasized is that the cognitive-biological interactions in depression must operate through evolved brain pathways and processes. Thus, certain evaluations, be these realistic or distorted, are likely to produce considerable biological disruption, if they activate mechanisms related to threats to survival.

Catastrophizing

The afore-mentioned patient examples demonstrate what some cognitive theorists call "catastrophizing" (Ellis & Whiteley, 1979). Rational emotive therapy, as developed by Ellis, points out how patients often grossly exaggerate the degree of actual threat that exists by linking fantasized outcomes. A. Lazarus (1977) demonstrates catastrophizing with a patient who suffered from speech anxiety. This patient believed that if he gave a bad talk he would be sacked; then he would lose money, then he would lose his friends, and his family would break up. Hence, the success or failure of his talk was linked to a host of catastrophic outcomes, which eventually focused on the loss of significant attachments and a fall in the social hierarchy.

In my view catastrophizing refers to the tendency to derive survival-relevant conclusions from events which, in reality, do not have such implications. To understand psychopathology it may be helpful to conceptualize catastrophizing as a form of amplification, that is, the content of the catastrophizing thoughts amplifies survival-relevant concerns. Hence, the biologically disruptive aspect of catastrophizing (amplification) arises from the degree to which it "fools" the brain to respond as if life is really threatened. In depression it is threatened in a particular way, that is, by individuals perceiving themselves as abandoned and isolated from other significant members of the group.

If catastrophizing is common in pathological states, then why is this so? This process may make sense when viewed against evolution. The brain has evolved as an "organ" to maximize survival, not rationality. Thus, many processes of psychological functioning are evolved to maximize survival and not rationality per se. Catastrophizing may be one innate tendency which is concerned with survival. In the case of depression, animals which are well motivated to stay close to the confines of their group, and are able to seek and obtain protection from their group in times of danger, are likely to have a better chance of survival than those that wander off or are not well integrated. It follows that processes which maximize the danger of losing group support and protection have survival advantage. It would seem possible, then, that "the tendency" to catastrophize, along specific dimensions, may have an innate basis. It also follows that if catastrophizing does have an innate basis there may be variations in the individual inheritance of this trait.

To understand catastrophizing in relation to depression, we need to focus on specific themes; that is, to examine the possibility that in depression there is catastrophizing "on a special theme." In very general terms, the following propositions can be made:

1. There is an innate basis for depression; that is, there is a prewired psychobiological system of responses which can be activated naturally. The natural conditions which activate this system of responses (brain state) are related to abandonment and isolation from significant others and the group.

2. Cognitive processes can amplify and modify the degree of genuine threat that actually exists (catastrophizing). Cognitive amplification and modification of the abandonment threat are capable of recruiting innate psychobiological response systems which are depressive in form.

3. The innate basis of depression can be activated by various processes, including those relevant to classical conditioning and endogenous biological disruption activating a depressive psychobiological response pattern.

In the following sections these propositions are examined, together with suggestions of possible psychobiological interactions. The essence of this approach is that irrational ideas, or maladaptive behaviors, do not of themselves produce depression. They produce pathology because they ignite (often inappropriately) innate, depressive predispositions. We can now begin to examine this in more detail.

Abandonment in the Adult

If the cognitive evaluations of depressed people focus on survival (abandonment) themes, then it is relevant to look very carefully at these themes, before proceeding with psychobiological considerations. In the first instance, it is important to note that the abandonment problems of an adult are not bound by the limits of childhood. In consequence there are related, but subtly different themes, occurring at different points in the life cycle.

One reason why it is important to consider the abandonment themes of the adult, and distinguish these themes from those of the child, is that most often adult depressive appraisals focus on peer-group loss. In other words, negative evaluations focus on the person's capacity to obtain support, love, and respect from a mate or a significant peer group (lovers, friends, and colleagues). Thus, the negative appraisals of depressives often involve conceptualizations of social status. Social status concerns are not noted for children until the development of peer-group relationships. Yet, as will be seen, depression cannot be fully understood without an awareness of the importance of social status evaluations.

The interaction between mother–child attachments and peer-group attachments is made clear by Harlow & Mears (1979):

> When monkeys are raised with agemates alone, without the mothering experience, they have no mother to encourage them to go out and play with their confreres. They have no mother to give them the sense of security to seek new adventures, to go out and explore and, incidentally, to find friends. Instead, they spend their time clinging insecurely to each other and they never do learn to play naturally and normally. By the time they learn to play at all, they learn too little and too late.
>
> When, on the other hand, monkeys are raised with mothers alone and denied the opportunity to play, they become withdrawn into themselves, do not develop into normal social animals, and also are unusually aggressive . . . [p. 197].

Harlow & Mears suggest that there are important developmental stages when the affectional bonding to a peer group becomes more important than bonding to the mother. During development there comes a time when the individual needs to secure care giving from his peers. This facilitates the development of group integration and cohesion for each new generation, allowing the proper development of sexual behavior and social organization. Some researchers have suggested that various neuroses are attempts to elicit care-giving behavior from a group or significant other. Henderson (1974) argued that various neurotic disorders can arise when an individual perceives himself as receiving insufficient caring behavior from others.

As Harlow & Mears (1979) suggest, "peer-group" love and affectional bonding become increasingly important during development from childhood to adulthood. Hence, it is the establishment of peer-group relationships which requires further consideration in depression. Although we cannot do justice to this highly complex issue here, many depressive evaluations have more to do with the loss of peer-group love than mother love. This does not deny the importance of mother love, since it may facilitate or handicap the development of important peer-group relationships.

Therefore, in addition to possible grief problems arising from unsatisfactory parental relationships (Bowlby, 1980), abandonment themes of depressives focus on the loss of peer-group support, love, and care. Hence, not only do depressives perceive themselves as being unable to obtain the love and respect they believe they need, but also these negative expectations are closely tied up with status evaluations. The depressive will often see himself as being different from others, unable to join in, rejected, weak, bottom of the pile, no use to anyone (e.g., his peer group), and so on. In effect, the individual perceives himself as losing, or having lost, important peer-group affectional bonds. He may believe this has occurred because of his own uselessness, his low-status position. The importance of the loss of peer-group affectional bonds helps explain why movement away from friends, or promotion to a new job, requiring the development of new peer-group relationships, can be depressing.

In some cases patients in therapy are worried about aspects of themselves in case the therapist rejects them. In these cases patients may harbor fears that if people "really knew" what they were like they would be rejected. It might be suggested that in so far as the therapist is attempting to facilitate the reinstatement of a peer-group affectional system, acceptance and empathy will be of crucial importance. Hence, as Mackie (1981) suggests, "being with" the patient can be as important as "doing to" the patient. There is much about psychotherapy which could be examined from this perspective.

The development of peer-group affectional bonds has many survival advantages. On the one hand sexual activity is in part determined by the teraction of group play, for it is in play that early dominance relationships e worked out, together with the development of relationships toward npparental members. It is also important that, at some point, the young dult learns to seek protection, support, and reinforcement from his peer oup. This prevents young adults from becoming too reliant on an old and, rhaps, sick parent, and increases the probability of survival. It also allows r another, often overlooked, capacity to develop. With the working-out dominance, the young adult may gradually become an important par- cipant in the "giving" of protection to others. Secure and dominant imals are able to offer protection and even food to other members awick-Goodall, 1975). Indeed, from earliest times, it seems that a con- derable amount of human activity has been to do with sharing, for cample, sharing the products of a kill. Another way to think of this is in the velopment of cooperation (Crook, 1980).

It seems, therefore, that group integration has two major components: are receiving and care giving. Although most theorists concentrate on the ss of care "receiving" in depression (a consequence of a perceived loss in terpersonal, peer-group attachments), it should not go unnoticed that a erceived reduction in care "giving" is also evident in some depressives. his may manifest as various ideas that the patient is "no good, no use to yone, a failure." More specifically, some patients speak in terms of social dundancy. A loss of peer-group bonds, and low-status evaluations, ignite e twin perceptions of a loss of care receiving and the capacity for care ving. Interestingly, some individuals in a predepressive state may appear "compulsive" caregivers; that is, they attempt to "buy into" their social oup by making themselves indispensable. Hence, threats to their capacity give care can be immensely threatening, since they may lose their social nding currency (e.g., see Blatt et al., 1982). Furthermore, many of the titudes of depressives (as discussed in Chapter 4) reflect beliefs about hat it is necessary *for them to do*, in order to ensure a stable flow of love, pport, protection, respect, and so on. It is understandable, therefore, at individuals who see their capacities to give to their peer group (or more ecifically, to be an active member of the family, group, or society) may vulnerable to depression. Retirement depressions, and depressions llowing children leaving home, may be examples of this. If care giving d care receiving are part of the same process—the facilitation of group tegration and cohesion—the perception of a loss of both care receiving d care giving may be prominent in depression. In that self-esteem is an ternal process which relates the individual to his group (Crook, 1980), lf-esteem will be vulnerable to a loss of both care giving and care ceiving opportunities.

However cognitive (abandonment) themes came into being, because oup bonding is so important for survival, individuals who perceive themselves as unable to secure peer-group integration may suffer biologic disruption. Armed with these suggestions, we can speculate on possib differences in abandonment themes. In general terms it can be suggeste that either the major premise of the depressive and/or the process of cat strophizing leads the individual to perceive himself as having lost pee group love, care, social reinforcement, and respect. It is this cogniti amplification and modification of reality which recruit brain mechanism evolved to deal with such a crisis. The suggestion is, therefore, that perceived loss of peer-group love, care, and support, real or imagine activates depressive (innately available) psychobiological respon patterns.

Self as a Reinforcing Agent

Before proceeding with a detailed psychobiological discussion of abando ment and depression, the interaction between care giving and care recei ing needs further exploration. The damage that can be done to th subsequent development of attachments, by distorted or broken attac ments early in life, has been eloquently outlined by Bowlby (1980). But the development of socialization, a species must enter into mutual rel tionships of care giving and care receiving. Indeed, we may go further ar propose behavioral interactions, such that social relationships are mai tained by the reciprocal enjoyment of reinforcement. My suggestion is th failures in an individual's capacity to see himself as a source of reinforc ment to others may pose as many problems for subsequent attachments failures in the capacity to elicit care and reinforcement *from* others. At th juncture the perception of "self as a reinforcing (care-giving) agent" r quires examination.

All human beings need to be recognized as individuals who not on require care and social reinforcement, but who are also able to *provi* reinforcement to others. The capacity to bring pleasure to another rests the center of our relationships; we have value. Moreover, individuals ma feel less lovable when they perceive themselves as having let others dow or when perceptions of being reinforcing to others fall, in spite of u changed or even consoling behaviors by others.

The capacity to give care and reinforcement to others forms an impo tant dimension of social interaction. It is probable that these lessons ar learned in childhood, from the time the baby recognizes that smiling i duces smiling in a parent. This learning process continues throughou childhood as parents show pride and pleasure in the achievements of the offspring. Importantly, however, parents may be very caring of their chil ren without necessarily allowing their children to be reinforcing to them!

The emotion associated with the perception of self as a reinforcemen caregiver is, I suggest, pride, pleasure, or "warm glow" (i.e., using Mischel et al.'s, 1976, concept). If a child tries, but fails to provide reinforcement for another, the emotion is disappointment and rejection. Because the need to give care and reinforcement is part of our inherited behavior patterns, linked to our emotional responses, some children may adopt unrealistic standards to be acknowledged as reinforcement givers. This links with the cognitive theories of Chapter 4. Negative, or weak self-schemata may develop when there have been few opportunities to experience self as a source of pleasure to others. In extreme cases a child's failure to be recognized as a reinforcing agent may activate (perhaps unconscious) fears of abandonment, because from the child's point of view he has no "power" to maintain relationships. In other words, he has no "goods" to trade with in his significant relationships.

This analysis has implications for the development of self-esteem. One pillar upon which a positive self-image would seem to rest is the perception of self as a reinforcing agent to others. Of course, this aspect can be overdone, leading to inflated perceptions of self and/or an overconcern that love is only maintained if one is always reinforcing. "Good enough" parenting allows an adequate mixture of care-giving and care-receiving perceptions, setting limits to a child's power in a relationship. Crucial to these aspects are those parental behaviors which reinforce the varied behaviors of children.

The emphasis on perceptions of self as a reinforcement giver is to make it plain that social reinforcement effectiveness depends on mutual interactions between the reinforcing properties of self to and from others. This adds an important behavioral dimension, by pointing out that behaviors are maintained not only by the reinforcement contingencies of others, but also by internal perceptions of reinforcing effectiveness on the outside world. This is an aspect of what Bandura (1977) has called "self-efficacy." Early psychoanalysts have been more interested in this aspect. Whereas behavior theorists have investigated the effects of external reinforcers on an organism—"the world acting on the self," psychoanalysts have been more concerned with the effects of "self acting on the world." In the work of Klein, the origins of the depressive position emerge from the time when the child fears that its own aggressive impulses might destroy the good object (mother). In this sense Klein emphasized that the child is not passive, but acts in a mutual exchange of behaviors (overt and covert) with another. In those early days, aggression and sexual impulses were seen as the forces to be tackled. In general, however, there has been a neglect of the importance of the positive interactions. As Bowlby makes plain, attachment networks are maintained by the positive and mutually reinforcing aspects of relationships. Hence, while we should not underestimate possible negative elements in early relationships, it is also important to emphasize that acceptance of aggression in a child may not be enough to secure a positive self-image. The child needs to experience its own positiveness. There is a long history of psychoanalytic thought which has suggested that difficulties navigating the depressive position produce a vulnerability to depression (Pedder, 1982). But in many ways there has been an under-evaluation of the degree to which a positive self-image depends on percep-tions of being reinforcing to others. This aspect becomes especially relevant for helping to understand how the transfer of affectional bonding, from parental to peer-group relationships, may produce difficulties, leading to subordinate peer-group perceptions. As mentioned in the last section, and as can be seen shortly, an analysis of depression must account for the low-status perceptions of depressed individuals. The essence of this approach suggests that individuals are maintained in relationships by at least two processes—the perceived reinforcement they receive, and the reinforcement they perceive themselves as capable of giving. Hence, although some depressions may arise from the failure of others to be caring and reinforcing, other depressions can arise when individuals perceive "themselves" as being unreinforcing or uncaring. Both sides of the equa-tion are needed, for social cohesion rests on mutual, reciprocal inter-actions. Hence, while some depressives may be helped by working through grief, associated with a loss of care receiving, others require help to change their perceptions of themselves as reinforcement caregivers, although in clinical practice it is rarely an either/or distinction.

In the next section we return to the consideration of abandonment appraisals, for it is abandonment appraisals which lie at the heart of the depressive problem. Before this, it is worth briefly pointing out how dis-torted, early attachment relationships may interfere with the development of a positive self-image. Early loss of a parent, or distorted early parental relationships, would seem to have at least three possible effects on the development of a positive perception of self as a reinforcement giver:

1. In the case of death of a mother, the child learns that his care giving behavior was totally ineffective in averting the death of his loved mother. Thus, the child learns that there is a serious limit to his effective power to maintain relationships. A perception of ineffectiveness may also arise from the various distorted relationships described by Bowlby (1977a). Families in conflict may be very insensitive to a child's efforts to be reinforcing. They are less able to show pleasure in the behaviors of their children. This reduces the opportunities for positive affects (pride, warm glow) to become conditioned to developing self-schemata.

2. Depression in other family members may also result in the child learning of his ineffectiveness as a reinforcement care-giver. This may be important when the death of a sibling submerges a family in grief and

depression in which the child finds his parents unresponsive to his efforts to be reinforcing.

3. Especially important is the possible impact of broken, or distorted, parent–child relationships on ongoing, and subsequent, peer-group relationships. Without a stable home there may not be adequate attachment figures to be reinforcing to (in addition to obtaining reinforcement from). There may be no one to turn to, to be reinforced as an agent of goodness, as an agent of reinforcement giving; no one to make the child feel important and of value. This may be especially needed when early peer-group relationships can be rejecting and often cruel.

In essence, secure attachments at home allow a child to cope with rejection from age-mates. The knowledge that the child is reinforcing to his parents may allow the child the opportunities for self-repair following the many, minor making and breaking of age-mate relationships. The child with a strong self-image may be more able to sit out rejection from age-mates, and wait for them to repair relationships. This allows children to handle and control social (peer-group) dominance problems more effectively. Children with doubts about themselves as reinforcing agents may be particularly vulnerable to the inevitable ups and downs of age-mate relationships. Most importantly, the child may adopt submissive, nondominant (subordinate) behaviors to deal with minor rejections. This greatly undermines the child's perceptions of his reinforcing capacity to his age-mates, and may set the stage for submissive, clinging behaviors later in life. A central issue will be the degree to which a child is forced to seek some sort of stable attachments with his age-mates. Unstable attachments at home may force a child to try to be accepted by his age-mates, even on the most unacceptable of terms.

In this thesis, a vulnerability to depression may reside in a distorted development of a self-image, which is not only incapable of eliciting care, but also of being reinforcing to others. A most important aspect of depression in adult life, following the breakdown of an attachment relationship, is that it deals a heavy blow to perceptions of self as a reinforcement giver. We are not as reinforcing as we thought we were, or hoped we were! Therefore, taking an ethological-behavioral position, vulnerability to depression is not so much a problem of internalized good or bad objects, but rather an internalized system of values about the self. Moreover, these values are associated with various emotions. Adaptive opportunities to have experienced one's own reinforcing capacity are conditioned to positive emotions (pride, warm glow) which may act as a buffer when self is threatened. Negative emotions of disappointment and rejection may be associated with various self-values, if there have been many experiences of having failed to be seen as sources of pleasure and reinforcement to others.

This analysis allows us to see that many different environments may be linked to depressive vulnerability; from loss of a mother on the one hand, to overprotection on the other. Overprotection may lavish care on a child, but fail to allow the child to experience his own reinforcing capacity. Importantly, however, the overriding damage lies in the development of a self-image which is vulnerable to abandonment perceptions. Individuals may be vulnerable to abandonment perceptions because they have been abandoned and/or because they have not developed a sufficiently robust perception of themselves as reinforcement givers. In both cases they will perceive their attachment networks as being maintained by significant others, having learned themselves that they have little personal power to maintain secure attachments. When attachments break down, or disengagement is called for, they may perceive themselves as being deficient in reinforcement power! Hence, without such power how are they ever going to obtain important social relationships to replace those that are insufficient or lost?

Variations in Abandonment Themes

The previous sections have highlighted the following:
(1) depressive appraisals focus on abandonment–survival concerns; and (2) these concerns have two elements: (a) negative perceptions of the amount and quality of care–reinforcement received (care–reinforcement flowing in from the outside world); and (b) negative evaluations of care reinforcement given to the world—the capacity to be of use and, hence, have some control over interpersonal interactions. This analysis suggests the model shown in *Fig. 6.3*.

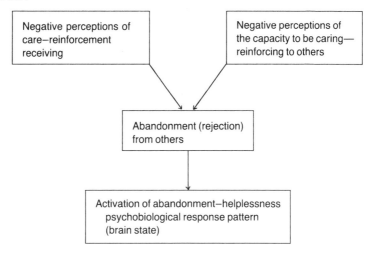

FIG. 6.3   Care-reinforcement perceptions.

Since the brain responds to "its" construction of reality and not reality itself, variations in the internal construction of reality may recruit various psychobiological response patterns. Individuals who construe themselves in the world as being deficient in care–reinforcement giving skills and/or perceive the world as being rejecting, may activate evolved, psychobiological response patterns (which exist as innately determined patterns) for responding to abandonment threat. At this point, consideration is given to the nature of possible psychobiological response patterns. Moreover, since they are psychobiological, these response patterns have cognitive-behavioral and affective elements, operating in unison with biological changes. We already know some of the biological changes that occur in response to helplessness and separation (see Chapter 5). At this juncture we can consider whether abandonment perceptions show variations in the themes which manifest in consciousness, and whether these point up possible subtle differences in depressive subgroups. The suggestions put forward here are speculations, based on a combination of clinical experience and available data.

In very general terms, it is possible to identify three abandonment themes in the depressed subject. They probably interrelate to a significant degree, but to aid discussion they are presented as separate constructs. The focus, or content, of these themes seems to be: (1) abandonment to die through physical injury, disease, or old age; (2) abandonment by a significant other; and (3) abandonment because of low social status.

1. *Abandonment to die.*   Physical injury, disease, or old age can make it very difficult for an individual animal to keep up with its own group, or collect enough food necessary for life. Diseased and wounded animals are sometimes left behind or wander off to die. The observation of injured and old elephants leaving the herd stimulated myths about an elephants' graveyard. Examples of such behavior are also observable in humans. In parts of Asia there are apparently tribes which leave their old behind to die, as they migrate from one pasture to another. Bushmen in parts of Africa are reported to leave the group to die when they perceive death is close. Similar stories can be found for various American Indian tribes. Although these are usually anecdotal stories, the behavioral disposition for physically inferior animals and humans to move out of the group when they regard themselves as injured, diseased, or just too old, may be related to some evolutionary mechanism.

It is of special interest, therefore, that some depressions, especially in the elderly, are associated with perceptions that death is all that awaits them. Elderly, psychotic, depressed patients may believe death is imminent and have various delusions concerning a change in body functioning (rotting bowels or brain, etc.) It is sadly the case that the suicide risk is higher for the elderly group of depressives, especially for those was live alone or are socially isolated.

Some depressed states also develop in conjunction with various phobias of bodily deterioration (e.g., cancer phobia), with various fears that the individual is suffering from a disease which will bring about death. Is it possible that this kind of pathology may relate to the activation of brain mechanisms related to the behavior previously described? My psychiatrist colleagues have informed me that, sometimes, patients who express the urge to wander off, pack up, and leave may be a suicidal risk. The "wandering-off urge" seems to indicate some activation of concepts related to dying. Also various fugue states, which involve wandering-off behavior, may be handled as if these individuals are a suicide risk. Fugue states which have a focus in the temporal lobe are sometimes associated with this behavior. It is not exactly clear how the theme of "abandonment to die" relates to depression or, indeed, to those fugue states mentioned. Are there pathways in the brain that mediate these themes and behaviors?

Seligman (1975) has pointed out that helplessness can be associated with reduced chances of survival—death via helplessness. We are, as yet, still unclear what the brain mechanisms are which mediate these responses. One line of evidence suggests that the degree of (perceived) social integration plays a part. Consider, for example, research by Myers & Swett (1970). They investigated the effect of bilateral anterior temporal neocortex lesions on free-ranging monkeys, compared to a control group given lesions to nontemporal areas. In conclusion to their study they said:

> Free ranging monkeys fail to rejoin their social group following removal of anterior temporal neocortex. They remain solitary and survive in the field on average only a few weeks. During survival they appear to express diminished reactivity and aggressiveness to other animals and to humans. Evidence was lacking for an active rejection of these operates by members of Group E. Rather, the operates appeared to manifest a major deficit expressed as a lack of orientation or affinity for their own family or group members. Eight control animals immediately rejoined their group on release. These and other current findings support the view that the anterior temporal neocortex plays a major role in the expression of social behavior in the primate . . . [p. 555].

At present we can but ponder over these observations with respect to depression. Are there pathways in the brain that relate to a loss of social interaction (real or perceived), that are capable of inducing significant disturbance to the extent that survival is reduced? Is psychobiological retardation an expression of the activation of these pathways? Why is death awareness so much a part of depression, especially in its more serious forms? All that can be said here is that, in various complex ways, abandonment to die may manifest as cognitive-behavioral elements of a psychobiological response pattern which has evolved over millions of years. During this time, humans have become social animals who are highly dependent on an integration with their social group for survival. Hence, abandonment appraisals may activate cognitive-behavioral patterns which focus the individual's attention on his reduced survival chances and his movement away from social, interactive opportunities. For psychobiology it is always the "interaction" between psychological elements and biological elements which demands our attention.

2. *Abandonment by a significant other.* In nonpathological cases abandonment by a significant other may manifest as grief. This theme does not center on attributes of the self which are old, injured, or diseased, but on a painful realization of the loss of attachment. Averill (1968) has discussed the biological and behavioral (mourning) response to grief. Grief does seem to involve some evolutionary mechanism. Freud (1917) made the distinction between mourning and melancholia central to his discussion of the affective disorders.

In pathological grief, there appears to be a depressive shift in addition to the grieving problem. Indeed, the presence of depression can significantly inhibit or interfere with grieving. It is clear that the direction of Freud's thinking was correct. Today, however, we have different ideas about the distinction between pathological and nonpathological grief. For example, Horowitz et al. (1980a) suggested that pathological grief results when loss of a significant other reinstates old, unresolved, negative views of self and role relationships. Generally, the depressive aspect of pathological grief centers on the individual's perceived inability to remain socially integrated within his group. In the presence of a fall in self-esteem and perceived, poor coping abilities, the individual sees himself as being abandoned by others, with no internal capacity to insure the love, attachments, and protection that he feels are necessary to his survival. Indeed, death of a significant other may lead to perceptions that the individual himself will soon die. The relationship between grief and sudden death is of great interest (Parkes, 1970, 1972; Seligman, 1975).

Again, learned helplessness explanations have been put forward to explain depression and death following loss (Seligman, 1975). However, what often emerges in these cases is a painful appraisal of low social status (not to be confused with economic considerations). The two abandonment themes stated earlier may well exert their biological impact by being related to the theme of low status. Although this remains unclear, abandonment perceptions, consequent to low-status evaluations, seem particularly relevant to depression. Moreover, this combination of stress evaluations (abandonment and low status) sets up powerful, conflicting problems for the individual.

3. *Abandonment through low status.*   Price (1972) argued that depression was an adaptive (evolutionary) response for an animal that had fallen in the social hierarchy. Depression following defeat reduces the chances of

the animal refusing to accept the outcome, and escalate fighting to a serious degree. There may also be submissive behaviors which inhibit subsequent attack, and ensure that the defeated animal is not killed. A combination of cognitive and more recent biological data allows us to reconsider these ideas from a slightly different perspective.

In depressed patients, low-status evaluations are common. These center on themes of low self-esteem, being a loser, a fake, an outsider, and so on. Such themes focus on a perceived loss of social support and social reinforcement, contingent on not meeting internalized, idealized standards. Allied to these perceptions are evaluations of increased needs, for example, to be loved and protected. (For Kovacs', 1980, patient, it was "I need others to survive.") The problem for the depressed individual is that these two perceptions, low status and increased needs, set up powerful approach–avoidance conflicts. In order to secure the social support and love that is felt to be needed, the depressive must avoid assertive (punishment) and withdrawal of support responses from others. However, this may only be achieved by passive compliant behavior. This passive behavior may invoke further negative ideas of weakness and low self-esteem, which further increase needs. These, in turn, further increase passive compliant behaviors and so on.

As we have seen in earlier chapters, there are various writers (e.g., Freud & Ferster) who have discussed such conflicts from different perspectives. However, by analyzing the cognitive content of the depressed individual, we can hypothesize that many of their negative constructs focus on low-status evaluations. This observation provides an important link with evolutionary, biological, and cognitive data. At the present time it is unknown whether the abandonment-to-die theme, to some degree, works through the same brain mechanisms governing the behavior of individuals who perceive themselves as having low status. Thus, at present, it may be useful to consider the above abandonment themes separately. What seems reasonable, however, is the suggestion that increasing needs, and low-status evaluations, run the individual into a host of problems. One major difficulty is in the handling of aggression. The discussion now focuses on this issue.

Biology, Low Status, and Depression

The biological relationship between low status and depression is obscure, but there are important reasons for considering such a relationship. First, Price (1972) suggested that depression was an adaptive response to a fall in status. Secondly, many of the cognitive themes of the depressed individual reflect ideas about low status, for example, not being good enough, being alienated from others, being weak and incompetent, a loser, not lovable, and so on. Thirdly, as Lewinsohn et al. (1980) demonstrate, depression is associated with a real decline in social skills and social functioning. Fourthly, many of the conflicts experienced by depressives center on concerns about the loss of support and social reinforcement contingent on assertive behavior. Fifthly, these conflicts may loosely be labeled as fear of attack or counterattack to assertive behavior, and the chosen response to such threats is passive compliance or avoidance.

For the sake of developing a line of thinking, we can equate passive avoidance and compliant behavior with submission. Although this presents some problems (see next section), it does provide some interesting avenues for thought. Until recently, the behavior of submissiveness was regarded as a type of defense. However, Adams (1979) suggests important differences between defensive behavior and submission. From a biological point of view, it seems that there are different brain pathways which mediate defensive, as opposed to submissive behavior. The exact wiring of the relevant internal structures is not our concern here (though there is some overlap with those suggested for depression). However, we should note that Decsi & Nagy (1979) suggest that the neurotransmitters mediating offense, defense, and submission may be cholinergically controlled. Importantly, the switching mechanism from defense to submission may be catecholaminergic. These observations suggest important sources of data when viewed against the discussion of Chapter 5 (i.e., that hypercholinergic function and hypoaminergic function may be biological substrates for some depressions).

The neuroendocrine response system may also differentiate aggressive behavior from avoidance of attack behavior. Leshner (1978) suggests that pituitary adrenal activity may increase avoidance of attack behavior, while other hormones regulate general aggressiveness. Furthermore, Starkman et al. (1981) suggest that the endocrine disorder of Cushing's disease, which includes disturbed cortisol and adrenocorticotrophin production, is accompanied by various manifestations of depression and heightened irritability and anger. Disturbances in cortisol production are now well observed in depression (Carroll et al., 1981; Depue & Kleiman, 1979). It is, therefore, of growing importance to consider a possible relationship between heightened aggressiveness (anger), low status, submissive behavior, and depression.

The biological interactions of these processes are highly complex, yet since the aim is to understand psychobiological relationships in depression, we are forced to juggle with many different strands of data arising from many different avenues of research. Leshner (1978) provides important insights into endocrine activity associated with avoidance of attack. He presents data supporting the view that endocrine changes differentiate between aggressive and submissive behaviors. Furthermore, changes in gonadal hormones may play an important role in the depressive aspect of the premenstrual syndrome, and such hormones have also been implicated in aggressive–submissive behaviors. Bowman et al. (1978) also point out that social status can have a significant impact on reproductive hormones. Hence, all in all, as Rasmussen & Reite (1982) suggest, subordinate animals may be particularly vulnerable to social stress because of the endocrine changes associated with low social rank. From a psychological point of view it is not the intention to suggest that depressives actually *are* of low social rank, only that in perceiving themselves to be so, they may activate the biological changes associated with low-ranking animals. Rasmussen & Reite note that animals of low social rank are particularly sensitive to separation depression.

The depressive perception of being "inferior" or, more scientifically, of low social status may provide important clues as to why aggression in depressives appears to be powerfully inhibited in most situations. It has been known for some time that status, or the dominance position, in social animals bears centrally on the expression of aggression. Various forms of elicited aggressive behavior (from frustration to direct electrical stimulation of certain brain areas) will produce attacks by senior-ranking animals on lower-ranking animals. However, aggressive attacks by low ranks on senior ranks are rare (Montagu, 1976). Nevertheless, elicited aggression will produce aggressive outbursts from low-ranking animals toward safe objects or even lower-ranking animals. Thus, in situations where there is an increase in anger or aggressiveness, perceived status plays a key role in determining how that behavior manifests. Low status is a powerful inhibitor of aggressive behavior toward others. Interestingly, fighting may be one response set which protects against monoamine depletion, following inescapable shock (Anisman, 1978). It can be suggested, therefore, that various situations may elicit anger or aggressiveness in the depressive, but there may also exist powerful, psychological inhibitors (perceived status) of the display of assertive and offensive behavior. Furthermore, different neurochemical systems may differentially control submissive and attack behaviors.

Adding the idea that depressives experience low-status evaluations with high fears of (social) abandonment, a simple model (*Fig.* 6.4) can be developed to describe the possible interactions. Clearly, this model is an oversimplification, but it offers an opportunity to consider possible psycho-biological interactions. The model suggests a relationship between the inhibition of assertive behavior and low-status (and low self-esteem) evaluation. Adding the biological dimension, we can see how these interactions may become interdependent. For example, the cognitive evaluations outlined for the depressive may activate biological pathways mediating avoidance of attack behavior. These biological changes may act to inhibit assertive behavior producing maladaptive interpersonal behavior. This increases the fear of social abandonment which produces further negative evaluations, and so on. Equally, of course, we could consider this chain reaction commencing in the biological pathways regulating submissive behavior. The greater the predisposition to behave submissively, the lower the perceived status, the greater the need for support, and so on. The point is, of course, that complex interactions of this order suggest a weakness in searching for simple cause–effect relationships.

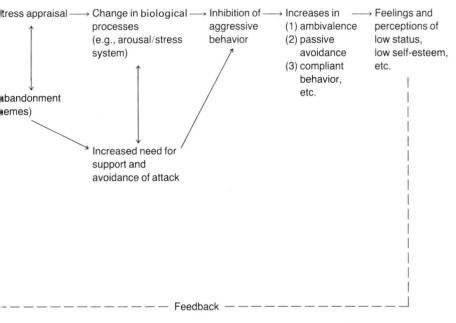

FIG. 6.4   Model of the interaction between stress evaluation, biological change, and cognitive-behavioral change.

If simple cause–effect relationships prove inadequate, then we are faced with the proposition of there being complex sources of vulnerability and triggering events. In discussion of this aspect we can identify three potential sources of vulnerability:

1. Genetic predisposition may regulate the capacity for individuals to defend or attack without receiving counter, inhibitory inputs from the submission system or network. The biological capacity to tolerate anxiety and stress arousal in the face of attack, or the threat of social support withdrawal, may be one controlling influence. Moreover, in that a catecholaminergic pathway may mediate the switch from defense to submission, then inherited instability in such a pathway may lower the

threshold for the occurrence of such changes or switches from one behavior to the other.

2. If it is true that specific neurochemical pathways mediate avoidance of attack behavior, or regulate the switch from aggressive to submissive behavior, then such specialized pathways are open to classical conditioning. The proposition here is quite straightforward. Simply, previous assertive behaviors, from significant others toward a child or young adult, may have led to submissiveness by the child. The biological pathways mediating this behavior would then (in theory) be open to becoming sensitized to cues associated with assertive behaviors from significant others.

3. Early learning of negative consequences of assertive behavior (e.g., punishment or withdrawal of love) may produce structuralized concepts and expectations. Whenever assertive behavior is required, the individual will have at hand an expectation of the outcome. If the outcome is feared, avoidance of the outcome may leave only a submissive response open. Thus, beliefs and attitudes governing the person's perceived needs, and the consequences of assertive behavior, will significantly influence the chosen response.

To complicate matters, these sources of vulnerability are probably differently combined and distributed in depression-prone individuals. In that we can only observe the final response, we may be incapable of knowing which sources of vulnerability are most important for each individual. This is because cognitive-behavioral-biological processes interact, each feeding the other.

Possible relationships between low status, biological change, and aggressive versus submissive behavior, indicate a further area of importance. If we consider that there is some switching mechanism from defensive to submissive behavior, then the importance of possible discontinuous changes in behavior is clearly seen. In fact, attack–defense discontinuities have been examined by catastrophe theory (e.g., Postle, 1980). If it is true that status is a psychological factor mediating this switching mechanism, then we may expect to find unstable attack–submission behaviors in some depressed individuals. This is indeed noted in some cases.

One patient whom I recently treated demonstrated these difficulties clearly. His depression (related to unresolved grief) resulted in heightened tension, which he described as a rage and tension within him. Small things made him angry, but he rarely expressed this anger. What he would do was to smash up his own model aircraft, which he had painstakingly made. He was very worried about his own "anger capacity" and feared he would lose the love of his family. The more depressed he was, the more he needed them, but the more irritable he became. He had dreams of himself as a burden to others and had a dread that he would get a disease and become dependent on his family for all his needs. At times he had very low feelings of self-worth. Other examples of depressed patients taking their anger out on safe objects (e.g., the washing-up) may also demonstrate this problem. (However, I would not suggest that all angry outbursts should be described in this way.) The way in which depressed individuals actually handle aggression is complex. Blackburn (1972, 1974), using questionnaire measures of hostility, found high intrapunitiveness in both unipolar and bipolar depressives. Unipolars, however, also had higher extrapunitive scores. Lyketsos et al. (1978) observed cultural differences in hostility patterns during recovery from depression. A reduction in intrapunitiveness was associated with recovery from depression. Weissman et al. (1971) found depressed women had greater hostility toward those who shared a close relationship with them. This pattern of hostility may reflect conflicting tendencies in that those close to the patient are "safe objects," that is, they are more likely to be understanding and less likely to counterattack. Yet hostility may also be inhibited, if patients believe that significant others can fulfil their needs and must not be driven away. In any event, the interacting processes are likely to be quite complex.

Nevertheless, it is clear that depressives are not adaptively assertive. If we suggest that there is a neurochemical disturbance in depression which produces heightened aggressiveness, then clearly we must ask: why, for most of the time, are depressives so unassertive or why do they behave in maladaptive ways? Cognitive-behavioral predispositions furnish important insights and neurochemical observations take us further. For example, if ACh and monoaminergic changes are consequences of uncontrollable trauma, and if these neurotransmitters regulate the heightened aggressiveness and influence its expression, then uncontrollable stress may (in the presence of cognitive-behavioral predispositions) produce heightened, but inhibited aggressiveness. Personally, I would not go so far as to consider that for some patients the only safe object to attack is the self, but there may be an element of truth to it.

If we are going to consider low-status evaluations, conflicts relating to assertive behavior, and passive compliance (submission), we cannot forget the biological dimension. For it is the biological dimension which gives the affective reactions their intensity and depth. The removal of the biological distortions, which inhibit adaptive responding, is a major concern. It does not follow, of course, that drugs are the only way to do this. Once we fully appreciate the complexities of psychobiological interactions, we can free ourselves to develop therapies aimed at removing the biological substrates of emotional suffering.

Very briefly, then, we can sum up the propositions outlined in the last few sections as follows:

1. Depressives have cognitive themes which center on abandonment and low-status evaluations. These (in some way) relate to evolutionary mechanisms.
2. These themes, in combination with learning and biological vul‑ nerabilities, trigger biological changes.
3. Because of the low-status evaluations and dependency needs, these biological changes may increase both aggressive (tension) and submissive tendencies, reducing adaptive interpersonal behavior. Anger is passive, and only expressed openly toward safe objects.
4. Such behavior may ultimately push away potential caregivers, re‑ inforcing the negative themes of the depressive.

Death and Depression

Animals which are low in status have reduced opportunities for coping with stressful situations. They may be less able to engage other members of their group in reciprocal relationships, with reduced opportunities for eliciting care, engaging in sexual activity, and food sharing. One of the effects of low-status perceptions mirrors these evolutionary facts, to the extent that depressives appraise themselves as having reduced social reinforcement opportunities—in the widest sense. Significantly, low status limits capacities for, and perceptions of, control (especially in intraspecies activities). Hence, the relation between status perceptions and helplessness is an important one.

In 1975, Seligman ended his exposition on helplessness and depression by pointing out that helplessness perceptions have significant effects on survival. In certain situations helplessness may be responsible for unexpec‑ ted death. In the pursuit of evolved psychobiological response patterns in depression, Seligman's observations may hold a most important key. There are at least three aspects to this key:

1. Although the exact mechanisms between helplessness and death are unknown, there is supporting evidence that helplessness can induce death, sometimes quite suddenly. Helplessness may reduce an organism's capacity to resist disease (e.g., via the consequent disturbance on immune-system functioning linked with cortisol change) and/or it may invoke parasympath‑ etic hyperarousal (Seligman, 1975). The latter suggestion is especially in‑ teresting because hypersensitivity of cholinergic control mechanisms may mediate parasympathetic hyperarousal and some depressions.
2. Freud noted that humans serve two purposes: self-preservation and preservation of the species. It may make evolutionary sense, therefore, that nature should provide psychobiological mechanisms which can be activated

n individuals, whose contribution to the gene pool would not be in the best interests of the species. As a general case, animals which find themselves under chronic stress, which is beyond their coping, are (from the species point of view) more usefully removed. A more specific case would be to suggest that animals which find themselves abandoned, with no means of reuniting, may be inhibited from passing on their genes by early death. Hence, attachment failures, of whatever origin, are selected against. This is a speculative position. None the less, it points to the evolution of psychobiological response patterns which operate to the benefit of a species, but not to that of the individual. Having a mechanism capable of bringing about early death, which is what Seligman's observations suggest, may make sense in terms of evolution.

3. The third link in the chain is even more controversial and speculative. This concerns the degree to which individuals, at some point in a depressive state, can be aware of psychobiological mechanisms (acting from within), which are working toward their own death. I am hesitant in suggesting this because it raises various, old problems of a death instinct. Bowlby (1973) points out that Klein believed that, right from birth, the baby had a "fear of annihilation" which became associated with various aggressive impulses toward the mother. Unfortunately, psychoanalytic thinking is now rather confusing on this issue. Nevertheless, we are faced with the possibility that perceptions of helplessness may activate psychobiological response patterns which threaten to bring the life of an individual to a premature end. Furthermore, we need to ask whether depressed individuals are aware of this.

One depressed patient who was treated by the author said that during his depression he had the "feeling" that some definite resolution was needed. It was a difficult and "dark" feeling to describe, but he sensed death was close. In his deep depression he was sure he would not make it. In a subsequent discussion, following his recovery, he said death was the wrong word, rather "non-existence" seemed more correct. Sometimes during his depression he planned various ways he could "bring the whole thing" to "its proper end."

At present the relationship between depression and some awareness of reduced chances of survival is vague and obscure. All that can be suggested is that somewhere deep in the brain there may be mechanisms which indicate (and are involved in) reduced chances of survival. These are activated under conditions of chronic stress, especially stress related to disengagement from social networks. This may be related to psychobiological retardation, which marks a phase where death can be brought closer. The genetic implications are clear. Furthermore, if there are psychobiological response patterns which underwrite helplessness death (as seems likely), some sense might be made of epileptic phenomena in which patients experience wandering and deathlike experiences. The degree to which individuals may have a conscious awareness of the relationship between their helplessness, low status, and reduced chances of survival is unclear. Parasuicides may be trying to say something important in experimenting with possible death as a means of eliciting care. The notion that there may be a psychobiological response system capable of terminating life, which switches in under certain conditions, is more than alarming. The idea that there is an attack on life, which comes from within—set up as an evolutionary mechanism to remove coping failures for the benefit of the species—adds an odd twist to psychoanalytic thinking!

This area remains clouded and vague. But once again we are forced to ponder how cognitive-behavioral amplification and modification come to ignite prepared psychobiological response patterns, producing perceptions of imminent death, rotting brain and bowels, emptiness, and nothing to live for. Anger against the self does not provide a sufficient basis for understanding these cognitive manifestations. The expression of an inbuilt psychobiologic program seems more in keeping with the data. Hence, helping depressed people to develop positive perceptions of their own skills and care-giving (reinforcing) capacities helps to reduce helplessness and low status (they are of value to their species or some member(s) of it). In the end the therapist is fighting, on behalf of the individual, the dictates of evolutionary pressure. Most times we can help them to win. Sometimes we cannot; even with the help of ECT or drugs, some are lost.

Dependency, Passive Avoidance, and Submission

The issues discussed so far have been considered in many ways by many writers. Freud talked of dependency needs and anger turned inward. Ferster talked of approach–avoidance conflicts and the conditioning of anger suppression. Cognitive theory has little to say about anger and irritability in depression, but does talk of negative schemata and expectations. The previous analysis suggested psychobiological interactions between complex variables, for example low status and abandonment themes, increased anger and submission, and evolutionary processes. To what extent do all these point to similar observations about the problems experienced by depressed people?

Generally, I suspect, there is a fair degree of overlap. However, there are also important differences. The relationship between passive avoidance and submission is complex. Passive avoidance suggests a general behavioral trait of which submission may be one of its manifestations. It may be more complete to consider passive avoidance as a general behavioral predisposition rather than selecting one aspect, for example, submission. On the other hand, this may overlook important biological and evolutionary mechanisms. For example, submissive behavior is only relevant to intra-species disputes and not predatory attack. The biological mechanisms governing intraspecies aggressive behavior are different from those governing other forms of aggressiveness. It is, therefore, open to discussion whether or not important sources of data are lost by investigating a more general behavioral trait—passive avoidance—instead of a more specialized aspect—submissiveness.

Freud's concepts of increased dependency needs and anger turned inward have been of enormous importance. Here, however, we discuss these questions from a different perspective which, I believe, has the following advantages:

1. It is not anger turned inward which is the problem for the depressed individual, but rather heightened irritability, which may be inhibited from expression toward significant others. This provides a neurochemical discussion of the problem and avoids energy transfer models, thus removing the notion of catharsis in recovery.

2. Dependency needs are not regarded as a regression, as Freud suggested, but rather as an associated change which occurs in conjunction with low-status evaluations. Thus, we do not need to rest the acquisition of vulnerability at some developmental period. These needs may manifest for any number of reasons, e.g., (a) endogenous biological shifts; (b) the activation of negative schemata; and (c) presentation of CSs associated with submissiveness (or passive avoidance), and so on.

These alternative views accord with Freud's basic proposition (and, indeed, Pavlov's) that psychiatry cannot, and should not, free itself from biological psychology. Moreover, as I have tried to show, there are now opportunities for integrating new data and ideas, which if not directly concordant with Freud's view, at least suggest he was on the right lines. This new integration has been made possible by taking some of Beck's ideas and reworking them with current neurobiological insight. Thus, the focus is on cognitive-behavioral-biological interactions; each part is necessary and contributes to our better understanding of depression.

Summary

It has been suggested that cognitive factors play an important role in the evaluation of the meaningfulness of a stressful event (primary appraisal). I have put forward the idea that some of the major premises, operative in depressive thinking, center on survival themes of evolutionary significance. It is, therefore, suggested that the emotional intensity experienced by some depressives is related not simply to the cognitive interpretation of various evaluations, but to their evolutionary and survival relevance. In this way the capacity for certain appraisals (determined by major premises) to produce excessive affective reactions is understood, via their capacity to activate biological patterns of responding mediating threats to survival.

It is suggested that there may be different, though interacting and overlapping, abandonment themes that can be detected in the cognitive schemata of depressed persons. These include:

1. Abandonment through deterioration in the physical abilities of the individual—the wander off to die theme.
2. Abandonment by a significant other, through loss, separation, or death—the loss of a source of major reinforcement (and/or attachment bonds) theme.
3. Abandonment through a real or perceived deterioration in status, associated with loss of social support, social reinforcement, and perceived movement toward the periphery of the group—the loss of status theme.

It is suggested that the loss of status theme (3) carries the most complications for the depressive. The interdependence of these themes and their relationship to depressive disturbance require further investigation.

Activation of the loss of status theme is complicated by approach–avoidance conflicts. As Lewinsohn et al. (1980) point out, depressives are often painfully aware of inadequacies. It is suggested that biological disturbances (perhaps in ACh and catecholaminergic pathways) regulating aggressive and submissive behaviors may further complicate the depressive's efforts to behave in a manner which will ensure a self-determined flow of social reinforcers. The biological pathways which mediate submissive (passive compliance and avoidance) behaviors may be sensitized by previous learning, thus presenting the possibility that some submissive behaviors are classically conditioned responses. It is implicitly suggested that the intensity of the "felt" or "experienced" aversive states associated with approach–avoidance conflicts are biologically mediated. Thus, biological changes, be these endogenous, conditioned, or secondary to negative appraisals, produce deep conflicts relating to internal (feeling) states of aggressiveness (sometimes experienced as tension and agitation) and feelings relating to a need to be submissive and, hence, not attacked or abandoned.

The low-status perceptions of depressed individuals cannot be understood without placing them in their social context. While some depressives may feel "inferior to everyone," it is more usual for there to be a particular type of group which the subject relates to, yet feels inferior in. The question of social status to group identification is important, but it is not discussed here. It is clearly impossible to outline all the possible implications of abandonment–low-status perceptions. It can be noted, however, that recent evidence suggests that some social hierarchies are maintained (in part) by dominant members avoiding subordinates (Crook, 1980). Hence, findings which suggest that depressives may be avoided by nondepressed individuals may further indicate some evolutionary dimension. In general, it seems that humans prefer relationships with those to whom they are closest in terms of status dominance (Hinde, 1979). In other words, relationships with individuals who are perceived as significantly more dominant, or significantly less dominant, may not be particularly rewarding. Furthermore, the introduction of strangers into a primate social group often invokes dominance behaviors. It is not unreasonable to suggest, therefore, that a "fear of strangers" (social anxiety) may relate to some innately activated mechanism, requiring the individual to dominate or be dominated when confronting strangers. Social anxiety is common in some depressions.

There is a considerable way to go before these speculations become anything more than that. What I have attempted to do here is to sketch out, in a rather primitive way, potential, psychobiological interactions, based on the data presently available. In regard to the psychological aspects of depression, there is a growing necessity to develop our theories along the dimensions of evolutionary biology. Evolution may well have provided for open and closed programs (Crook, 1980), but it is their interaction which is important for psychopathologists to illuminate. Hence, we return once again to the idea that there are innate, prepared, psychobiological response patterns to various events and stimulus configurations. The task for the psychologist is to understand how psychological factors (behaviors, thoughts, and events) act as amplification and modification mechanisms which are capable of recruiting maladaptive psychobiological response patterns (maladaptive, that is, for 20th-century individuals).

As far as possible this discussion has focused on stress evaluation. It was suggested that the quality and content of the depressive's stress-evaluating mechanisms center on dominant themes and premises, which focus on survival and evolutionary dimensions. The questions and problems relating to submissiveness were also introduced although, more correctly, these are coping behaviors. Implicit in this analysis is the idea that depression is a problem relating to interpersonal, or intraspecies interactions. We can now focus on another important aspect of depression: coping.

COPING

Secondary Appraisal

Secondary appraisal is shaped by perceptions of coping-resource availability. Research has shown that it is this dimension—the availability of an effective coping response—that determines the severity of monoamine depletions, and not primarily the stress itself. The discrimination between the biological consequences to a stressor, and those following some coping response to it, is useful to psychopathological research. It may help us to understand why various psychiatric patients appear to have similar aversive conceptualizations about themselves and the world, but manifest varying forms of pathology. Basically, they have different patterns of coping behavior. Many negative cognitive elements such as low self-esteem, fears of abandonment, rejection, and so on are observable in a variety of patient groups (e.g., alcoholics and anorexics), but they manifest different coping responses. Some seek to drink away their poor self-perceptions, and some give up and become submissive, hoping for needs to be met by others. The importance of the discrimination between types of stress and the coping options to them has been highlighted by Bandura (1977, pp. 141–142).

For depression, some workers suggest that the depressive does not just have maladaptive coping behaviors. Rather, he sees himself as having none at all. This may well be one of the factors that, in response to stress, marks some depressives—the overwhelming sense of hopelessness and helplessness. Lazarus (1966) suggested that: "... real hopelessness is here proposed as a condition of inaction in the face of threat ... The affect associated with such a condition of hopelessness is depression. Fear and anger will only occur when the individual is not totally resigned to the hopelessness of his plight ... [p. 263]."

Seligman (1975) also suggested that depression replaces anxiety when the individual realizes that trauma cannot be controlled. Thus, the depressive is in a state of inaction in the face of threat or loss. It is this inaction—inhibition of coping behavior—which places the depressive in a highly vulnerable (biological) state; this follows directly from animal data already discussed. As Lazarus makes clear, however, other affects can be present to a significant degree, depending upon whether resignation is total or not. Total resignation is also associated with severe behavioral inhibition and may be of some importance in retarded depressed states. In agitated depressed states, coping behavior may have fallen to zero, but the individual is not "totally" resigned to his plight, thus other affects are manifest (see Chapter 7).

There seems little doubt that cognitive factors significantly determine coping behavior (Abramson et al., 1978; Bandura, 1977; Beck, 1976). What is far less clear is whether these constitute the sole basis for discriminating coping behavior, or whether biological factors also play an important role. It is an obvious point, of course, that cognitions do not occur in a vacuum, but are represented in some neurobiological code. It is also fairly clear that the biological state of an individual, for example, level of fatique, state of exhaustion, or physical illness, can significantly undermine perceptions of coping. Attention to internal fatigue levels may well play some role in perceptions of being unable to cope. Therefore, any biological change which signals to the person a reduction in functioning may act as additional source data for perceiving problems as being beyond coping. Moreover, to be able to cope with stress, individuals must be able to generate various options, work out the implications, weigh up the costs, and so on. If there is a poverty of options, either because they do not exist (environmental restraint) or because the individual has never learned to generate important coping responses, then it could be expected that coping behavior will be limited.

What is sometimes overlooked in discussions of coping behavior is that coping goes on over time. People may struggle to cope with stress for days, weeks, or even years. Whereas the evaluation of what needs to be coped with can occur fairly quickly, actually putting coping responses into action can take time. Thus, when we observe coping failure in depressed patients, this may be the product of endless attempts which have not worked out. They have not, in the long run, succeeded in terminating self-generated aversive states. This simple point may help us to understand why, for some, depression suddenly appears to take hold. For some depressives, the arousal of self-generated aversive states eventually becomes too demanding to the biological system. Exhaustion or neurochemical depletion finally begins to emerge in individuals who have appeared to cope up until that point. Clinical data would tend to suggest that the point at which this happens may be gradual or sudden.

It could be argued that there is a point of "cognitive realization," when the individual suddenly realizes that he can no longer cope. One patient, who had been struggling with a difficult job, believed he had to prove himself to himself in this job. He told me that he suddenly woke up early one morning and realized he just could not go on. The job was beyond him. He experienced a most unpleasant panic attack at that point and was admitted to hospital some days later. There was little doubt that many of his cognitive schemata (I must be strong, efficient, make good decisions, etc.) sowed the seeds for a good deal of the stress he was experiencing. However, the actual point at which he had become pathologically depressed seems to have reflected a point at which some significant biological change had occurred. That his biological system had been under high demand was clear. For some weeks before his actual depression, he found his concentration failing, sleep became a problem, he had minor anxiety feelings and, most important to him, he was easily fatigued. The harder he tried the less he did. Whether or not he would have been diagnosed as depressed during those weeks is unknown. But what became clear was that, following his realization that he was "all washed up", there was, within days, a marked intensification of symptoms in the depressive direction. A negative cognitive triad appeared in full force. Whereas before sleep had been a problem, now he woke early, his appetite left him, concentration became almost zero, and he was tired all the time.

This case seemed to offer some support for the uncontrollable stress → neurochemical change model. What was interesting about this man was that he had been troubled with self-doubts for years, but, by his own accounts, he had coped with them. Until this particular job he never really felt he had been "put to the test." When faced with his own psychology in a stressful situation, however, his biology simply could not cope. Sadly, after a number of admissions and temporary relief from various physical treatments and cognitive therapy, he committed suicide. This was precipitated by finding his ex-wife living with another man and not wishing to have anything further to do with him. It seemed that once his biological capacity to cope with stress had been overloaded he became highly sensitized to moving into extreme pathological states under provocation. The event that finally precipitated his suicide is highly relevant to our earlier discussions concerning abandonment.

In many cases it is possible to see how depressives have struggled with various stresses for long periods. Often, stress is self-generated by high psychological demands, or emotionally impoverished environments. In view of this, it is surprising that recovered depressives do not show any marked tendency toward more negative conceptualizations than control groups (Gilbert, 1980; Lewinsohn et al., 1981). This is an interesting paradox because, when treating depressives, it is clear that few appear out of the blue. This may suggest that vulnerability and precipitating stress (cognitive or otherwise) are different. More research is needed on this, and it is likely to be quite difficult to separate the two. Nevertheless, it does appear that either a change of circumstances and/or a gradual accumulation of events can overload the stress system. If not before, then certainly at this point of overload, biological factors do become extremely important in understanding depression. The breakdown in coping mechanisms in the helpless direction does seem to coincide with an intensification of the disturbance. It is here that the stress → neurochemical change model has much to offer, for it is at this point that (theoretically at least) neurochemical depletion begins to take its toll. Before this point various neuroendocrine and neurotransmitter systems may have been put into unstable states, but at the point of coping failure serious pathology emerges.

The relations between the unstable and depleted states are obscure. It is unlikely that the same relations pertain to all depressives. Moreover, genetic factors probably play an important role in determining the capacity of any system to be maintained in an aroused, unstable state without, as it were, going into reverse. Although we might suggest that neurotic depressions may constitute an unstable state and endogenous ones a depleted state (which might fit with Akiskal et al.'s, 1978, data), this may be too gross a simplification. Nevertheless, we have to entertain seriously the idea that at the point when the individual can no longer make any viable coping response to stress, various biological changes not present in the coping state will now emerge. However, it may also be that in some cases the only coping options available are maladaptive ones, for example, the adoption of passive avoidance. But these behaviors may not succeed in reducing internally generated distress, especially that distress originating from self-doubts and low self-esteem. Thus, to all intents and purposes, maladaptive coping behaviors are as pathogenic as no coping response.

Coping in an Interpersonal Context

There is little doubt, as Lazarus & Launier (1978) observe, that laboratory studies of coping behavior are significantly limited in their power to elicit information on how people actually cope in the real world. It is also clear that outpatients and those not presenting to medical agencies do succeed in coping with their lives to a considerable degree. They continue to work and function socially, more or less, in spite of feeling unwell. Not all depressions are associated with a complete breakdown in coping mechanisms. Thus, while the uncontrollable stress model is highly illuminating, for these and other reasons (see the concluding comments of Chapter 5 and also Chapter 7) depression is not simply coping failure.

We need, then, to consider coping failure within a context, and to ponder how, in the context of the person's life, coping efforts are not reducing distress. We need to consider the interpersonal context of depressives' coping efforts. In the earlier discussion of stress evaluation, I put forward the hypothesis that depressed individuals attempt to cope with stress, which relates particularly to low-status evaluations. Thus, distortions in coping will relate primarily to an interpersonal (or intraspecies) behavioral dimension. The social context of depression was, therefore, implicitly implied. Indeed, in many of the psychological theories discussed, distortions in psychological processes focus on how the individual is relating to other members of his species or group. If depression is related to pathological processes (either psychological or biological), which mediate interpersonal behavior, then we would expect this dimension of behavior to point up important differences between coping efforts of depressed versus nondepressed people. This is indeed the case.

Coyne (1976b) proposed a model of depression which was entirely interpersonal in form. He suggested that depressed people seek support and comfort from others in ways that are maladaptive, and produce guilt and ultimate rejection from potential support-givers. The major hypothesis of Coyne was that the depressed person is engaged in maladaptive, person–environment interactions. It is not so much that the individual fails to cope with internal distress, but rather that the coping behaviors employed actually enhance the person's distress.

More recently, Coyne et al. (1981) have provided important work on how depressives (in the real world rather than in the laboratory) set about coping. They make the important distinction that human coping behavior is aimed at two outcomes: solving problems and reducing emotional distress. Their data suggest that for depressed and nondepressed people: "Differences in problem-focused coping and self blame were conspicuously absent, but depressed persons sought more emotional and informational support from others and engaged in wishful thinking [p. 445]."

Coyne et al. also note (unpublished data) that "depression is associated with perceptions of lower emotional and tangible support from others, both concurrently and prospectively. The implication is that depressed people do more seeking of support and perceive themselves as receiving less [pp. 445–446]."

What is emerging is that while coping is a complex set of behaviors, it forms an important aspect for understanding depression. Moreover, it may be coping centered on (1) obtaining support from the social group; and (2) reducing emotional distress, which has special relevance for depression. The problems for depressed individuals are many. In the first place, the people who exist within their support systems may not be the best people from whom to seek support. As Bowlby (1980) makes clear, spouses may have been selected with a good deal of "defensive exclusion" of the bad aspects of the spouse. Thus, depressives may find themselves needing to increase attachments to unsuitable partners or, at least, to partners who do not really understand the depressed person's needs.

Secondly, trying to simply reduce emotional distress may not always be a good idea. As suggested before, disengagement is sometimes a good coping response. But disengagement is not cost free. Thus, sometimes depressives find themselves in vicious circles, where they cannot face the emotional cost of disengagement (be this from an incentive or person), but to continue with it (or the person) is also emotionally distressing. Maternal overprotection may be one sensitizing, early life influence which hinders the person's adaptive ability to work through and face the unpleasant consequences of (healthy) disengagement.

Clearly, this is not the case for all depressions, but then depression is a very heterogeneous disorder. What does seem to be the case, however, is that the coping difficulties of the depressive focus on interpersonal (or intraspecies) conflicts. Disengagement from incentives can be similarly regarded, because often the emotional cost is perceived as being a failure in the eyes of others. Failure is regarded as being associated with a significant reduction in social support and reinforcement opportunities. Moreover, there is growing awareness that depression constitutes problems relating to person–environment interactions. The person's behavior may actually shape aversive environments. In this case, it is not sufficient to regard depression as a process or processes that are completely internal to the individual, be these cognitive or biological. As has already been pointed out, Tennant et al. (1981a) have shown that neutralizing life events can reduce neurotic difficulties in up to one-third of cases. Thus, as Lazarus & Launier (1978) make clear, it is what happens in the real world that requires our attention (see also Rippere, 1979, for a discussion of this issue).

Coping with rejection and abandonment problems.   Earlier, it was suggested that the stress evaluations of depressives focus on low status and fears of abandonment. It was also suggested, following Ferster's and Bowlby's work, that many of the avoidance tendencies of depressed people are coping efforts aimed at evading withdrawal of support, or punishment responses, from significant others. Assuming that survival themes are present in depressed patients' conceptualizations, then biological changes which are consequent to the activation of such themes may place limits on the use of particular coping responses. If the biological changes are related to an increased need for support (social integration, protection, etc. from significant others) and the avoidance of attack, then clearly, certain behaviors for coping (e.g., assertiveness) may be inhibited. The inhibition of certain coping behaviors, in response to specific stresses, will be dependent on complex cognitive-behavioral-biological interactions. These may include beliefs and attitudes about the social consequences of certain behaviors, dependency needs, and learned behaviors for dealing with stress. Biologically, neuroendocrine and neurochemical differentiation of submissive, compliant behaviors and aggressive behaviors may act as a conditioning substrate for certain behaviors. In other words, neurochemical changes associated with submission (avoidance of attack) may be conditioned to certain stimulus events. If these suggestions have validity, then we may expect superior learning from depressives, especially in those situations where they are trying to avoid rejection and abandonment.

There is evidence that the avoidance of attack is an important coping behavior for depressives. Forrest & Hokanson (1975) investigated the propensity for depressives and nondepressives to use self-punishing behaviors, in response to interpersonal conflict (confederate aggression). They examined the rates of self-administered electric shock in response to aggressive behaviors. It was found that baseline rates of self-punishing responses were much higher for the depressed group. They suggest that this indicates a previously established repertoire for dealing with aggressiveness from others (although it cannot be ruled out that such behaviors become manifest as a consequence of the biological change associated with depressed mood). They also found evidence to suggest that self-punishment, or the emission of a friendly response, in the face of agression from another, had significant arousal-reducing properties. In other words, "avoiding attack responses" reduced the arousal associated with confrontation in the depressed, but not the nondepressed group. Forrest & Hokanson (1975) state:

> ... The experimental findings indicate that the greatest plethysmographic arousal reduction takes place in the depressed group when a self punitive (or friendly) counterresponse is made to the aggressive confederate. The nondepressed group exhibited comparably rapid reductions only following an aggressive counterresponse [p. 355].

Animal conditioning work has shown that noxious events can become reinforcing, if they are associated with the avoidance of even more aversive events. Animals can learn to direct their behavior to the lesser of two evils. Forrest & Hokanson suggest that such learning has been developmentally important in depressives. In other words, depressives have a learning history in which the reinforced behavior toward aggression from others has been self-punitive or friendly (i.e., submissive). They suggest that:

> ... depressed patients have learned to cope with environmental and interpersonal stresses with self-punitive and/or nonassertive behaviors and these behaviors have been successful in dealing with their normal day-to-day existence. At times when situational stresses become great, this limited behavioral repertoire may be invoked to a degree that may seriously impair adequate functioning and these people may manifest a clinical depressive or masochistic episode [p. 356].

Schwartz & Gottman (1976) have provided further data on this issue. They demonstrated that compared to high- and moderately assertive subjects, low-assertive subjects seemed to be inhibited in delivery of an assertive response to an unreasonable request. The cause of this difficulty was not a lack of knowledge of what to say or do. Rather, it lay in their significantly higher degree of intrusive negative thoughts about responding assertively. Low-assertive subjects had much higher scores on a questionnaire designed to measure positive and negative self-statements. Low-assertive subjects scored significantly higher for responses such as "I was worried about what the other person would think of me, if I refused: I was thinking that it is better to help others than to be self-centered: I was thinking that the other person might be hurt or insulted if I refused" [Schwartz & Gottman's test example, p. 913].

Schwartz & Gottman raised a number of important points relating to the transfer of assertive skills in therapy situations. However, from our point of view we can suggest that low-assertive subjects may well be fearful of even further assertive (rejecting) behavior on the part of the other. If this is so, then such a fear (relating to low-status perceptions and all they entail) would need to be handled directly. For the patient to simply know what to do, and practice the response(s), may not actually remove the fear that the person will be rejected if he is assertive in his everyday life.

The relationship between Schwartz & Gottman's work and depression is not as straightforward as it is for that of Forrest & Hokanson (1975). Physiological variables did not discriminate the groups in Schwartz & Gottman's study, but Forrest & Hokanson did find changes in arousal, associated with submissive responding for the depressed group. Although these are only two studies, the data suggest that in depression there may be important interactions occurring between perceptions of low status and avoidance of attack in assertive situations. An important area to investigate is how biological changes, associated with low mood (of whatever cause), can undermine assertive responding. Uncontrollable stress may shift the biological substrates of assertive responding toward a submissive style. In this situation operant and classically conditioned predispositions are interactive vulnerabilities.

It can be seen that there is a good deal of overlap between the views expressed in earlier discussions and those outlined above. Ferster (1974) argued that depressives demonstrate significant passivity in response to aversive events. In the discussion on achievement and failure (see Chapter 4), it is suggested that self-blame could be used as a response by a child, to avoid the anger of parents in a perceived failure situation. In addition, there is growing evidence that depressives are highly dependent on external sources of support and reinforcement. Hence, depressive coping strategies are aimed at minimizing possible aversive consequences to assertive demands.

The implications of avoidance of attack responses in a social animal like the human must be seen against the backdrop of evolutionary processes. For it is not simply that avoidance of attack may succeed as a coping response. Rather, it is the fact that such responses carry significant information about one's standing in the social hierarchy. The relationship between depressed or angry moods when one is forced to "eat humble pie" bear close examination! The experience of "having let oneself down" or "sold oneself short," especially in interpersonal situations, can produce powerful, unpleasant emotions. For most of us, cultural or social inhibitors, fears of rejection or outright punishment, do not allow us to give full vent to feelings in interpersonal conflict or competitive situations. How we see ourselves as a result of such inhibitions, be they internally or externally imposed, can have a powerful impact on mood state, depending upon the importance we place on the encounter. Thus, although the depressed individual may feel relieved by his self-punitive responses, his self-esteem and perceived place in the hierarchy are likely to suffer. This will be counter-productive since it will increase dependency needs.

There are many aspects to these considerations. For example, the earlier discussion of achievement and failure, and the relationship between achievement strivings and self-esteem, will bear critically on this issue. Fear-of-failure motivation is associated with various unpleasant symptoms. Indeed, I believe that there is much in the fear-of-failure research which could be investigated from the point of view of "avoidance of attack." Thus, fear of failure may well be influenced by the type of processes we have been discussing above, for example, trade-offs between pushing for success, being assertive, "getting the just rewards," and fear of losing love, support, and protection.

At this present time, the potential for synthesizing many different theoretical positions now exists. The interactions are manifold and complex. A complete understanding of these processes will not be forthcoming without a considerably greater interdisciplinary approach than exists at present.

Biological Factors

Unlike those of the rat, human coping responses are difficult to evaluate for effectiveness on the basis of behavior alone. It seems, therefore, that their effectiveness may need to be judged (at least in part) by their physiological cost. Those behaviors which reduce arousal and avoid negative biological outcomes may be regarded as viable coping behaviors. Ursin (1980) suggests a similar view. History shows that some individuals, who are propelled by their own self-doubts, sometimes produce great works or services. If successful, great effort as a means of coping with self-doubt is rarely criticized. For others, sadly, their biology is not up to the demands placed upon it. This issue is complex, however, because, as we have seen, some coping behaviors (e.g., submission) may reduce arousal (Forrest & Hokanson, 1975), yet also put the subject at greater risk.

The biological constraints to certain styles of coping require further research. The capacity of rats to cope with novel or fearful environments is subject to genetic factors, as shown by the breeding of reactive and non-reactive rats (Gray, 1971). Stolk & Nisula (1979) point out that various mechanisms governing basal levels of catecholamine synthesis and deamination are determined by inheritance, and that the qualitative nature of such changes is determined by genetic factors. However, as they make clear, such factors do not necessarily predict the animal's capacity to deal successfully with challenge. This may incline us to the view that it is genetic–learning "interactions" which act as the most potent sensitizing base for a biological vulnerability to psychopathology.

Since biological constraints may develop in response to learning (as discussed in the last chapter), significant constraints may be programed into the system as a process of sensitization and/or conditioning. We need to consider the possibility that some individuals have biological systems which, as a result of early learning and/or genetic predispositions, are overly sensitized to disruption by certain events (Meyersburg & Post, 1979). The role of cognitive variables in this context may act as amplifying, rather than causal mechanisms. Thus, for some individuals, rejection and cues associated with it may ignite directly various biological changes, which have to be coped with, in addition to various negative cognitive predispositions. The biological changes triggered by rejection cues are probably to do with social integrative behavior. Thus, genetic differences in separation-mediated behaviors will play a significant role in learning–environment interactions.

The biological aspect is important in attempts to cope with abnormal affect. When patients say they "feel bad" about this or that event (often some personal rejection), they may be reacting biologically to the event, in addition to cognitively appraising it. The intensity of their "bad feelings" is due to biological change, and not solely a response to cognitive appraisal. It is the capacity to cope with the consequences of such biological change, on functioning and subjective experience, which may place some constraints on coping. Thus, we should question the view that emotional responses are "nothing but" specific reactions to cognitive appraisal. Although the coping response (based upon secondary appraisal) has a very real influence on the biological (and emotional) reactions to stress, we need to consider that the biological disequilibrium caused by the stress may vary between individuals as a response to a specific inheritance or conditioned biological systems.

The major point of concern must be, therefore, how such directly ignited biological change interferes with coping evaluation and effectiveness. If these biological changes are able to reduce the threshold for the recall of negative memories, interfere with attention and adaptive responding, increase submissive dispositions, alter the subjective experience of other events, produce fatigue, and increase anxiety and anger, then coping effectiveness may not only fall as a result of negative secondary appraisal, but might also suffer at the hands of a directly changed biological system. These considerations do not undervalue the role of cognitive processes in coping and emotion. Rather, in some cases, cognitive processes have to deal with disturbed biological states. In other words, the evaluation of how one can cope or should cope with certain events is partly determined by one's biological state. This explains why a series of stresses are often a problem, because each stress subtly changes the biological state of the individual, even if that person appears to be coping well. It also suggests why some depressions take hold following physiological trauma, such as serious infections or childbirth.

THE ENVIRONMENT

Life Events

We have discussed the major premises of depressed individuals and various aspects of coping behavior. However, stress evaluation and coping take place in a context. It was suggested that one way of thinking about depression is in terms of evolutionary processes governing interpersonal and socially integrative behaviors. It follows, therefore, that the context of depression is social, and that environmental constraints on socially integrative behavior could be significantly related to depression onset and recovery. This moves us into the complex area of life events, and socially determined vulnerability (constraints).

The role of life events in the causation of depression has become an increasingly important area of research over the past 15 years or so. During this period of time methodologies have become increasingly complex. Many of the early studies, which relied on life-event inventories, have been criticized (Brown, 1979a; Tennant et al., 1981b). Tennant & Andrews (1978) pointed out that life events are "pathogenic" in neurotic conditions because of their emotionally distressing impact, and not simply because of the change in lifestyle that they require. Coyne et al. (1981) demonstrated that it was coping with emotional distress, rather than solving problems, that differentiated depressed from nondepressed subjects. Thus, the evaluation of idiosyncratic stress, determined by the specific appraisals (meaning) and coping options available to the individual, acts as an important interface between life events and pathology.

In an effort to overcome such difficulties, which are not easily handled by inventories, Brown & Harris (1978a) developed a measure of contextual threat. This was derived by the use of trained interviewers allowing any event to be considered as potentially stressful and then rated blind by other workers. Tennant et al. (1979) have evaluated this procedure and found it to be "highly satisfactory." Clearly, it is not possible here to go into detail about the adequacy of research design, but there are several papers that the interested reader should consult (Bebbington, 1980; Brown & Harris, 1978b, 1980; Cooke, 1980b; Harré, 1980; Paykel, 1978, 1979;

ennant & Bebbington, 1978; Tennant et al., 1981b; N. Tennant &
Thompson, 1980). To proceed in this area in a straightforward way, we first examine
whether life events ever cause symptoms to emerge in people exposed to
them. Later it can be asked whether symptoms cluster into recognizable
syndromes, which can be labeled depression. To answer the question, "Do
life events ever produce symptoms?," the answer is clearly, "Yes, they do."
At the extreme, severe life events and major crises produce symptoms in
the vast majority of subjects exposed to them. Tennant et al. (1981b)
suggest that: "When subjects are exposed to the horrific sequelae of a
disaster involving personal threat to life, death or serious injury of friends
and relatives, loss of personal effects, and disruption of social bonds, the
risk of psychological morbidity may approach 100% in the short term [pp.
385 and 387]."

Seligman (1975) also reviews evidence which demonstrates that major
disasters can produce significant disturbances in functioning. He attributes
this to helplessness. Generally, major disasters ignite symptoms by their
capacity to threaten, or actually disrupt or destroy, the social, integrative
fabric of people.

Less extreme, but still major events which focus on the individual also
produce disturbances in functioning. Grief is one example (Averill, 1968;
Parkes, 1972). Horowitz et al. (1980b) have provided important data on the
sort of symptoms that emerge following traumatic stress. They have
demonstrated that various symptoms of depression, anxiety, obsessive-
compulsive, anger–hostility, and somatization, are consequent to traumatic stress. Often these symptoms appeared in over 90% of cases. Again it
turns out that the most serious stresses invoking these symptoms are "the
loss of a relationship with another, the loss of self-esteem, or the loss of a
physical aspect of the self [p. 91]." Horowitz et al. (1980b) note particularly
the intrusive and avoidance episodes that characterize these syndromes.
They point out that the engagement of psychological processes necessary
for adapting to these aversive events plays an important part in these stress
syndromes.

It is clear that major life crises do provoke symptoms. More specifically,
severe disturbances in social (interpersonal) life and attachments produce
symptoms for the vast majority of people. Armed with this general finding
we can now ask the question, "Can life stress, occurring within certain
social contexts, produce depressive illness?" It is clear that major disasters
are not the life events which interest researchers. Nevertheless, as we shall
see, the combination of events and vulnerabilities associated with depression is major in that they carry specific implications for the individual's
ability to derive support and comfort from significant others in particular,
and the social group in general.

Life Events and Depression

To answer the question, "Are there life events associated with depressiv illness?," it is useful to bear in mind our earlier discussions of the possibl evolutionary (intraspecies) aspects of depression. We can then, theoret cally, expect the answer to be in the affirmative. However, the question i: in pragmatic terms, complex. There is little doubt that some psychiatris remain wedded to disease notions of depression. I have already discusse the historical reasons for this and believe such views to be inadequate (se Chapter 1). The notion that there is a disease entity called depression, tha exists in a Platonic sense bound only by its biological substrates, is prot lematic. Rather, we need to recognize that there may exist patterns (symptoms, which tend to cluster together, to which we can apply the ter "depressive illness." In other words, in the absence of any biological lesior which in its presence produces a syndrome, and in its absence no syndrom is manifest, it is necessary to ask, to what set of phenomena should we appl the term "depression"? We should not ask, is this syndrome or tha syndrome *true* depression. Depression is defined by its symptom patter (including duration and frequency). For these reasons we have descriptiv psychiatry, which has provided the DSM III, the ICD 9, Feigher's criteri: and so on. Diagnosis based on careful description and identification (symptoms is different from diagnostic procedures investigating a biologic: lesion (e.g., as for Cushing's disease). Whether or not psychiatry will eve be able to diagnose depression in the absence of careful description, fc example, using tests like dexamethasone suppression, is unknown. Bic logical disturbances which are secondary to psychological, or life-ever processes further complicate questions of causality. What is clea however, is that life-event stress does not allow useful distinctions to b made between endogenous and neurotic depressions (Akiskal et al., 197 Paykel, 1979).

I raise these issues again here because one of the most common criticism leveled against life-event notions of causality is that life events cause di: tress, but not depressive illness. As long as the syndrome that is unde investigation is carefully defined, there can be no argument on this score Paykel's work, however, has been criticized for failing to adequately de: cribe syndromes associated with life-event stress (Slater & Depue, 1981 Tennant & Bebbington (1978) have criticized Brown & Harris' (1978a work for their identification of cases, and Brown & Harris (1978b) hav answered their critics. However, the area remains a controversial one.

Brown & Harris (1978a) have provided the most comprehensive invest gation of the role of life events in depression. Their results are fascinatin and important. They investigated the relationship of life events to depres: ion in two populations—a depressed female patient group and identifie cases from a female working-class population in London. Most importantly, Brown & Harris made major efforts to identify true cases of depression, using generally accepted descriptive psychiatric phenomenology. This was achieved with trained interviewers using a structured interview, based on the Present State Examination (PSE). As Brown (1979a) makes clear, it was the symptom cluster and not simply depressed mood, no matter how severe, that identified cases as true cases of depression. (Bipolar patients were not included.) Furthermore, for cases identified from the nonpatient population, it was generally agreed that had those individuals presented themselves to medical agencies they would have been regarded and treated as depressed.

In general, then, it seems fair to conclude that Brown and his colleagues did identify true cases of depression, and did develop a measure of contextual threat which is highly satisfactory. We can now consider the findings of this major study. These are presented as findings concerning the events themselves, and findings concerning vulnerability factors.

The events themselves—provoking agents. It is only long-term, threatening events which play any role in depression. Short-term threatening events play no role in depression onset. The long-term threatening events were generally those that involved disturbances in the socially integrative relations of the person. These were threats or actual losses, and included loss of a significant other (e.g., separation from husband), an unpleasant discovery forcing reassessment of major relationships, a threatening illness to someone close, material loss and disappointment, and miscellaneous stresses concerning redundancy following a period of secure employment (Brown, 1979a, p. 270).

The stresses and major difficulties outlined by Brown and his colleagues are labeled "provoking agents." However, Brown makes it clear that the social context within which these events occur has a significant bearing on the probability of developing a depression. Thus, it is suggested that provoking agents themselves need to be considered against a background of ongoing vulnerability. Provoking agents affect depression onset, but it is the combination of vulnerability factors and provoking agents that is most associated with depression.

Tennant & Bebbington (1978) have raised technical and statistical arguments against the idea that vulnerability factors and provoking agents can be regarded separately. In spite of this, Brown's model does make good sense. Actually, the vulnerability factors outlined are of two types, though they interact. To make our exposition clear, I have labeled these "social vulnerability factors" and "psychological vulnerability factors." Brown does not discriminate these factors in quite this way.

Social vulnerability factors. The probability of becoming depressed, in the presence of provoking agents, is increased if a woman does not have, within her social network, a close, confiding relationship. The most important relationship, which looking at it positively confers some protection, is a confiding relationship with her husband. Other vulnerability factors include having no full- or part-time employment, having three or more children at home, and having lost her own mother (especially by death) before the age of 11. This last factor, Brown believes, may also have a significant bearing on the form the depression takes. He relates this factor to symptom formation.

Brown (1979b) suggests that none of the vulnerabilities in themselves are capable of triggering depression, but do significantly increase risk in the presence of a provoking agent. The combination of provoking agents and vulnerability factors goes some way to explaining major social class differences in the prevalence of depression. Working-class women are more likely to have severe life events and difficulties, and to have significant social vulnerability as described by the factors outlined.

Psychological vulnerability factors. The contribution of vulnerability working through psychological processes is a more speculative part of Brown's work. Nevertheless, it makes good sense. Brown (1979b) says: "I believe that present evidence suggests that clinical depression is essentially a social phenomenon in the sense of being usually the result of a person's 'thoughts' about his or her world [p. 253]." He goes on to say that he would not make the same claim for schizophrenia. In view of the arguments put forward earlier, concerning the social and evolutionary aspects of depression, it is possible to see a considerable degree of agreement between those ideas and Brown's, although each set of ideas was reached via different paths.

Brown suggests that the two most important perceptions that provoking agents and vulnerability combine to produce, are low self-esteem and hopelessness. He suggests that if there is a tendency toward generalized perceptions of hopelessness and low self-esteem, then depressive symptoms manifest. The relationship between the causes of low self-esteem and vulnerability factors is obscure, however. Sometimes Brown suggests that self-esteem might be low "before" a depression occurs, at other times the provoking agents and vulnerability factors appear to bring about low self-esteem. This is an important point, I suspect, since ongoing, low self-esteem may significantly influence the type of relationship a woman chooses, together with the style of interaction. Low self-esteem women may pick low self-esteem husbands, who may be less capable of providing a confiding and secure relationship. This is unknown, although I have seen some cases clinically which might support this view.

Further Evidence

It is becoming increasingly clear that the impact of life events on pathological styles of responding is complex. Hong et al. (1979) point out that individuals are not simply passive recipients of life events, but to some degree actively shape their environment. Recent models, describing the mechanisms that translate life events into illness behavior, usually outline social support and resource availability, psychological and biological processes. Rahe & Arthur (1978) offer an interesting model for understanding the intervening processes between life change and illness. Andrews et al. (1978) point out that coping style and social support influence risk of psychological impairment. But they suggest that coping and social support are independently related to neurosis and do not primarily exert their effect by detoxifying the effects of high stress. Nevertheless, their data suggest that: "In those without stress, with good coping and good support, the risk of psychological impairment was 6 per cent, while in those under stress, without support and with poor coping, the risk was raised 5-fold to 30 per cent [p. 313]."

With specific reference to depression, there is evidence that depressives tend to appraise life events as more threatening than nondepressed subjects, and perceive them as requiring significantly greater readjustment (Schless et al., 1974). Paykel and his colleagues have contributed greatly to our understanding of life-event relationships in depression (Paykel, 1979) and psychiatric illness (Paykel, 1978). Unfortunately, the various measures used by Paykel have been criticized (Slater & Depue, 1981; Tennant et al., 1981b). Nevertheless, his work has demonstrated a consistent finding that the quality of life events is related to depression. Exit events, especially those that threaten or involve real, important, interpersonal losses, are the most significant events associated with depression.

Paykel et al. (1978) examined the relationship between social adjustment and severity of symptoms. Social maladjustment did not correlate well with severity of symptoms during an acute disturbance. The reasons for this are obscure, but suggest that illness severity and interpersonal coping should be regarded as separate processes. On the other hand, Paykel et al. (1978) point out that mild depressives may have significant social maladjustment. Life events also adversely affect relapse (Paykel & Tanner, 1976). Indeed, the importance of social and interpersonal variables on relapse is clinically well noted. It is not uncommon for recovering hospitalized patients to return from a weekend with an intensification of their symptoms or even outright relapse.

Warheit (1979) also investigated complex interactions between life stress, coping, and depressive symptoms. A large sample was interviewed, of which 517 cases were reinterviewed three years later. His general finding was that symptoms at first interview had a better predictive capacity of symptoms at second interview than life stress or losses. However, other findings suggest important associations between depression and social-psychological processes. Amongst the findings were: (1) the presence of a spouse was significantly correlated with level of depression regardless of (other) losses; (2) life-event losses were higher for the higher depression-scoring subjects; (3) for the high-loss individuals, having friendships was associated with lower depression scores; (4) losses and the absence of resources were significant variables when used to predict depression scores. Warheit suggests, therefore, that the effects of life-event losses are mitigated somewhat by the availability of personal, familial, interpersonal, and other resources.

Such data again suggest important interactions between life events, social support, and psychological processes. McC.Miller & Ingham (1976) confirmed the importance of social support, especially that of a confidant, in the manifestation of various symptoms. Moreover, as in Warheit's study, friendship was found to be important. An examination by Slater & Depue (1981) of suicide attempts in primary depressives led them to conclude: "... the occurrence of serious suicide attempts in primary depressives is strongly associated with an increased rate of independent events in the year preceding the attempts and that a particularly high density of events between episodic onset and the attempt may further enhance the probability of an attempt [p. 282]."

Furthermore, the significance of events was that they tended to represent a loss of an important, confidant relationship. Slater & Depue (1981) suggest similar mechanisms to those which Brown suggests as being important; that is, adverse life events increase perceptions of hopelessness. Moreover, this would seem to confirm Paykel & Tanner's (1976) work, since Slater & Depue (1981) suggest that life events, especially those involving loss of support, may overwhelm coping resources and lead to relapse. On the positive side, Tennant et al. (1981a) have demonstrated that neutralizing events can lead to a remission of symptoms in up to one-third of neurotic conditions.

The few studies outlined here represent the tip of an ever-growing iceberg of research which demonstrates important associations between life events, social support, and coping. Bebbington et al. (1981) offer further support to these associations and a good review of some current findings. Although methodologies can be criticized, and the relationship between distress reactions and illness is uncertain (Tennant et al., 1981b), the results are in the main consistent enough to safely conclude that the environment does play a significant role in at least some depressions.

Clearly, the environment does not exert its impact magically and it is well demonstrated that depression is associated with various biological disturbances. Consequently, the negative environmental characteristics outlined must (via various mechanisms) affect biological functioning. Separation and isolation are emotionally and biologically disruptive (McKinney, 1977). Recovery from neurotoxin insult to catecholamine systems is affected by the housing conditions of animals. Recovery in socially housed animals is better than for isolates (Diaz et al., 1978). Furthermore, social housing versus isolation has a significant effect on disruption produced by inescapable shock (Anisman & Sklar, in press). Valzelli (1977) has reviewed the biological effects of social experience on normal behavior and drug effects. In general terms the evidence tentatively suggests that integrative, social environments are in some way biologically protective to various stresses.

At this time we do not know whether adverse environments contribute to depression because they are unstimulating and produce nonspecific detrimental effects on coping, or because they exert specific effects on specific behaviors. Clearly, the view taken here very much suggests specific relationships. Thus, adverse environments are depressing when they involve specific losses, or threats to the social integrative framework, at both the individual level (e.g., loss of a significant attachment) and the group level (loss of friends, tied to the house, loss of employment). What seems to be emerging is that life events, which are perceived as moving the individual to the periphery of the social group—in effect into a more emotionally and socially isolated position—are positively associated with depression. The exact nature of the psychobiological mechanisms that mediate the translation of environmental events into illness(es) is still under investigation. This is examined in Chapter 5.

Some General Comments

Brown and his colleagues have provided a major and valuable contribution to our understanding of depression. Brown does have a fairly liberal psycho-biological or, at least, socio-psychobiological concept of depression. Writing for a neuroscience journal Brown (1979b) says:

> Clearly, clinical depression must have a biological basis (and in this sense be potentially treatable by physical means); but it must be recognized that biological correlates of depression are not necessarily aetiologically significant in the sense of explaining population differences in prevalence of depression or, indeed, why a particular person became depressed at a specific time. This is not to deny the possible aetiological implications of recent biological research, nor the possible aetiological role of genetic and constitutional factors [p. 254].

In stressing the social dimension of depression, Brown is in line with many ideas on preventive medicine. For example, it is known that diet, alcohol consumption, poor exercise, executive stress, and so on are all lifestyle (vulnerability) factors that increase the risk of heart disease. An approach for evaluating changes in risk associated with life events has been proposed by Paykel (1979). He also discusses the issue of evaluating the "magnitude of effect" of life events. Using his index of risk, Paykel suggests that an exit event increases the risk of depression 6.5-fold in the subsequent six months. Indeed, taking any of the events he examined, the increased risk for depression is 5.6. Like Brown, however, Paykel makes it clear that events themselves are not sufficient to understand causality. He suggests that the translation of life events into final pathology is determined by mechanisms that are both internal and external to the individual.

The model that Paykel (1979) derives is simple and helpful. He outlines various sources of interaction between social support and stressors, vulnerability to events, specific illness vulnerability, and treatment-seeking factors. The major points of disagreement between Brown and Paykel would probably be over the exact mechanisms of "vulnerability of events" and "specific illness vulnerability." Brown would suggest that specific illness vulnerability is determined by the combination of provoking and vulnerability factors. Paykel tends to load his concept toward biological factors. At the present time more work is required in this area.

There seems to me one important aspect of these issues which has tended to be overlooked. This is the "failure to recover" aspect. There is considerable evidence that, for most, the events implicated in depression are, indeed, depressing, suggesting an evolutionarily-relevant dimension. However, most disturbances are mild or, even if severe, transitory. So, perhaps not only do the social vulnerability factors increase risk of onset of depression, but they also reduce the chances of recovery.

Two points are in order here. First, many life-event models do not allow for feedback processes. Feedback may occur between psychological and biological processes. For example, uncontrollable stress may produce biological changes which interfere with adaptive responding and, thus, reduce further the subject's ability to cope. Alternatively (or in addition), subtle changes in mood and functioning in the affected person may drive unsympathetic others away, thus increasing distress. This may be why it is not the appraisal of a stress which has the most important implications, but coping behavior, and why Paykel chooses a six-month time-scale between life event and onset of depression. In this sense a confiding relationship may act as a recovery mechanism in coping with the emotional distress of an adverse life event, that is, helping the person to weather the storm. Coyne et al.'s (1981) data do suggest that depressives can solve problems, but that they seek more emotional support from others and see themselves as receiving less.

Secondly, if we take an evolutionary view of depression, then clearly the social context of depression is important. We have already discussed how induced biological changes in monoamine pathways affect the status position of the animal; but also how socially housed animals recover faster than isolates following some biological changes. Clearly, in these cases we are discussing processes of recovery and not vulnerability. Thus, we can suggest that whether or not genetic vulnerability plays a role in depression, recovery can be adversely affected by the degree of social and emotional isolation that the person experiences. In very general terms, the social environment has an affect on vulnerability *and* recovery. If depressed humans can socially reunite, then given the evolutionary arguments I have put forward, their chances are much better for coping with stress.

As we have learned more about the functioning of the body, it has been possible to increase the health of the Western world. In the main these benefits have derived, not from high technology medicine, but from better housing, sanitation, and education. I would humbly suggest, therefore, that in these days of increasing adolescent suicide and distress caused by ever-growing pressures to compete and the need to succeed, we should learn the social lesson well. It is probable that no matter how good a socially integrative environment may be, there will always be some who sadly suffer serious depression. But as we begin to understand depression in its social and evolutionary contexts, we can begin to consider no less radical changes in our mental life to those that occurred in our physical environments at the turn of the century. We should oppose the philosophy that any psychosocial environment is acceptable and that those who are going to get depressed will do so anyway. Such a philosophy is a betrayal of the better traditions of preventive medicine and flies in the face of reason. The brain has evolved with an increasing capacity and need to function in a socially integrative way. To forget this in our educative and preventive endeavors is a grave error for which some will pay dearly.

Thus, as with heart disease, preventive medicine is aimed at increasing the thresholds for illness. Education and dietary changes, together with psychological advice on the harm of stress, are becoming more available. As we begin to understand environmental factors implicated in reducing population thresholds for depressive disturbance, we can begin to consider important preventive options, for the individual and the group.

CONCLUDING COMMENTS

The ideas that have been developed here are derived from the work of Beck, Bowlby, Brown and many others. Much of this work was examined in detail in previous chapters. What I have attempted to do is to present certain data in ways which facilitate our thinking along integrative lines. As suggested at the beginning of this chapter, such integrative formulations are bound to be artificial to some degree and no claim is made to offering a comprehensive theory. Nevertheless, we can, for clarity, suggest three major propositions which flow from this particular organization of data:

1. Depression, normal and abnormal, relates to mechanisms which have evolved over eons of time in the human brain. The mechanisms that seem especially important, judging from psychological and sociological data, are those concerned with the social integration of the human group. As Bowlby suggests, a considerable amount of our affective experience relates to relationships (attachments) we share with other members of our species.

2. The cognitive themes of depressives need not make sense in any logical way. This is because, as Jung and others observed, "thinking" is only one aspect of human consciousness. However, cognitive distortions are easily understandable when viewed against an evolutionary background. Patients who feel they need others to survive are, in this sense, responding to true primitive needs. In a primitive state without others, many humans would not survive.

3. Depression, therefore, involves disturbances in many aspects of social integration. These include (a) how individuals view themselves in relationship to others; and (b) how individuals perceive their needs (for love, protection, and comfort) and how they perceive themselves as able to fulfil these needs (social skills, submissiveness) and the capacity of others to fulfil them.

At the present time we have only sketched rough outlines of the sort of psychobiological interactions which may be important in depression. One suggestion is that adult depression is related to the breakdown of peer-group attachments. Moreover, as I have mentioned, this ignites twin appraisals of loss, focusing on care giving and care receiving. If it is true that it is peer-group attachments that are disturbed in depression, then what should we make of the psychotherapeutic suggestion that therapists act as "good parents"? This is a fascinating question because it shows an over-concern with parent–child attachment difficulties. Consider, for example, the work of Lawick-Goodall (1973, 1975). She has shown that defeated chimpanzees do not always seek comfort from their parents. Sometimes they approach dominant members. They can become quite distressed if the dominant animal does not respond with stroking (Lawick-Goodall, 1975). Also, Ellenberger (1970) points out how early hypnotists were fascinated by the importance of rapport between patient and therapist. While masters could hypnotize their servants, the reverse was rarely true. Does the perceived status of a therapist play a role in therapeutic effectiveness?

Early, and so-called primitive, societies often had shamans to cure various illnesses. It is important to note that these healers were not so much seen as being parental, but rather as powerful mediators with dominant status (secret powers). Ellenberger may be correct in relating psychotherapeutic qualities to the same types of process. In other words, the therapist is seen not necessarily as a parental figure, but rather as a dominant member of the peer group who provides protection and acceptance of the person, enabling a reintegration of peer-group relationships. Although it is not the intention to throw out the idea of therapist as parent, we should also seriously consider that therapists may be behaving in ways more to do with shaman qualities than parent qualities.

Another important issue we should consider is that of self-awareness. Crook (1980) has given an important and fascinating evolutionary view of this. It seems reasonable to propose that only human beings can perceive themselves as a burden on others and this reflects their capacity to be aware of self in relation to others. Dobzhansky (1975) also points out that death awareness and self-awareness are related. In other words, it is unlikely that animals, without self-awareness, are aware of their own capacity for death. Humans clearly are, however, and in depression perceptions of hopelessness are tied in with death awareness, inner emptiness, nothing to live for, and being of no use to anyone. Thus, the development of self-awareness opens up new dimensions of experience for positive and negative states. The negative (depressed) states reflect both the loss of care receiving and the loss of care giving. This is not to say that the experience of depression is simply an epiphenomenon of self-awareness. But the human subject can be more positively or painfully "aware" of himself in relationship to his group. Thus, the capacity for self-awareness undoubtedly opens up new dimensions on depressive phenomenology which animals do not have. This "extra" capacity of humans is profound, and animal models of psychopathology often fail to note the implications of self-awareness in the human subject.

To suggest that depression is in some way related to evolutionary mechanisms holds out important questions. As we have seen for anxiety, the concept of preparedness in the development of phobias is now very much with us (Eysenck, 1979). An evolutionary hypothesis of depression also suggests some form of preparedness. In fact, we may go so far as to suggest an archetypal concept of the notion of preparedness. At the present time it is not clear how the behaviorist notion of preparedness and the concept of archetypes, believed by Jung to be products of the collective unconscious, are related, though I think they are. As Jung (1972) suggests, the inherited structure of the "psyche" breeds true to the species. Further, the predispositions for specific forms of experience—cognitive-affective patterns—are inherited. They are not individual, but universal, which are acted upon and developed by the personal-cultural experience of the individual (see Tart, 1980). The commonality of depression, leaving aside normal versus abnormal presentations, suggests some inherited pre-paredness, or archetypal constellation, which is activated under certain conditions. This fits with Beck's suggestions that the content of depressive thinking is much the same across subgroups of depressed individuals.

Within fairly wide limits, this chapter has attempted to focus on the social meaning of depression and the implications for stress evaluation and coping. It has highlighted the fact that stress and coping difficulties of depressives center on intraspecies relationship concerns. This approach offers a psychoevolutionary perspective which links cognitive-behavioral and biological data. I do not offer any grand theory of depression, for the heterogeneity of depression rules that such an endeavor is unlikely to succeed, given our present knowledge. Rather, I hope that this chapter throws light on possible patterns of interaction.

As a psychological inquiry we now need to proceed with a further discussion of the individual. In this effort we can move into more detailed consideration of the depressed brain state.

7
The Depressed Brain State

The previous chapter examined the possibility that there is an innate predisposition to depression. This being so, there is the probability that the threshold for the activation of this predisposition is subject to the laws of inheritance and genetic variability. But it is not only genetic variation which may facilitate the activation of various brain–behavior response patterns. Psychological processes are essentially concerned with structuring reality, allowing meaning to be derived from stimulus events and actions to be planned. It follows, therefore, that in some cases internal constructions of reality can activate innate predisposed styles of responding, which are maladaptive to the extent that these internal constructions are not "true" reflections of reality. The idea that depression is the result of a divergence between internal reality and external reality forms an essential part of Beck's cognitive theory. However, cognitive distortions do not cause depression because they are irrational, but because they recruit brain–behavior patterns of responding which have a prepared innate basis, and these have evolved within the human brain. Put simply, internal constructions which produce perceptions of emotional isolation and abandonment, together with appraisals of insurmountable obstacles and/or unobtainable incentives, may activate various (inherited) prepared styles of biological response patterns. Under these conditions there is an activation of multiple response systems which have their bases in the evolved structure of brain function.

There are a growing number of psychologists who regard as folly the notion of the "tabula rasa" view of man. Eysenck (e.g., 1979) has always stressed the importance of the physiological basis of experience and behavior. He has consistently argued that psychological theories should accord with what is known about the evolved biological systems of the brain. The more eclectic cognitive theorists have also begun to show some interest in the biological basis of learning. Mahoney (1974) puts it well:

To contend that most human behaviors are learned is not incompatible with the assumption that learning is biologically mediated. We presume that there are neurochemical changes underlying the process. Given a biological organism and a presumably neurochemical substratum for learning, it seems only reasonable to concede the posssibility that the current physiological state of the individual may influence his ability to assimilate, retain, or utilize experiential information [p. 253].

This line of reasoning suggests that we cannot consider the variation in cognitive-behavioral capabilities of the depressed person without some conceptualization of the "physiological state" of the individual. Indeed, without such a conceptualization it would be difficult to provide a rationale for the efficacy of biological treatments, or for the emergence of symptom variation (e.g., diurnal variation of mood, loss of energy, early morning waking, and so on). Equally, the clear evidence that the vast majority of depressions are related to various psychological difficulties, together with the evidence for the efficacy of nonphysical treatments (Weissman, 1979), suggests that psychological mechanisms which distort and amplify innate predispositions must be an important part of any holistic understanding of depression.

For these reasons we may conceptualize depression as constituting a change in cognitive-behavioral-biological interactions. Because it is the interactions which are important, we need to examine these in more detail. They do not share one-to-one relationships, but have complex feedback systems. Weingartner et al. (1977) and Reus et al. (1979a) have suggested that depression should be regarded as a change in "brain state." Hence brain state may be regarded as a descriptive term for the interactions of cognitive-behavioral-biological variables.

In this chapter we look more closely at a few psychobiological interactions and feedback systems which occur in depression once the disorder has started. It is useful to bear in mind that there are multiple levels of interaction, including those between causal, maintenance, and recovery mechanisms. Furthermore, by regarding depression as a change in brain state we can confront an important aspect of brain function. This concerns the evolved capacity for the brain to switch from one state to another, sometimes in a rapid manner. By acknowledging the capacity for the brain to switch states, we can introduce another dimension of change, which has implications for various disorders. This dimension is one of brain-state stability–instability and this dimension itself can be affected by genetic and psychological mechanisms.

To accommodate these two aspects of discussion this chapter is divided into two parts. In the first part, various cognitive-biological interactions are discussed. In the second part, the importance of brain-state discontinuities is considered. Arguments are put forward to highlight the importance of changes in brain states for models of psychopathology.

BRAIN STATE INTERACTIONS

Depression exerts important effects on many aspects of information processing (Miller, 1975). These effects have been studied from different perspectives. Some studies are derived directly from cognitive theory (e.g., Blackburn & Bonham, 1980; Teasdale & Fogarty, 1979), and others from state-dependent learning theory (Weingartner et al., 1977, 1981). In an early experiment Lloyd & Lishman (1975) investigated changes in memory function associated with depression. They found that increasing levels of depression, in a clinical population, were associated with a change in the latency ratio for the recall of pleasant and unpleasant memories. Typically, depression led to a faster recall of unpleasant memories. Teasdale & Fogarty (1979) investigated this relationship using a mood-induction procedure with normal subjects. The main effect of induced mood was to increase the latency of recall for pleasant memories. Changes in the recall of unpleasant memories were relatively unaffected. Teasdale & Taylor (1981) suggest such findings relate to induced mood change, rather than the induction procedure. Breslow et al. (1981) obtained similar results using a different technique with hospitalized depressives. They found that deficits in the recall from a story could be attributed to the fact that the depressives tended to show decrements in the recall of positive themes within the story. Recall of negative and neutral themes was not affected. As these authors are aware, however, positive themes may have been remembered but not mentioned because of a mood discordant state.

The idea that mood may have asymmetrical effects on cognitive processes is further highlighted by Mischel et al. (1973, 1976). They found induced perceptions of success affected selective attention to positive information about self, but subjects experiencing failure did not significantly differ from a control group in their allocation of attention to self-relevant information. Isen et al. (1978) found that the induction of positive or negative moods (via manipulations of outcome on a game) affected the recall of positive material but the recall of negative material was unaffected. Gilbert (1980) found that depressives were less sensitive (as measured by GSR) in response to positive (success) cues but not more sensitive to negative (failure) cues, when compared to an anxious control and normal control group. Such data may support Mischel's idea that normals have a "warm glow," or positive bias of information processing. Rather than becoming more negative, depressives may lose this warm glow distortion (Lewinsohn et al., 1980).

These studies point to the importance of further investigations on cognition and mood interactions. The relationships between mood, cognition, and biological change are more difficult to evaluate, though of some importance to a psychobiological perspective. Teasdale & Rezin (1978a) found that although the presentation of external stimulation at a high rate reduced the frequency of negative thoughts in nine out of fifteen depressed patients investigated, effects on mood were only significant for two patients. Teasdale & Rezin (1978b) also examined the technique of thought stopping and found it to have no significant impact on mood, or corrugator EMG. (Corrugator EMG is a psychophysiological measure believed to be sensitive to depression [Teasdale & Bancroft, 1977].) In a single case study of five depressed subjects, Blackburn & Bonham (1980) examined cognitive coping strategies with depressed patients provided with happy and unhappy thoughts. They investigated a number of psychophysiological response patterns in three conditions—distancing from unhappy thoughts, involvement in unhappy thoughts, and happy thoughts. Although there were differences between cases, their data supported the view that cognitive coping strategies had a significant influence on mood and two psychophysiological variables—corrugator EMG and heart rate. These were significantly correlated with mood. Thus, Blackburn & Bonham provide useful evidence on the interaction between mood, cognitive activity, and biological change. Of course, a number of studies have shown relationships between styles of cognitive coping with stressful stimuli and psychophysiological change (e.g., Lazarus, 1966). Blackburn & Bonham's study is of special interest, however, because these relationships were examined in diagnosed depressives in a depressed state.

These data point to the growing recognition that cognitive-mood interactions operate in both directions, with various feedback systems (Isen et al., 1978). As Wright & Mischel (1982) point out, affect can bias information processing and information processing can influence affect (see also Bower, 1981). Hence, the simple cognition → affect equation, presented by some cognitive theorists, is incomplete. Moreover, the above data imply that direct changes in affect will alter cognitive bias. This fits clinical observations that changes in cognitive distortion may ebb and flow with changes occurring in the affective disposition of the individual.

Weingartner et al. (1977) indicate that the manner in which life events are encoded, stored, and retrieved may be greatly influenced by the prevailing brain state. Since various affective experiences involve changes of brain state, it follows that the biological substrate, upon which memories are encoded, will be intimately linked with affective experience. Thus, different brain states are associated with different attentional predispositions and discrete encoding strategies (Reus et al., 1979a). The data point to a highly interactive system.

The brain state approach allows for the investigation and integration of endogenous biological changes in the biological substrates of cognition behavior and affect. For example, variations in MAO activity during the menstrual cycle carry the possibility that these changes invoke changes in nformation processing, and the retrieval of mood-relevant memories. The overall qualitative effect of these changes will be significantly influenced by whatever current concerns and cognitive schemata are embedded in the psychological organization of the individual. If MAO changes feed negative self-appraisals, invoke past memories of rejection and failure, then the affective reaction is likely to be more pronounced. A similar feedback system could be described for biological changes associated with uncontrollable stress and/or abandonment threats coming from the environment. There is a further aspect to brain state interactions in the depressive. We have seen that the "quality" of information processing (e.g., what is recalled from memory) is affected by mood and vice versa, but also the actual capacity for information processing is altered in depression. Beck et al. (1979) have argued that depressives exhibit primitive thinking. It is unclear, however, whether this refers to quality or capacity. Aside from issues of what memories are recalled or what stimuli are attended to, depression, especially when severe, significantly inhibits "the capacity" to process information. There are two aspects to this issue. The first seems to relate to a general loss of capacity for complex thinking and the second to an interference effect.

Loss of Information Processing Capacity

Cohen et al. (1982) suggest that the more difficult a task and the greater the level of effort required, the greater the probability of deficits being manifest in depressed individuals. They suggest that in depression there is a general deterioration in the capacity to structure and organize responses. This may be in response to general cognitive efficiency change, and/or general changes in a central motivational system. Weingartner et al. (1981) examined both qualitative and quantitative changes in information processing in depression. Generally, depressed patients exhibit difficulty in structuring inputs for recall, but when provided with structure, learning deficits were not significant. Hence, both studies support the view that the depressed brain state is also an inefficient brain state. These data may link with the evidence presented in Chapter 5; that is, disturbance in brainstem activity makes it difficult to "switch analyzers." This may also have an effect on "interference."

On the biological side, drugs can significantly affect information-processing capacity (Davis et al., 1976; Warburton, 1979). Henry et al. (1973) and Glass et al. (1981) demonstrate that depression–drug–information-processing interactions are highly complex. Findings suggest that antidepressant drugs may improve brain state efficiency before affecting mood. This area is controversial, however, as a recent review demonstrates (Thompson & Trimble, 1982). For example, the cognitive functioning of normals given nonMAOI antidepressants tends to deteriorate, while for depressives it tends to improve.

An Interference Effect

It has been known for some time that stress is often accompanied by painful repetitive thinking, which some individuals find difficult to terminate or inhibit. Horowitz & Wilner (1976) and Horowitz et al. (1980b) point out that these ruminative aspects are often painful, focusing on the stress, and are sometimes experienced as difficult to control. Sutherland et al. (in press) have also demonstrated that negative moods exert complex influences on an individual's ability to control and dismiss intrusive thoughts. In a different vein, Braden & Ho (1981) found that "racing thoughts," which are difficult to control, are common in depression and mania. Furthermore, schizophrenics who had racing thoughts met the criteria for schizoaffective disturbance. They suggest that racing thoughts are involved in poor concentration and relate to an affective dimension. It has also been known for some time that loss–bereavement is associated with painful, sometimes constant ruminations on the lost person.

The interference effect offers a new twist to the uncontrollable stress research. If it is argued that a large degree of stress is related to the content of an individual's thoughts, then repetitive, stress-arousing thoughts that cannot be controlled may operate as an "internal" uncontrollable stress. In other words, an individual may be brought to a state of NA depletion because he cannot control the constant, repetitive source of his arousal— his painful thoughts. Furthermore, animal work may be of limited value here, if the biological disruption found in humans is due to a ruminative aspect. Helpless animals may fail to learn escape responses, either because their brain states are too inefficient for new learning, or because there is something equivalent to ruminative processes interfering with new learning. Neither explanation requires a "belief that the stress is uncontrollable."

Taking these data together suggests three issues relevant to the cognitive changes in depression. Depression affects what is attended to and recalled; depression affects the *capacity* to attend and structure information; depression invokes uncontrollable, repetitive ruminations. Presumably the level of depression affects the severity of each aspect. Hence, depressed individuals are going to find themselves significantly handicapped if, when attempting to cope with problems, they cannot think straight and are being constantly reminded of their unfortunate state. In this situation aversive cognitive-affective-biological feedback systems are likely to emerge. If the biological system does become significantly disturbed, then the depression may become self-perpetuating. Hence, recovery may depend on a changing biological process, which in turn increases brain state efficiency and helps control the arousal generated by ruminative thinking. It is of some interest to speculate that some drugs may be most effective in controlling the ruminative aspects of a depression, thus freeing the central nervous system from "internal" uncontrollable stress and facilitating recovery. In this sense, such drugs would not be truly antidepressant, but would work by inhibiting cognitive-biological feedback systems. Their antidepressant (mood-elevating) properties would be something of a secondary effect. The extent to which some antidepressants can help panic attacks and obsessional states may suggest this as one of their actions. Drugs with specific 5-HT actions may be especially relevant for this, though this is a speculation. Perhaps 5-HT dysfunctions act to keep things going, inhibiting the switch from one brain state to another, in effect acting to freeze or "lock in" specific states.

Psychobiological Models of Depression

It has been suggested here that depression constitutes an amplification and modification of specific psychobiological response patterns. These specific patterns of responding have evolved as a response set to separation–abandonment in social animals. The structure of this response set is biphasic, namely protest–despair. The learned helplessness model is also capable of being viewed in evolutionary terms, and it too points to a biphasic response pattern, namely invigoration–helplessness. Although some have tried to explain separation–abandonment responses in terms of learned helplessness (Seligman, 1975), this is not altogether satisfactory. An important difference between the models is the degree to which depressed affect can exist during the first response phase to either uncontrollable shock or separation. In the learned helplessness model, depression is a consequence of helplessness, so depressed mood cannot exist during invigoration. For Seligman (1975), depression replaces anxiety as the stress comes to be perceived as uncontrollable. This limitation is not evident for the separation–abandonment model. Dysphoria can be present during the very first stages of protest. Thus, as in grief states, crying, sadness, and labile affect can all be marked during the protest stage, when a major loss first occurs. Hence, as Mineka & Suomi (1978) indicate, protest may relate to agitated depressed states.

The possibility that dysphoric moods exist during both phases of responding to specific stresses suggests an interesting set of hypotheses: (1) the psychobiological response patterns to abandonment are biphasic; (2) a lowering of mood exists during both phases; and (3) behaviorally, a distinction can be made between the first-phase response pattern—agitation—and the second-phase response pattern—retardation.

The model shown in *Fig.* 7.1 (based very loosely on the ideas of Solomon, 1980) thus presents itself. We shall assume that the brain is programed to exhibit and experience two (state) response patterns in relation to abandonment–separation stress. The A-state is a fast building state, which is ignited by the perception of loss of important interpersonal relationships. This may be termed "protest," but may include the affective experiences of sadness and lability of mood. There is a focusing of attention on the lost object, coupled with heightened activity, designed to increase the probability of reunion. The R-state is a state which independently is also activated by separation and loss of a loved object. This state is associated with a turning-in on the self and a (reduced) retarded level of activity. It builds more slowly than the A-state, hence in the early stages of abandonment A-state predominates.

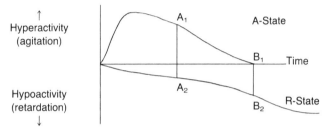

FIG. 7.1   Phasic activity model to abandonment stress.

Figure 7.1 suggests that A-state extinguishes if it is not reinforced by cues signalling reunion. Cues that signal reunion may inhibit both A- and R-states, but A-states are more rapidly extinguished in the absence of reunion cues, whereas R states are facilitated by such absences. Additionally, A states can be prolonged by certain cues which indicate a potential for reunion, in the absence of reunion itself.

In regard to depression it is assumed that both A- and R-states are experienced as dysphoric. The syndrome exhibited will depend upon the relative balance between the presence of A-state patterns and R-state patterns. Patients who are at points A_1–A_2 may experience hyperactivity (agitation) labile mood; they may be high reassurance seekers, and cognitive content and rumination will focus on loss in the world (loss of reinforcement receiving). If the individual is unable to make a satisfactory reunion with significant others, the A-state may extinguish and a full R-state will manifest (B_1–B_2). In this situation the individual experiences retarded psychobiological activity and hides away from others (not to be confused with social anxiety). Cognitive content and ruminations focus on the loss of feeling, experienced as flattened affect and inner emptiness–deadness; there is a loss of the capacity to see oneself as reinforcing to others. Any individual lying between (say) A_1–A_2 and B_1–B_2 will show mixed patterns because both states can coexist. Patients lying beyond B_1–B_2 will show greater degrees of retardation, but little agitation.

This model may fit Lader's (1975) view that the psychobiological state of depression is basically one of retardation; agitation, if it exists, is super-imposed on basic retardation. Furthermore, the second phase of re-sponding to uncontrollable shock is seen as an R-state, associated with a specific form of depression, that of retarded depression. Hence, as Depue & Monroe (1978a) suggest, the learned helplessness model may be more relevant to endogenous depression. This is because the learned helplessness model equates depression with the second-phase response pattern to un-controllable trauma, and ignores the importance of the first, invigorated phase. It also highlights the fact that the "type of stress" is an important determinant of the affective consequences to it. Dysphoria may not be invoked by shock, but can be invoked by significant losses.

TABLE 7.1
Variations Between A-State and R-State Depression

	A-State	*R-State*
neurochemistry	5–HT ↓ ? NA ↑ Ach? DA?	5–HT ↓ ? NA ↓ Ach ↑ DA?
Type	Agitated—anxious (neurotic? unipolar?)	Retarded—depressed (bipolar? psychotic?)
Affect	Labile, crying, unstable anger control; complains of instability of affect; depression focusing on feelings of loneliness—absence of relationships, etc. (empty world)	Flattened affect; lacks reactivity; loss of any feeling, can't cry; complains of deadness, emptiness, can't love, or get angry (empty self)
Behavioral	Fails to extinguish to: (1) Cognitive—biological interactions; ruminates on losses in the world. (2) to aversive stimuli (e.g., loud noises) Seeks external reinforcement (e.g., reassurance from staff); wants love, care, protection	Extinguishes to external stimuli, e.g., loud noises; experiences ruminations on inner state of emptiness, deadness of feeling Hides away, does not seek external reinforcement; believes self to be unconsolable, unhelpable.
Cognitive	Self lacks skills but may perceive self as having some positive attributes (e.g., tries to be trustworthy)	Less emphasis on an absence of skills, more on negative attributes of self, e.g., bad, wicked, no use

This is a speculative model, but having come this far it is worth seeing whether the model does suggest differences in depressive type. *Table 7.1* outlines possible differences between A-state depressions and R-state depressions. These are highly speculative distinctions, but are made in a logical fashion on the basis of the data reviewed in this book.

Clearly, it is rare that only one state dominates. In depression, mixtures are far more common. It is also clear that some individuals remain in the A-state throughout most of their depression, whereas some depressives appear to show relatively little A-state but exhibit gross R-states. Why should this be?

As I have emphasized, both A-states and R-states are psychobiological response patterns which have evolved as prepared response systems, to be triggered by certain environmental (or perceived) outcomes. Hence, genetic and/or classically conditioned variations in the biological codes mediating both A-states and R-states will give rise to variations in their degree of recruitment at times of stress. Those more prone to retarded depressions, we may assume, have biological mediators of R-state patterns which are readily accessible. Hence some individuals are biologically more vulnerable to shift into R-states under the relevant provocation.

The control mechanisms are in some part clearly biological. This, however, should not be taken as ignoring the role of psychological factors. The animal work reviewed by Mineka & Suomi (1978) suggests that A-states can be prolonged following separation or, indeed, shortened. Also, in as much as psychological differences are detectable in A-state and R-state depressions, individuals who have very negative perceptions about the probability of regaining meaningful relationships (perhaps for reasons described by Bowlby) may be psychologically predisposed to exhibiting R-state depressions (i.e., the A-state is mild or easily extinguished). Perhaps negative perceptions of personal attributes also act as a factor. In other words, firmly held, negative beliefs that the self is unlovable (coded in memory) may act against efforts to rejoin the world and seek reunion with others. Blatt et al.'s (1982) description of dependency depressions and self-critical depressions may also provide a clue. The more self-critical the individual, the less value there may be in searching in the external world for reinforcement. At this time the model proposed here is too speculative to make any firm distinctions. However, it does recommend itself for future research and makes some sense of variations between depressives, on the basis of variations in the amplification and modification of specific, evolved, psychobiological response patterns.

A model for depression. Taking the data presented in previous chapters together, we are able to outline the model shown in *Fig. 7.2.* This model seeks to sketch possible interactions between cognitive-behavioral-biological components. In some sense it hides more than it reveals for no

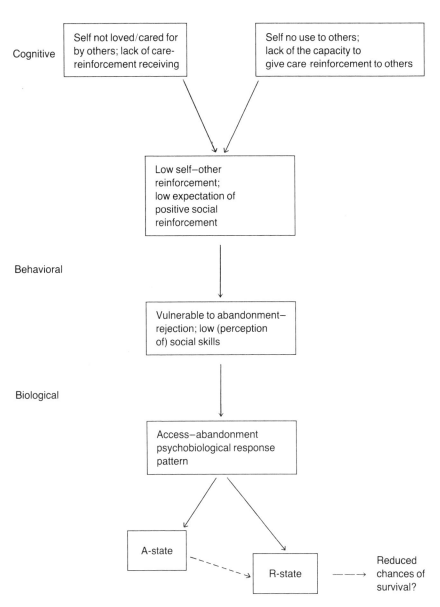

FIG. 7.2 Possible interactions between cognitive-behavioral-biological components.

attempt has been made to show the various feedback processes involved. Amplification and modification of the basic psychobiological response patterns can exist at any or all of the different levels. As the brain responds to the inner construction of reality, and not reality itself, various cognitive schemata and memories may predispose some individuals to grossly amplified perceptions of abandonment threat. In these cases A-states and R-states may be inappropriately recruited under minor provocation. The essential element of this thesis is that the capacity to manifest A-states and R-states exists as inherited potentials. Moreover, since the brain has evolved these potentials, variations in the biological codes mediating A-states and R-states will further influence their accessibility, amplification, and modification. Hence, genetically controlled sensitivity of (say) NA or ACh will play a role in the timing and manifestation of the depressive episode. Further, variations in genetically controlled dominance–submissive biological profiles will influence the individual's sensitivity to abandonment threat and will thus influence the interpersonal behavior of the individual throughout life.

The extent to which R-states are involved in reduced chances of survival remains controversial. Various physical traumata may involve neurochemical response patterns which increase the accessibility and availability of R-states. More research is need on this aspect.

These models do not rely on variations in symptoms to suggest differences between depressive types. Rather the emphasis is on variations in underlying psychobiological responses and the evolved nature of their predetermination. Although these models are speculative, they are derived in the light of current data from a number of research efforts. It is hoped they will be of some value for research purposes.

To add further speculation we can suggest three final points. Firstly, difference in the predisposition to A-state or R-state depression may reside in the focus of negative appraisal. Those that seek comfort from the world (significant others) relate to the anxious, labile, depressed group. Under stress their first coping efforts are to look to others for support. In other words, there is a movement outwards. This vulnerability may relate to early maternal over protection. On the other hand those that are more vulnerable to R-state depression tend to believe that love and comfort from others must be earned. Under stress their first movement is inwards—to look for the necessary "performances" that will earn them a place in meaningful social relationships. This vulnerability may relate to the adoption of harsh ego standards as the means to securing love and respect. As children their histories are marked by the conditional love given by their parents. Such a predisposition relates to histories described by Cohen et al. (1954), the ego-analytic theories, and to processes discussed in Chapter 4.

Secondly, those vulnerable to bipolar affective illness have most in common with R-state depressives. In the hypomanic state there are invigorated efforts to unite with significant others. But this is not an agitated seeking of support, but rather a magnified effort to be of value and of use to others. The hypomanic, in various disorganised ways, tries to be as useful and helpful as possible; money spent is normally on others; they may get angry with those who interfere with their good ideas and projects. All in all they are literally full of their own self-importance to their species. This behavior may be seen as a gross amplification of social interactive behavior relating to a need to be useful to others (see Chapter 6). It is possible to see how a vulnerability to R-state depression and hypomanic vulnerabilities may share common histories. The dimension of vulnerability for both exists as negative schemata relating to the "earning of love and security." For the very reason that our need to see ourselves as useful to others and others as caring of us are innately available predispositions, it follows that neurochemical changes in brain may lead to an amplification of these social behaviors. Whether or not the control of these twin aspects (care reinforcement giving and receiving) reside in different areas of the brain is unknown. In view of recent evidence demonstrating the dispersion of control centers in the brain this seems a likely possibility. Hence, it remains quite possible to perceive oneself as being loved, but still be profoundly depressed because one's own judgment of one's value to others is negative.

Thirdly, we can speculate about what may happen if an individual acquires harsh ego standards but inherits a low status biological profile. To what degree will his psychology amplify the risk of a depression? In a society which places so much emphasis on achievement, success, assertiveness—I leave the reader to make his own speculations!

This presentation fits some of the classification data (Chapter 1). It allows for various combinations of symptoms to exist and for changes over time to occur within any one individual. Furthermore, because these states rest on biochemical parameters then changes in these parameters (e.g., changes in MAO with age) may facilitate the activation of these states. This model may also fit biochemical work (e.g., Schildkraut et al., 1978a,b). A-states may relate to hyperactivity of NA while R-states may relate to both NA hypoactivity and ACh hyperactivity. Hence, rather than thinking in terms of diseases, it seems more useful to regard depression as the amplification of specific psychobiological response patterns.

THE BRAIN STATE STABILITY–INSTABILITY DIMENSION

One of the problems for models of psychopathology centers on the tendency to view human subjective experience as on a continuum. When confronted by a rapid switch from mania to depression, or of sudden explosive rage in a patient, it is clear that sometimes changes can occur rapidly. There is good reason to believe that under some conditions the brain has evolved the capacity to switch states rapidly. For example, the presentation of a danger stimulus, e.g., a snake, can lead to immediate arousal in many species, including the human. The important aspect of this argument is that the whole psychobiological response pattern (including cognitive, behavioral, and biological components) may change all at once.

A common experience of brain state discontinuity is that following sexual orgasm. Stimuli that were pleasant and arousing before orgasm may not be so immediately afterwards. Invigorated behavior ceases, with a switch into a more passive state. Although these changes are associated with the physiological changes of the sexual act, the final state (tense, relaxed, anxious, guilty) will depend on a variety of psychological factors, e.g., the security of the relationship, fears of performance anxiety, place of the act, and so on. In regard to depression, these considerations raise two related issues. The first concerns discontinuities of affective experience; the second concerns the forces that are operating to engender instability in certain psychobiological response patterns.

Discontinuities of affective experience are noted in depressives. These may be associated with the presentation of certain stimuli or signals (e.g., failure or rejection signals), with the occurrence of automatic thoughts, or with subtle changes in physiological state. Sometimes the person is described as "overreacting." Some patients in the depressed state can experience a sudden worsening or lifting of their depression. One schizoaffective patient described to me how her depression would suddenly lift for up to three hours at a time. When it returned it was sudden, expressed as "flooding back." Some patients with diurnal variation can experience sudden changes in state during the course of a day. Sutherland (1976) describes how his own depression suddenly started to dissipate on hearing a certain piece of music. Clearly, any model of brain state instability must account for this "switching" of states. Interestingly, multiple personality disorder (Hilgard, 1977) might also be investigated with a brain state approach.

The idea that the biological basis of depression is one of instability has been suggested by Maas (1979). Hence, there is the possibility that under certain conditions changes in brain state are not gradual, but sudden. This points to important psychobiological information about how the brain functions in states of high arousal. In other words, discontinuity of function may be built in. Both patients and therapists can gain from this knowledge, for it helps us to understand that during recovery some patients will experience sudden returns of their depression. These relate to a breakdown in homeostatic processes governing the equilibrium of brain state function. Because these homeostatic mechanisms are under psychobiological control, this allows patients and therapists to deal with relapse without either feeling pressured to "work harder." Before becoming aware of this, I often regarded mild lapses as probably due to some automatic thoughts. It became clear that sometimes the automatic thoughts were consequences of mood change, and that this affective change could itself become a focus for depressive cognitions (why am I like this, why aren't I getting better, maybe I'm doing something wrong, etc.).

In addition to the issue of discontinuity, it is necessary to know how this instability has come about; what is the source of the instability? In order to answer this, it is necessary to have a model. Such a model must fulfil the role of representing the interactions of psychobiological components in a dimensional form, yet demonstrate how such interactions can produce discontinuity and instability of functioning.

A Model for Instability

The model which seems especially suitable is that derived from catastrophe theory (Zeeman, 1977). Zeeman points out in his introduction to catastrophe theory (CT), that CT "is particularly applicable where gradually changing forces produce sudden effects. We often call such effects catastrophes, because our intuition about the underlying continuity of the forces makes the very discontinuity of the effects so unexpected and this has given rise to the name [p. 1]."

Catastrophe theory depends on complex mathematical theorems developed by the French mathematician Rene Thom. However, we are able to use the geometric forms of CT without an in-depth understanding of the complex mathematics involved. CT offers a means by which we can understand discontinuity and the sources of instability arising from the interaction of processes, which of themselves are not discontinuous.

There are a number of "catastrophes," each capable of describing the interactions between various dimensions. The larger the number of dimensions, the more complex the catastrophe. Here we shall be concerned with just one model, known as the "cusp catastrophe." This is a relatively simple model to understand, and provides a useful starting point for the examination of discontinuity in psychopathological processes. It has already been applied to schizophrenia (MacCulloch & Waddington, 1979), bipolar illness, and anorexia nervosa (see Zeeman, 1977).

For psychological theories the clearest example of a discontinuous cusp catastrophe at work is in an approach–avoidance conflict. In these situations the organism is confronted with two, behavioral motivations (to avoid and to approach) to the same (set of) stimuli. When both motivations are low, or when one is significantly stronger than the other, the expected behavior will be determined by the strongest motivation. But when both motivations are strongly aroused, the organism moves into an unstable state, where a small increase in one motivation, not equally matched by an increase in the opposing motivation, may cause a sudden switch or jump in behavior.

The example used by most theorists applying CT to behavior is a slight variant of the approach–avoidance model (Postle, 1980; Zeeman, 1977). In this case the competing motivations of fear and anger are described. In that the behaviors arising from the activation of these two motivations are different (fight-flight), these motivations, when dimensionally represented, are called "splitting factors." It is helpful to examine this example in more detail.

Let us suppose there are forces working on an animal that increase anger. As long as this is not opposed, then the more angry the animal, the more aggressive the behavior. Equally, the more frightened the animal, the greater the strength of avoidance behavior. We can see the relationship between these two processes in *Fig.* 7.3; the lower surface represents the opposing motivations of fear and anger, and the upper surface represents a three-dimensional behavior surface. Starting from point A, an increase in fear increases avoidance (flight) behavior, shown by the path AC. An increase in anger, however, increases flight behavior, shown by the path AB. But when both fear and anger are strongly aroused, this model predicts neutral behavior, AD. Clearly, this is not likely.

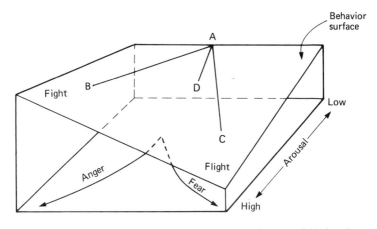

FIG. 7.3.   Changes in fight–flight behavior as shown by a non-folded surface.

The CT solution to this dilemma suggests we fold the front edge of the behavior surface so that we have a shape as shown in *Fig.* 7.4. Now, examining the problem again using this catastrophe model, we have the following situation. As before, high fear produces flight, and high anger produces fight. But when both are highly aroused the animal moves toward the front surface of the plane, along or near the axis of the fold or cusp. In *Fig.* 7.5 we can see how this works.

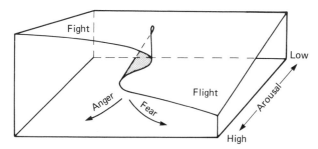

FIG. 7.4.   A cusp catastrophe model of fight–flight behavior.

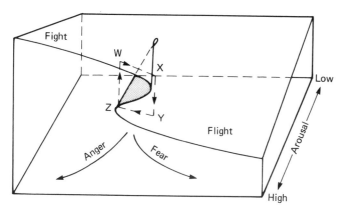

FIG. 7.5.   Discontinuous changes in fight–flight behavior shown as paths on the cusp catastrophe surface.

Suppose that the animal is at point W and exhibits fight behavior. As fear is increased, without any further increase in anger, the animal moves toward point X. Any further small increase in fear will result in the animal turning tail and running away (flight). This is represented by a discontinuous jump from point X→ Y. If, however, fear reduces again, the animal now moves along the path Y→ Z. This continues until point Z is reached, where anger is significantly stronger than fear and the animal turns and fights.

This is obviously a very stereotyped example and various complications can be introduced. But this very brief outline of CT allows us to make some important observations:

1. It approximates to a reasonable description of what actually happens when two conflicting motivations are strongly aroused.

2. It provides one possible model which aids our understanding of discontinuities in behavior.

3. Perhaps most importantly, it suggests that entry and exit from one behavior to another do not occur at the same level of anger and fear. In other words, once the animal has moved from X → Y, before it will fight again, it must move along the path Y → Z. Thus, even if fear is decreased, it will not attack again until fear has decreased well beyond point Y, to point Z.

In depression, some of the motivations which resemble the approach–avoidance conflicts described above, are those to do with (a) the avoidance of failure and the need for success; and (b) the avoidance of a loss of support and attachment, and the need to be independent and assertive. In the latter case, we have spent some time examining these opposing motivations. In Chapter 6 the important sources of conflict were those relating to the fear of counterattack contingent on assertive behavior versus the need to be assertive and secure positive reinforcement. Let us look first at (a).

Figure 7.6 demonstrates how these two opposing motivations, when strongly aroused, can produce unstable states. As before, changes in the relative strengths of these motivations at or near the fold (cusp) produce unstable states. We can see that when these motivations are strongly aroused, individuals might oscillate between high (fear) avoidance behavior or high (success) approach behavior.

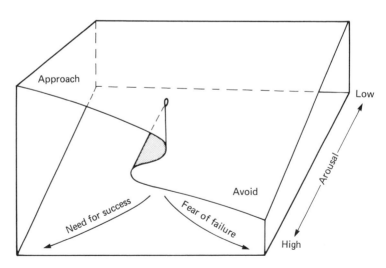

FIG. 7.6. A cusp catastrophe model of approach—avoidance behavior related to the opposing motivations to approach success and avoid failure.

Because both motivations are involved, we would not expect stable behavior near the fold. In these situations, hypersensitivity to failure cues may produce radical shifts in behavior. Thus, we may find some individuals "suddenly" giving up when the approach to success starts to become difficult. Giving up near the cusp is not stable, because the individual still has a strong need to succeed. Moreover, the radical shift in behavior will be associated with radical changes in affect. To understand this we must return to our psychological theories and be aware of the "meaning" the individual derives from giving up. In other words, giving up is associated with the loss of the possible advantages of success. Individuals who hold success as the key to social and self-acceptance are likely to experience this discontinuous change in behavior as grossly distressing. At this point the analysis becomes complex, for we need an in-depth understanding of why the individual's fear of failure got the better of him. CT can help us understand the relationship between various dimensions, but it cannot throw light on the factors which produce high fear of failure and high success needs in the first place. All we can do is note the instability that is introduced into the individual's response system when these motivations are operative at a high level. Both Ferster's (1973, 1974) discussion of approach–avoidance conflicts and various suggestions of how individuals come to fear failure and worship success, must enter the discussion.

We can make a very similar analysis for the fear of loss of attachments and the need for assertive independent behavior. These interacting forces are outlined in *Fig. 7.7.* We can see that considerable instability is intro-

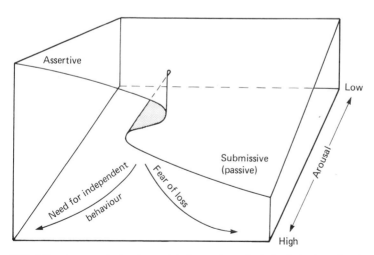

FIG. 7.7.   A cusp catastrophe model of assertive–submissive behavior related to the opposing motivations for independence and fear of loss of social support.

duced once these two needs or motivations are strongly aroused. If it is true that the passive compliant mode of behavior is the behavioral correlate of depression, then activity near or around the fold will not only lead to unstable behavior, but unstable affect. It follows that this problem exists only when the two conflicting motivations are operative. Individuals who are quite happy being passive, or who do not fear the consequences of being assertive (counterattack and loss of support), would not have these instabilities built into their repertoire. Again, we would have to return to our psychological theories to understand why these motivations are aroused, how they developed, and so on.

Apart from demonstrating the principle of instability and providing a model for analyzing it, CT demonstrates a most important point in regard to therapy. It follows from CT that any point near or around the catastrophe fold or cusp is unstable. We should not attempt to find solutions for our patients' difficulties by having them change surfaces. Rather, we need to get them away from the cusp (points of instability) altogether. This means one of two things. First, we can either reduce the strength of one motivation, allowing the other to dominate more or less all the time or, secondly, we can reduce the power of both motivations. For various reasons the second option is by far the better. In CT this means helping patients move away from the cusp altogether; in effect, facilitating movement to the back, unfolded part of the surface.

The importance of this issue must be emphasized, and in many ways cognitive-behavioral therapies attempt to do exactly this. They help patients to fear the consequences of failure less, while at the same time showing them that their high needs for success are based on faulty ideas and premises.

This solution is less clear when it comes to drug treatment. It may be that, for some cases, drugs produce an unreliable stability near the cusp. The biological activity which mediates fear, or depression responses, may be restrained but, nevertheless, the individual remains highly vulnerable. The question is complex for it is possible that drugs *are* capable of reducing the power of two conflicting motivational states, by reducing arousal. For some individuals certain dimensions of instability may have a significant biological basis (e.g., bipolar illness). However, certain individuals may be given an artificial protection by drugs (which may be very useful to reduce certain symptoms), but removal of this protection allows the potential damage of having two powerfully conflicting motivational systems to re-emerge. The question is, whether drugs offer temporary relief, which then allows the individual to work on various conflicts, that is, to give up and disengage from unrealistic incentives, attachments, or ideas; or whether these remain, ready to cause havoc again at some point in the future.

Biological Instability

In Chapter 5 it is noted that when stress first occurs there is an increased turnover of noradrenaline. An increase in synthesis matches demand. If the stress cannot be controlled, there comes a point at which utilization outruns synthesis, resulting in depletion. Thus, with high levels of stress, biological systems are placed under high demand. If the animal can cope with the stress, invigorated behavior may result. But biological systems are limited in their capacity to sustain this high demand without some resolution of the stress. Thus, there must come a point where the biological coping mechanisms begin to break down. To derive a CT approach for these events the noradrenergic system will be used as an example. We can postulate that there are endogenous variables controlling synthesis–utilization rates of NA. We can also assume that as the individual begins to reach his point of biological overload, there is a counteracting process which is responsible for bringing disengagement. These two processes—invigoration and disengagement—are conflicting processes (Klinger, 1977). Invigoration may represent a biological state of NA synthesis exceeding NA utilization; disengagement may represent a biological state of NA synthesis falling below utilization.

It is clear that the model depends upon the selection of the independent and dependent variables. Here we shall assume that the biological processes are independent variables. This is not altogether satisfactory since psychobiological interactions are important. Nevertheless, if we assume that genetic inheritance plays some role in determining the biological capacities of the animal to deal with stress, then we can derive the model shown in *Fig.* 7.8. This model suggests that as the animal moves into a high-stress situation there will be endogenous processes controlling NA synthesis and utilization rates. At point P, near the fold, the animal's NA system is just managing to meet the demands of stress. However, it is an unstable point and any endogenous process which reduces the capacity of the animal to maintain synthesis at this high level will result in utilization outstripping synthesis. The factors responsible could include a breakdown in the synthesis processes, possibly through a reduction in the availability of tyrosine hydroxylase, or there may be faulty uptake mechanisms or a "leaky membrane." The actual mechanisms can only be derived from biological research.

Whatever the mechanisms are, the suggestion of the model is that at high levels of stress some degree of instability may be present in the individual's psychobiological response system(s). In this example, instability is biologically mediated. Hence, under some conditions we may find animals (and people) showing invigorated behavior which appears to suddenly stop and a disengagement, giving-up phase becomes apparent. It follows that endogenous changes near the fold or cusp can produce highly unstable states.

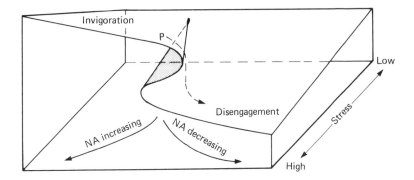

FIG. 7.8.   A cusp catastrophe model of invigoration–disengagement relating to processes which excite and processes which inhibit NA activity.

As with the psychological models presented previously, CT offers one way of conceptualizing various interactions. To use this model further we would need to know more about the biological mechanisms which facilitate increasing synthesis rates of NA and those that inhibit them. It needs to be emphasized that the CT approach presented here is highly simplified. Zeeman (1977) has described a very complex model for instability of bipolar illness. More recently, King et al. (1981) suggest that the action of the dopamine system in schizophrenia can be described using a CT approach. Unfortunately, these complex models are not easily understood. Nevertheless the fact remains that some model of discontinuity is probably essential for a full understanding of the psychobiological interactions in psychopathology.

In Retrospect

This analysis indicates how interacting processes which, of themselves, appear continuous, can produce discontinuous effects. The source of these discontinuities may be biological or psychological (most often both) and they can arise from the operation of at least two competing processes. This analysis allows us to begin to investigate the brain's capacity to switch from one brain state to another. It allows us to investigate how small stresses in people's lives may act as "the last straw." Hence, it helps us to understand how small changes in one process can produce "catastrophes." Importantly, whether big switches or mild switches occur depends on the nearest to the front edge of the fold. Not all patients will be right at the front edge—some may be halfway along and experience only mild discontinuities.

In seeking the causes of discontinuity and instability, we need to look at the splitting factors to decide which are the most important for each case (e.g., NA instability under stress and/or the arousal of two conflicting motivations, e.g., fear of failure and need for success). In some cases of severe disturbance, individuals may have inherited biological systems which become highly unstable in certain stress situations. Ellis (1977b) suggests that borderline psychotic and psychosis-prone individuals have inherited biological systems which become highly disturbed under minor provocation. Thus, maybe in these cases the biological dimensions which give rise to brain state instability need special attention.

In the milder forms of depressive illness, the primary source of discontinuity may arise from the arousal of two competing needs or motivations. These in turn may relate to various cognitive misrepresentations of reality; for example, "I must have love and I must not get angry. Yet I feel very bad when people walk all over me because I don't stick up for myself." The relevant competing motivations will be determined by the patient. For both mild and severe states, however, causality cannot be understood without some model which handles discontinuity and instability.

The implications of CT for the maintenance of, and recovery from, a depressive disorder are important. In the first case, factors within the individual (ruminations and preoccupations) may operate to keep the individual in a high-stress, noncoping state. The loss of interpersonal bonds may keep prominent the activation of biological responses, innately determined, dealing with loss and abandonment. Negative cognitive schemata may ensure that various appraisals are distorted. The lack of social skills may limit the individual's ability to readjust to life crises. Such factors can be seen to operate both in a causal and maintenance fashion. Depending on where the person is in relation to his depression, it is useful to decide how various processes should be viewed. For example, the individual who becomes depressed having lost a significant other, may find his lack of social skills a real handicap when he seeks to repair this loss. But lack of social skills may or may not have been responsible for the loss in the first place. Alternatively, becoming depressed may be a matter of various negative appraisals, but the depression may be maintained by disturbed and unstable biological systems. It is important that, at some point, treatment decisions are made as to the similarity or differences between causal and maintenance factors.

In regard to recovery, CT demonstrates that points at, or near the cusp are unreliable and unstable. Thus, the individual remains vulnerable. In this case, recovery must include, where possible, the removal of vulnerability; that is, we need to help the patient to a position at the back of the catastrophe surface. This will involve reducing the strength of any competing motivation. This may include reducing high fear of failure *and* reducing a high need to succeed. In the fear–anger example, individuals are angered by their own fear, and fear the consequences of their own anger.

Of particular interest are Jung's observations that the self needs to balance conflicting aspects of the psyche, and it is this resolution that dissolves their power, that is, the resolution of opposites. CT demonstrates this by pointing out that it is often two highly aroused, conflicting tendencies that need to be resolved. The individual can only resolve the degree of instability by moving out of the cusp area. Moreover, as Jung noted, conflicting aspects of the psyche feed off each other. To translate in terms of the models used here, fear of failure, or anger are fuelled by overidealized needs to succeed or to be loved.

In summary, the following points emerge:

1. The brain has evolved the capacity to switch from one state to another. This has survival advantage allowing animals to accommodate rapid changes in behavior when the need arises.
2. Under some conditions this rapid switching of brain states can be observed when two conflicting motivations are highly aroused. Although these are not the only processes which facilitate brain state changes, and biological processes need full consideration, for the majority of depressions they are probably among the most important.
3. Acknowledgment of brain state discontinuity and instability requires a model to handle this phenomenon. CT has been derived especially to deal with discontinuities arising out of continuous processes. It therefore recommends itself for this type of analysis. Here only the cusp catastrophe has been examined, but there are a number of more complicated catastrophes which may prove more useful. Unfortunately, these require a greater understanding of the mathematics involved in deriving their geometric form.
4. CT suggests that therapy should aim to remove the person from the cusp area. When psychological processes are involved as the most important sources of discontinuity, this requires identification and resolution of both splitting factors. In severe depressive states, instability may rest on an underlying biological vulnerability. It may also be the case that psychologically produced discontinuity may ignite so great a disturbance in biological systems that the individual is unable to switch out of the depressed brain state without some modification of the disturbed biology. For example, animals exposed to inescapable shock cannot learn the necessary escape

responses until the availability of NA returns to adequate levels. Such a finding does not suggest that the "cause" of a failure to learn escape responses is a lack of adequate NA, since clearly it is the uncontrollable shocks that produce a disruption of NA transmission in the first place. But it is the case that the animal is "maintained" in a noncoping state because of the changes in NA. This highlights one example where causes and maintenance factors need to be distinguished.

Finally, the enormous heterogeneity of brain states in depressives needs to be underlined. On the one hand, this reflects differences in symptom patterns. On the other, it reflects the variety of responses that may occur to the same challenge. For example, Silberman et al. (1981) investigated responses of depressives to dexamphetamine infusion. Not only did responses tend to be highly variable between subjects, but changes associated with this procedure can occur relatively independently of each other. Differences were also found in patients' attitudes to the procedure. Some viewed a dysphoric effect positively, while others viewed an antidepressant effect negatively. Euphoric reactions were more often associated with bipolar illness. Reus et al. (1979b) demonstrated that baseline levels of noradrenaline in depressives had a significant influence on memory change in response to dexamphetamine. Mood change, however, did not correlate with cognitive change, or the indices of baseline noradrenaline function. Although some responded with an euphoric mood, others experienced a worsening of their depression.

This type of data suggests important differences in the source of splitting factors. In other words, the most important factors affecting discontinuity are differently represented among depressives. Clearly, for some patients dexamphetamine produced jumps or switches in mood, indicating the crossing of a fold or cusp area. For others, depressed mood was intensified, indicating that dexamphetamine, for these patients, pushed them away from, rather than toward, a mood-switching cusp. Presumably, this reflects differences in the physiological substrate of the mood disorder; that is, whether the mediating systems are hyper- or hypofunctioning. Increasing activity in already hyperfunctioning systems may make the disorder worse. Increasing activity in hypofunctioning systems may produce drastic changes in mood. This analysis fits some of the data presented by Schildkraut et al. (1978a,b), in terms of high and low D scores (see Chapter 1).

At this point in time we do not have enough information to allow clear identification of splitting factors in all depressives. All we can suggest is that discontinuities do arise in some depressions, but these discontinuities may have different origins. The goal for the future might be to try to match biological and psychological sources of discontinuity for specific groups of patients. In any event, the models presented here are examples of the type of approach that might be useful for understanding psychobiological interactions. They are far from complete, but are simply presented to highlight the possible importance of discontinuity arising from interacting processes which appear continuous.

SOME IMPLICATIONS OF A BRAIN STATE APPROACH

Some of the implications of a brain state view of depression can be outlined. First, a brain state approach facilitates the analysis of psychobiological interactions. The manner in which psychological and biological processes can interact, in terms of the affective-biological bases of organization, encoding, and retrieval of information, has been well outlined by Reus et al. (1979a). Interestingly, this approach may have something in common with Russian concepts of set theory. Unfortunately, the language difference makes it difficult to evaluate this approach (see Rollins, 1974).

Certain brain states (or patterns of psychobiological interaction) are inefficient as information processors. They can invoke degrees of interference within systems, producing maladaptive feedback loops, for example, ruminations and racing thoughts. Drugs which alter affect will change cognitive-behavioral processes to some degree, because of psychobiological interaction. Hence, antidepressant medication cannot be viewed as having a specific effect on emotional systems only. The capacity to interrupt maladaptive psychobiological feedback systems and introduce a degree of stability into the various systems may be an important component of these drugs (for example, by reducing interference and the capacity for thoughts and memories to produce catastrophic changes in affect). In cases where a depression is biologically "stuck" or locked-in, drugs may offer one key to unlocking maladaptive interactions maintaining the disturbance.

Secondly, the susceptibility for brain states to become unstable reflects genetic–learning interactions. Some biological systems can be sensitized for disruption. This may arise from genetic sensitivity (e.g., to separation–loss) and/or from learned (e.g., classically conditioned) sensitivity. Background levels of ongoing stress may also act as sensitizing influences for instability. Raw (1978) discusses his own depression, arising from a personal rejection, occurring against a background of overwork.

Thirdly, entry and recovery from depression may be marked by a high degree of brain state instability. This subjective experience can be profoundly painful. It may be experienced as changes throughout a day or as a sudden worsening of a depression during a recovery. Although sometimes linked to real events (e.g., weekend leave), these states can be experienced as uncontrollable, and in themselves may provoke feelings of hopelessness.

I have known patients become suicidal when, thinking they are recovering, they are faced with the pain of some relapse into a depressed brain state. Helping patients to understand that instability of affect is common for some cases, can be biologically mediated, takes time to heal, and does not represent the ineffectiveness of their therapy, can go a little way to removing this form of hopelessness. It allows patients to "distance" themselves from these changes.

Fourthly, in order to more fully understand depressed brain states, we should investigate cognitive, behavioral, and affective components in depressions with known physiological causes, for example, cognitive-affective changes associated with thyroid dysfunction, Cushing's disease, various infections, childbirth, and so on. We need to know whether the cognitive constellations are similar to those of "true" depressive illness. If they are not, in what ways are they different? If they are similar, then what does this tell us about depressed brain states?

Finally, we can note some recent developments in the "fringe area" of psychobiology. MacKarness (1976) has provided some provocative ideas on the interaction between food allergies and mental states. Rippere & Adams (1982) suggest that clinical ecology has a place in psychiatry. Although controlled trials are few, there are some that provide positive support to MacKarness' basic proposition (e.g., King, 1981). In a similar vein there have been various claims that we should return to "natural foods." Although this view is gaining ground in physical medicine, it has not, to my knowledge, been taken seriously by psychiatry. This is indeed strange given the recent knowledge on the interactions between diet and neurochemical processes (Anderson, 1981; Growdon & Wurtman, 1979) and Crisp's (1980) work examining the role of diet on mood, sleep, and neurotransmitter (e.g., 5-HT) activity.

One of the arguments against taking seriously the role of dietary factors on mental distress is the fact that effects may be small. However, if discontinuity is a real phenomenon of brain–behavior interactions, then this argument may have less strength than at first appears. Dietary changes in relaxed, laboratory conditions may have subtle, but significantly different effects to the same changes in an individual under stress. In the latter case, the biological system may be operating at, or near a point of discontinuity. Very small changes in biological functioning may have catastrophic effects. This argument would suggest that vulnerability to dietary-induced effects may depend on the background physiological state of the individual. There are many other examples where rather obscure processes do seem capable of changing biological processes and producing significant effects. The atmospheric influence of small air ions is a further case in point. Negative ions have been shown to influence human performance (Hawkins & Barker, 1978) and have an effect on 5-HT systems in animals (Krueger & Reed,

1976). Electro-acupuncture is another area which appears to offer promise as a treatment for certain disorders (Schmit, personal communication). It is very difficult to investigate any of the above if it is believed that mental distress is either a disease or is learned. The point is that psychobiology is capable of examining these fascinating areas, not to find simple causes but to add further pieces to the jigsaw of interactions that is responsible for mental distress. In this sense psychobiology is holistic in its approach. Moreover, a greater awareness of how biological processes may be amenable to change, outside of drug treatments, opens doors to a fuller approach to human suffering.

CONCLUDING COMMENTS

The study of the psychobiology of the depressive disorders is likely to be very rewarding, though fraught with problems. At this stage it is the approach which is important, rather than the details of any derived model. Models are useful for organizing data, but must remain flexible. The very complexity of brain–behavior interactions provides numerous avenues for model building. For example, there is growing interest in the neuropsychological approach to depression (Tucker, 1981; Tucker et al., 1981). These data suggest that depression is associated with asymmetrical shifts in brain function. Mandell (1979, 1980) has also raised the issue of depression being associated with asymmetrical changes in 5-HT systems. Such data indicate that the clues to depression lie in the patterns of change associated with this disorder.

In addition to the interactions outlined in this chapter, two further points stand out. The first relates to the social inhibition of ruminative processes. In other words, how do emotional support and comfort act as discriminative stimuli, capable of inhibiting painful, intrusive ideas? It seems to me that comfort from another can act as a kind of safety signal. The exact mechanisms involved are unclear, but they probably relate to the various perceptions of needs described in Chapter 6. The second point relates to internal processes, and is concerned with how individuals themselves have learned to terminate intrusive thoughts and distress arising from these thoughts. To what extent have they come to rely on others to do this?

In some ways we can speculate that the general laws of learning (acquisition and extinction) of anxiety responses may provide interesting clues to the control of intrusive thinking. In other words, individuals who have received constant comfort from an overprotective parent develop S–R-type connections between the termination of emotional distress and a safe other. The individual has not been exposed sufficiently frequently to emotional distress, without an external safe other, to allow internal processes to become conditioned to the termination of emotional distress; that is, internal processes do not develop sufficient inhibitory control over distress. The processes governing this conditioning may be of a form outlined by Solomon (1980). In particular, Gray's (1971) excellent presentation of a safety signals hypothesis for the maintenance of avoidance behavior could be adapted to apply to the depressive situation.

In more psychotherapeutic language we could say that the internal world of the subject remains weak under stress, because of a failure for inhibitory control to become internalized. Safety is conditioned to significant, external others. Under stress, the individual seeks out others to terminate his distress, not because he is incapable of solving problems necessarily, but because he cannot terminate his own internal distress and internal preoccupations, without the necessary external safety signals. Fears of being abandoned, being cut off from safety, would be threatening indeed for these individuals.

Equally speculatively, we could also suggest that the absence of an early, safe, significant other inhibits the subject's movements toward self-control over internal processes and distress states. Early, mild stress would be overpowering because the individual had no ready way (proximity to a safe caregiver, safety signal) to turn off the distress. Thus, there is a developmental arrest. The individual becomes prone to moving into extreme states of distress under minor provocation and invests much effort in finding a safe other. Both these views are consistent with Bowlby's ideas.

This rather simplistic behavioral approach has the advantage of making certain analytic observations more manageable. The ideas are easily tested by finding out whether significant others (who are trusted and loved) can terminate distress reactions in depressives. We already know that avoiding aggression from significant others does reduce arousal in depressives, but not nondepressed people (Forrest & Hokanson, 1975; see Chapter 6). It would be useful to link some of the observations made in Chapter 6 concerning dependency needs, fears of abandonment, and conflicts between anger expression and submission, with conditioning formulations that take into consideration evolutionary and genetic–learning interactions.

The last three chapters have attempted to highlight why brain state, psychobiological formulations provide a useful way to further our understanding of depression. We need desperately to break the shackles of mind–body dualism in the study of psychopathology, and to be extremely cautious with qualitative versus quantitative arguments about diseases. Many of the interactions examined are governed by the psychobiological relations of the brain as it has evolved over countless millions of years. At this point in time, I am all too painfully aware that our understanding of these processes is still far short of the mark, but the future looks very exciting.

Conclusion

It is now clear, from the arguments put forward, that depression relates to the amplification of response patterns which have their origins in the (social) evolution of humans. In computer language, interest has been in the interaction between "software" and "hardware." Understanding the psychological influences on biological processes allows recognition of the biological basis of suffering, and the degree to which disturbed biological activity can influence symptoms and inhibit recovery. The interactions outlined, however, are far from complete.

DEPRESSIVE PROGRAMS

There is growing evidence that a considerable amount of learning is predetermined. For example, Kagan (1982) suggests that, provided a child grows with people and objects, various competencies (cognitive-behavioral patterns) are determined by biological maturity. In other words, there is a predisposition for the human child to acquire information about the effect his behavior has on others and, it would appear, to develop a sense of morality. Hence, the idea of there being innate predispositions for thought and action is gaining support (Crook, 1980). It would seem that learning provides the "software" or data which allows the brain's innate structure to develop programs for action, both covert and overt. It is, therefore, not unrealistic to suggest that the experience of life develops, modifies, and amplifies prepared, psychobiological response patterns. What may begin as rather crude, unsophisticated psychobiological response patterns (crying, distress calling, proximity seeking) are, through learning, welded into complex patterns of affective-cognitive and behavioral responses. These are coded in various neurobiological codes. Hence, endogenous- or exogenous-induced changes in brain chemistry will produce changes in the probability of one (or more) psychobiological response pattern(s) being invoked at the expense of others. This is not a particularly new view (e.g., Mandler, 1975).

One aspect of learning, which occurs in association with stimulus discrimination learning, is the selection of predetermined psychobiological responses, be they modified or not by previous use. Suppose we assume that two innate psychobiological response patterns are (1) goal seeking–exploration and (2) avoidance of abandonment–proximity seeking. Then, to a greater or lesser degree, learning involves the capacity to discriminate between situations which require one or other of these response patterns. Poor discrimination learning may produce one of two outcomes. Either the child has imprecisely coded conditions for inhibiting goal-seeking and selecting proximity-seeking behavior, in which case behavior may become unpredictable, or overgeneralization from stimuli which elicit proximity seeking may produce inappropriate switches to proximity seeking in novel environments. In this case, one psychobiological response system develops considerable inhibitory control over another (e.g., proximity seeking inhibits explorative behavior).

The observation that depressives fail to extinguish various action patterns (covert and overt) suggests there might be something happening in the brain which keeps maladaptive psychobiological responses (e.g., ruminating on loss) switched on. It is the interaction between hardware and software or, more precisely, between brain states and codes of learning and retrieval, which bears further thought.

Such considerations allow us to ponder how it is that some psychobiological responses, in some conditions, gain precedence over others. Furthermore, since the brain operates its programs of thoughts, behaviors, and emotions in neurochemical code, changes in the biological functioning of component systems can affect the selection of various psychobiological responses. For example, uncontrollable stress changes the neurochemistry of the brain in such a way that overriding behavioral inhibition (or a switch into an invigoration–problem-solving pattern) is exceedingly difficult. In effect, the brain state is so altered that an invigoration response pattern is not available. Hence, maladaptive (inhibitory) response patterns may get stuck in the "on" position, because the chemical laws of control have broken down.

In the complex world of reality, experience, mediated via the changed patterns of neuronal growth at synapses, allows for amplification and modification of innate predispositions. (Note that synaptic changes have no equivalent in the computer. The computer can only change its operations via changes in its software.) In essence it seems that the brain begins life with some degree of predetermination for development, laid down by genetic laws,which themselves have developed in response to the pressures of evolution. (Incidentally, as discussed in a previous chapter, this was Jung's point of view.)

Precise identification of the psychobiological response patterns which have become maladaptively amplified and modified in depression-prone individuals, is not yet available. Nevertheless, approximations can be made. As discussed throughout this book, the most severely disturbed aspect of the psychology of the depressive has to do with appraisals of powerlessness (helplessness) to operate within (the evolutionary important aspect of) a secure intraspecies attachment network. We have covered, in detail, how this comes about. So strong is the predetermination to be influenced by attachment relationships, that individuals will give up their own lives to protect others. Indeed, as Dixon & Lucas (1982) make clear, it is the loyalty of the individual to his group, and not innate aggressiveness, which threatens the world with the mass sacrifice of war.

It is, therefore, reasonable to assume that the human brain is equipped for a highly interactive (intraspecies) life. Furthermore, that many of the emotional systems of the brain are wired up to encourage this development, facilitating positive emotional experience for high attachment security (love, friendship, joy), and negative emotional experiences for low attachment security (loneliness, sadness, depression). But, as we have seen, perceptions of attachment security are both self-determined and world-determined; that is, they relate to (1) the perceived amount and quality of care and reinforcement flowing in *from* others; and (2) the perceived capacity to be of use, give care and reinforcement *to* others. This suggests that there are innately determined predispositions to form schemata, or construct systems capable of evaluating, organizing, and storing information which has relevance to both "self on the world" and "the world on self." The information coded in both construct systems provides the data base for the individual to locate himself within his social group (attachment network), evaluate the degree of possible threats to attachments, and assess various psychobiological responses for dealing with such threats. Hence, subservient to these construct systems are numerous psychobiological response patterns (e.g., submissive–dominance) which are innately available. In the adult, these patterns will have been developed, amplified, or modified by life's experience.

It is not difficult to see, therefore, that all of the data discussed in the psychology chapters provide insight into the maladaptive development of schemata of self as a care reinforcement giver and receiver. Fear of failure; learning that love is only supplied if various standards are maintained; it is the fault of self if others are rejecting, or efforts do not work out—these are all examples of how the construct systems, which provide information about the security of attachment networks, may become highly sensitized to activating abandonment psychobiological response patterns when the individual is threatened.

One of the most controversial aspects of this presentation concerns the true nature of the psychobiological response pattern for dealing with abandonment–helplessness. What does the brain do when all efforts fail? Seligman's (1975) account of the American prisoner of war, who made major efforts to obtain release, is harrowing. Finding his efforts for release had failed (he was not to be released and reunited with his loved ones) provoked a depressive stupor from which he died. His last statement concerned his love for his family. If there is a psychobiological response pattern(s)—a particular brain state—which, when activated, significantly reduces survival chances, then this must be of some evolutionary advantage. Such a mechanism may be advantageous to the species, for it serves the function of removing from the gene pool (and food supply) those that are not secured to the group, either because the group rejects them or because, in spite of their own efforts, they are unable to (re)unite.

One is tempted to say that the severely retarded depressive is preparing for death, for the brain is acting on a genetic imperative. But this is a humble attempt at what is an immensely complex issue. All that can be said here is that under certain conditions of perceived abandonment–helplessness, brain states change in such a way that either the chances of survival are reduced and/or patterns of behavior emerge which actively bring death by suicide. Sociobiological discussions of suicide are of some interest (deCatanzaro, 1980), especially in the light of data showing that exit (interpersonal) life events are the most common events preceding suicide attempts (Slater & Depue, 1981). Furthermore, there is no other psychiatric dimension of change, apart from depression, where a patient so seriously entertains the idea of dying, fading away, not existing.

It is suggested that whatever neurochemical mechanisms are discovered, which illuminate the intimate relationship between death and depression, in the psychological domain it will be found that the individual perceives himself as either not loved and/or of no use to his species. These are the perceptions which, in complex ways, have been entangled in the depressive psychobiological response pattern. It should not be forgotten that in a severe depression, the individual needs to overcome his perception of abandonment–helplessness. He is fighting for his survival and his unconscious mind may well know it, even if his conscious mind does not. Moreover, because (as we have previously discussed) brain states can become so disturbed in depression, leading to inefficiency, there comes a point when external stimulation may be incapable of breaking into a depressive psychobiological response pattern which has been activated.

I believe that an understanding of the brain state which is associated with negative perceptions of self in relation to others (not being loved, or of no use, a burden to others and society) will advance our understanding of how psychological factors can inhibit healing. Why is the "will to live" so important in many cases of physical disorder; why can recovery often be influenced by feelings of being cared for and of being wanted (of use)?

Spiritual Aspects

It may seem strange to close this work with a brief discussion on spiritual aspects. This was prompted by a discussion on the radio some months ago, in which sociobiology was attacked for being unspiritual and offering an overly reductionist view of human beings. Also, in my discussions with students, I have noted this aspect lurks behind a reluctance to adopt a psychobiological approach. (For a rather different view to the reductionist interpretation of sociobiology, see Crook, 1980.) The fact of the matter is that evolution is a process which invites change. Sophisticated theologians now subscribe to a pull–push model of evolution; that is, we are pulled forward to spirituality, but are pushed back by biological constraints. Moreover, there is growing awareness that spiritual experience itself may be coded in brain states, that is, coded neurochemically (Mandell, 1980). Thus, it is perfectly possible to have a spiritual view of ourselves and be psychobiologists.

In terms of psychotherapy, this aspect is important. As a psycho-biologist, I believe that mental distress is not a failure to be pulled forward to God, but rather a result of being pushed back, by the activation of psychobiological response patterns whose origins lie in our past. Wilber (1982) describes this aspect well, and notes the not inconsiderable danger of attempting to aid distressed individuals by putting them on a "spiritual path." It seems likely that many of those who gain comfort from religious sects do so because of their capacity to (potentially) offer a social reunion of individuals with other members of their species. As Wilber suggests, however, a strong ego, not disturbed by conflicts relating to evolutionary mechanisms in the brain, is a necessity before commencing a spiritual quest. In Jung's terms, individuation arises from a resolution in the psyche of its archetypal opposites. This is part of the life process.

Psychobiology not need be reductionist. If this were so, then we would welcome any drugs for relieving distress. On the contrary, if in 100 years' time drugs become so sophisticated that any emotional state is repro-ducible, psychobiologists would have problems indeed. Already the vast overuse of drugs like Valium is a cause for concern. This is simply because we know that it is social and psychological processes which amplify and modify innately available psychobiological response patterns. A belief in psychobiology is not an excuse to march for ever onward to Huxley's Brave New World.

Our attitudes and beliefs are focused and clustered by biological predis-positions. Our sense of morality, our need to identify with groups, our need to form attachments, our need to relate to a social hierarchy, are all examples of these. Indeed, many of the strongest unions between people are formed on the basis of the similarity of beliefs. We go to war, not because we are aggressive, but because our belief system, manipulated by the dominant members of the species, activates various psychobiological programs relating to threats to biological needs. (For example, the enemy is the out-group, they threaten members of our group with whom we share some sort of attachment, etc.) Hence, the pathology of nations is a mirror to the pathology of individuals. Both represent, not the imperfection or aggression of human beings, but the enormous capacity for the amplification and modification of innate psychobiological response patterns, by beliefs and attitudes. This knowledge can be used for psychotherapy of the individual and, I hope one day, with education of these facts, for nations.

To the students of psychology who appear put off by psychobiology's reductionist overtones we can say, fear not, it is an illusion. What lies in front of us is far more mysterious than what lies behind, but illness and distress reside in influences from our own life histories meeting the biological history of our past. As Jung would point out, in treating the disordered mind, we cannot say what will be, only what has been.

Acknowledgments

This work represents in no small part the impact of numerous influences in my life. As an undergraduate I studied economics. It was a subject which stimulated my interest in interactions between complex processes and events. In many respects my approach to psychology has been shaped by this exposure. Following this, I was fortunate to be able to study experimental psychology at the University of Sussex. I am deeply indebted to the many tutors who, with patience and encouragement, guided me through my courses and opened up the fascinating areas of learning and biological psychology. It had always been my intention to study clinical psychology eventually and a year spent as a psychiatric nurse stimulated this intention further.

Fortune smiled on me again when I was able to continue my research studies on the MRC Unit at Edinburgh University. Dr Ivy Blackburn guided my first explorations and research into the cognitive theory of depression, while members of the psychiatric team gave up their time to try to educate me in the biological basis of depression. Special thanks go to Dr John Loudon for his kind help in introducing me to psychopharmacology. This interest was further stimulated by links with members of the University Department of Psychopharmacology. Following an invitation to give a lecture to that department in 1976, I got the foolhardy and rather arrogant idea that my feeble psychobiological synthesis on depression could be improved upon. For a few years this idea lurked in the background, but it never went away.

From Edinburgh I was given the opportunity to study clinical psychology, and new individuals took over the role of trying to educate me. The ward rounds of Dr Roy Devine and his teaching seminars were invaluable. My special thanks also go to Dr Bill Hughes for providing many opportunities to explore psychoanalytic theory, and a forum to debate, modify, and amplify my own ideas. Mr David Castell and Mrs Catherine Lawrence have been most supportive. They have been invaluable in reading various drafts and putting at my disposal a fund of knowledge and insight. Also I would like to offer my appreciation to the many patients who have shared openly their depressive experiences and have gently attempted to refine my therapy skills. They have provided a wealth of insight not expressible in this, or any other book.

It is impossible to thank all the many friends and colleagues who have listened (sometimes endlessly) to my ideas with kindness and support (though not necessarily with agreement). Special thanks go to Dr Elspeth Seddon, for her "contagious enthusiasm." Last and first, my deep affection and thanks go to Jean and my family for giving me the experience of a loving relationship and providing a secure base from which to explore this work and many other things; also, for quietly putting up with my obsessions and grumbles.

Mrs Elizabeth Brown typed the manuscript, some parts of it many times. She did so patiently and kindly and her work is greatly appreciated. The efforts of Mrs Bridget Cole and, latterly, Kate and Sue, in obtaining numerous papers have made my work much easier than it might have been, and I am most grateful to them. Special thanks go to Catherine Carpenter for her excellent work on the drafts and to Michael Forster of LEA who worked hard to see this project through.

The idea that would not go away has found a sort of expression. Any errors of information are clearly due to my own misunderstandings. Psychobiology is a fascinating street to work. As a psychologist, I have been less able to examine how biological changes cause psychological ones, but rather have considered traffic moving in the opposite direction, from psychology to biology. This remains the more mysterious to me. Consequently, this work is heavily oriented toward an investigation of how psychological processes produce biological changes. I hope this endeavor will highlight the biological basis of suffering, invoked by beliefs and perceptions, as they operate on and through the evolved mechanisms of the brain. There is much that has had to be left out and this work is no more than the roughest of sketches. It is but one step on a long journey of understanding.

Paul Gilbert
February 1983

Dedication

To Jean, Hannah and James.

REFERENCES

Abraham, K. (1911/1927) Notes on the psycho-analytic investigation and treatment of manic depressive insanity and allied conditions. In Abraham, K. (ed.) *Selected Papers on Psycho-analysis*. London: Hogarth Press (1927).

Abramson, L. Y., Seligman, M. E. P. & Teasdale, J. D. (1978) Learned helplessness in humans: Critique and reformulation. *Journal of Abnormal Psychology*, **87**, 49–74.

Adams, D. B. (1979) Brain mechanisms for offense, defense and submission. *Behavioral and Brain Sciences*, **2**, 201–241.

Akiskal, H. S. (1979) A bio-behavioral approach to depression. In Depue, R. A. (ed.) *The Psychobiology of the Depressive Disorders: Implications for the Effects of Stress*. New York: Academic Press.

Akiskal, H. S. & McKinney, W. T. (1973a) Psychiatry and pseudopsychiatry. *Archives of General Psychiatry*, **28**, 367–373.

Akiskal, H. S. & McKinney, W. T. (1973b) Depressive disorders: Toward a unified hypothesis. *Science*, **182**, 20–29.

Akiskal, H. S. & McKinney, W. T. (1975) Overview of recent research in depression: Integration of ten conceptual models into a comprehensive frame. *Archives of General Psychiatry*, **32**, 285–305.

Akiskal, H. S., Bitar, A. H., Puzantian, V. R. et al. (1978) The nosological status of neurotic depression: A prospective three-to-four year follow-up examination in the light of the primary-secondary and unipolar-bipolar dichotomies. *Archives of General Psychiatry*, **35**, 756–766.

Akiskal, H. S., Rosenthal, T. L., Haykal, R. F. et al. (1980) Characterological depressions. *Archives of General Psychiatry*, **37**, 777–783.

Altman, J., Brunne, R. L. & Bayer, S. A. (1973) The hippocampus and behavioural maturation. *Behavioural Biology*, **8**, 557–596.

Amsel, A. (1958) The role of frustrative non-reward in non-continuous reward situations. *Psychological Bulletin*, **55**, 102–119.

Amsel, A. (1962) Frustrative non-reward in partial reinforcement and discrimination learning: Some recent history and theoretical extension. *Psychological Review*, **69**, 306–328.

Anderson, G. H. (1981) Diet, neurotransmitters and brain function. *British Medical Bulletin*, **37**, 95–100.

Andrews, G., Tennant, C., Hewson, D. M. & Vaillant, G. E. (1978) Life event stress, social support, coping style and risk of psychological impairment. *Journal of Nervous and Mental Disease*, **166**, 307–316.

Anisman, H. (1978) Neurochemical changes elicited by stress: Behavioral correlates. In Anisman, H. & Bignami, G. (eds) *Psychopharmacology of Aversively Motivated Behavior*. New York: Plenum Press.

Anisman, H. & Sklar, L. S. (1979) Catecholamine depletion in mice upon re-exposure to stress: Mediation of the escape deficits produced by inescapable shock. *Journal of Comparative and Physiological Psychology*, **93**, 610–625.

Anisman, H., Suissa, A. & Sklar, L. S. (1980a) Escape deficits induced by uncontrollable stress: Antagonism by dopamine and norepinephrine agonists. *Behavioural and Neural Biology*, **28**, 34–47.

Anisman, H., Pizzino, A. & Sklar, L. S. (1980b) Coping with stress, norepinephrine depletion and escape performance. *Brain Research*, **191**, 583–588.

Anisman, H., Glazier, S. J. & Sklar, L. (1981) Cholinergic influences on escape deficits produced by uncontrollable stress. *Psychopharmacology* (in press).

Anisman, H. & Lapierre, Y. D. (1981) Stress and depression: Formulations and caveats. In Burchfield, S. (ed.) *Physiological and Psychological Interactions in Response to Stress.* New York: Hemisphere (in press).

Anisman, H. & Sklar, L. S. (in press) Social housing conditions influence escape deficits produced by uncontrollable stress. *Behavioral and Neural Biology.*

Anisman, H. & Zacharko, R. M. (1982) Depression: The predisposing influence of stress (plus commentary). *Behavioral and Brain Sciences,* **5,** 89–137.

Antelman, S. M. & Caggiula, A. R. (1977) Norepinephrine–dopamine interactions and behavior. *Science,* **195,** 646–653.

Anthony, E. J. & Benedek, T. (eds) (1975) *Depression and Human Existence.* Boston: Little Brown.

Arieti, S. (1977) Psychotherapy of severe depression. *American Journal of Psychiatry,* **134,** 864–868.

Arieti, S. (1978) A psychotherapeutic approach to severely depressed patients. *American Journal of Psychotherapy,* **32,** 33–47.

Arieti, S. & Bemporad, J. (1980a) The psychological organization of depression. *American Journal of Psychiatry,* **137,** 1360–1365.

Arieti, S. & Bemporad, J. (1980b) *Severe and Mild Depression: The Psychotherapeutic Approach.* London: Tavistock.

Atkinson, J. W. (1964) *An Introduction to Motivation.* Princeton, N.J.: Van Nostrand.

Averill, J. R. (1968) Grief: Its nature and significance. *Psychological Bulletin,* **70,** 721–748.

Bagshaw, V. E. (1977) A replication study of Foulds' and Bedford's hierarchical model of depression. *British Journal of Psychiatry,* **131,** 53–55.

Baldessarini, R. J. (1975) An overview of the basis for the amine hypothesis in affective illness. In Mendels, J. (ed.) *The Psychobiology of Depression.* New York: Spectrum.

Bandura, A. (1977) *Social Learning Theory.* Englewood Cliffs, N.J.: Prentice-Hall.

Basch, M. F. (1975) That encompasses depression: A revision of existing causal hypotheses in psychoanalysis. In Anthony, E. J. & Benedek, T. (eds) *Depression and Human Existence.* Boston: Little Brown.

Bebbington, P. (1980) Causal models and logical inference in epidemiological psychiatry. *British Journal of Psychiatry,* **136,** 317–325.

Bebbington, P., Hurry, J., Tennant, C., Sturt, E. & Wing, J. K. (1981) Epidemiology of mental disorders in Camberwell. *Psychological Medicine,* **11,** 561–580.

Beck, A. T. (1963) Thinking and depression: I. Idiosyncratic content and cognitive distortions. *Archives of General Psychiatry,* **9,** 324–333.

Beck, A. T. (1967) *Depression: Clinical, Experimental and Theoretical Aspects.* New York: Harper & Row.

Beck, A. T. (1970) Cognitive therapy: Nature and relationship to behavior therapy. *Behavior Therapy,* **1,** 184–200.

Beck, A. T. (1973) *The Diagnosis and Management of Depression.* Philadelphia: University of Pennsylvania Press.

Beck, A. T. (1974a) The development of depression. In Friedman, R. J. & Katz, M. M. (eds) *The Psychology of Depression: Contemporary Theory and Research.* New York: Winston-Wiley.

Beck, A. T. (1974b) Cognition, affect and psychopathology. In London, H. & Nisbett, R. E. (eds) *Thought and Feeling.* Chicago: Aldine Publishing Company.

Beck, A. T. (1976) *Cognitive Therapy and the Emotional Disorders.* New York: International Universities Press.

Beck, A. T., Ward, C. H., Mendelson, M., Mock, J. & Erbaugh, J. (1961) An inventory for measuring depression. *Archives of General Psychiatry,* **4,** 561–571.

Beck, A. T., Weissman, A., Lester, D. & Trexler, L. (1974) The measurement of pessimism: The hopelessness scale. *Journal of Consulting and Clinical Psychology,* **42,** 861–865.

Beck, A. T., Rush, A. J., Shaw, B. F. & Emery, G. (1978) *Cognitive Therapy of Depression: A Treatment Manual.* Philadelphia: University of Pennsylvania.

Beck, A. T., Rush, A. J., Shaw, B. F. & Emery, G. (1979) *Cognitive Therapy of Depression.* New York: J. Wiley & Sons.

Becker, J. (1960) Achievement related characteristics of manic-depressives. *Journal of Abnormal and Social Psychology*, **60**, 334–339.

Becker, J. (1974) *Depression: Theory and Research.* New York: Winston-Wiley.

Becker, J. (1977) *Affective Disorders.* New Jersey: General Learning Press.

Becker, J. (1979) Vulnerable self-esteem as a predisposing factor in depressive disorders. In Depue, R. A. (ed.) *The Psychobiology of the Depressive Disorders: Implications for the Effects of Stress.* New York: Academic Press.

Bibring, E. (1953) The mechanism of depression. In Greenacre, P. (ed.) *Affective Disorders.* New York: International Universities Press.

Bignami, G. & Michalek, H. (1978) Cholinergic mechanisms and aversively motivated behaviors. In Anisman, H. & Bignami, G. (eds) *Psychopharmacology of Aversively Motivated Behavior.* New York: Plenum Press.

Birney, R. C., Burdick, H. & Teevan, R. C. (1969) *Fear of Failure.* New York: Van Nostrand-Reinhold.

Bishop, S. (1980) Private communication.

Blackburn, I. M. (1972) *A Psychometric Study of Unipolar and Bipolar Affective Disorders.* Unpublished PhD Thesis, University of Edinburgh.

Blackburn, I. M. (1974) The pattern of hostility in affective illness. *British Journal of Psychiatry*, **125**, 141–145.

Blackburn, I. M. & Bonham, K. G. (1980) Experimental effects of a cognitive therapy technique in depressed patients. *British Journal of Social and Clinical Psychology*, **19**, 353–363.

Blackburn, I. M., Bishop, S., Glen, A. I. M., Walley, L. J. & Christie, J. E. (1981) The efficacy of cognitive therapy in depression: A treatment trial using cognitive therapy and pharmacotherapy, each alone and in combination. *British Journal of Psychiatry*, **139**, 181–189.

Blakemore, C. (1977) *Mechanics of the Mind.* Cambridge: Cambridge University Press.

Blaney, P. H. (1977) Contemporary theories of depression: Critique and comparison. *Journal of Abnormal Psychology*, **86**, 203–223.

Blatt, S. J., Wein, S. J., Chevron, E. S. & Quinlan, D. M. (1979) Parental representations and depression in normal young adults. *Journal of Abnormal Psychology*, **88**, 388–397.

Blatt, S. J., Quinlan, D. M., Chevron, E. S., McDonald, C. & Zuroff, D. (1982) Dependency and self criticism: Psychological dimensions of depression. *Journal of Consulting and Clinical Psychology*, **50**, 113–124.

Blumenthal, M. D. (1971) Heterogeneity and research on depressive disorders. *Archives of General Psychiatry*, **24**, 524–531.

Bonhoeffer, K. (1909) Exogenous psychoses. In Hirsch, S. R. & Shepherd, M. (eds) *Themes and Variations in European Psychiatry.* Bristol: J. Wright.

Bonhoeffer, K. (1911) How far should all psychogenic illness be regarded as hysterical? In Hirsch, S. R. & Shepherd, M. (eds) *Themes and Variations in European Psychiatry.* Bristol: J. Wright.

Bower, G. H. (1981) Mood and memory. *American Psychologist*, **36**, 129–148.

Bowlby, J. (1969) *Attachment: Attachment and Loss, Vol. 1.* London: Hogarth Press.

Bowlby, J. (1973) *Separation, Anxiety and Anger. Attachment and Loss, Vol. 2.* London: Hogarth Press.

Bowlby, J. (1977a) The making and breaking of affectional bonds: I. Aetiology and psychopathology in the light of attachment theory. *British Journal of Psychiatry*, **130**, 201–210.

Bowlby, J. (1977b) The making and breaking of affectional bonds: II. Some principles of psychotherapy. *British Journal of Psychiatry*, **130**, 421–431.

Bowlby, J. (1980) *Loss: Sadness and Depression. Attachment and Loss, Vol. 3*. London: Hogarth Press.

Bowman, M. K. & Rose, M. (1951) A criticism of the terms psychosis, psychoneurosis and neurosis. *American Journal of Psychiatry*, **108**, 161–166.

Bowman, L. A., Dilley, S. R. & Keverne, E. B. (1978) Suppression of oestrogen-induced LH surges by social subordination in talapoin monkeys. *Nature*, **275**, 56–58.

Braden, W. & Ho, C. K. (1981) Racing thoughts in psychiatric inpatients. *Archives of General Psychiatry*, **38**, 71–75.

Brady, J. (1975) Conditioning and emotion. In Levi, L. (ed.) *Emotions: Their Parameters and Measurement*. New York: Raven Press.

Breslow, R., Kocsis, J. & Belkin, B. (1981) Contribution of the depressive perspective to memory function in depression. *American Journal of Psychiatry*, **138**, 227–230.

Bronowski, J. (1977) *The Ascent of Man*. London: BBC Publications.

Brown, G. W. (1979a) The social etiology of depression—London studies. In Depue, R. A. (ed.) *The Psychobiology of the Depressive Disorders: Implications for the Effects of Stress*. New York: Academic Press.

Brown, G. W. (1979b) Depression—a sociologist's view. *Trends in the Neurosciences*, **2**, 253–256.

Brown, G. W. & Harris, T. (1978a) *The Social Origins of Depression*. London: Tavistock.

Brown, G. W. & Harris, T. (1978b) Social origins of depression: a reply. *Psychological Medicine*, **8**, 577–588.

Brown, G. W. & Harris, T. (1980) Further comments on the vulnerability model. *British Journal of Psychiatry*, **137**, 584–585.

Bunney, W. E., Jr & Davis, J. M. (1965) Norepinephrine in depressive reactions. *Archives of General Psychiatry*, **13**, 483–494.

Burns, D. D. & Mendels, J. (1979) Serotonin and affective disorders. In Essman, W. B. & Valzelli, L. (eds) *Current Developments in Psychopharmacology: Vol. 5*. New York: S.P. Medical and Scientific Books.

Buxton, D. A., Brimblecombe, R. W., French, M. C. & Redfern, P. H. (1976) Brain acetylcholine concentration and acetylcholinesterase activity in selectively-bred strains of rats. *Psychopharmacology*, **47**, 97–99.

Byrne, D. G. (1981) Sex differences in the reporting of symptoms of depression in the general population. *British Journal of Clinical Psychology*, **20**, 83–92.

Carlton, P. L. (1969) Brain-acetylcholine and inhibition. In Tapp, J. T. (ed.) *Reinforcement and Behavior*. New York: Academic Press.

Carney, M. W. P., Roth, M. & Garside, R. F. (1965) The diagnosis of depressive syndromes and the prediction of E.C.T. response. *British Journal of Psychiatry*, **III**, 659–674.

Carroll, B. J., Greden, J. F., Rubin, R. T., Haskett, R., Feinberg, M. & Schteingart, D. (1978) Neurotransmitter mechanism of neuroendocrine disturbance in depression. *Acta Endocrinologica Supplement*, Part **220**, 14.

Carroll, B. J., Feinberg, M., Greden, J. F. et al. (1981) A specific laboratory test for the diagnosis of melancholia. *Archives of General Psychiatry*, **38**, 15–22.

Clarke, A. M. & Clarke, A. D. B. (1976) *Early Experience: Myth and Evidence*. London: Open Books.

Cohen, M. B., Baker, G., Cohen, R. A., Fromm-Reichman, F. & Weigert, E. V. (1954) An intensive study of twelve cases of manic depressive psychosis. *Psychiatry*, **17**, 103–137.

Cohen, R. M., Weingartner, H., Smallberg, S. A., Pickar, D. & Murphy, D. L. (1982) Effort and cognition in depression. *Archives of General Psychiatry*, **39**, 593–597.

Colotla, V. A. (1979) Experimental depression in animals. In Keehn, J. D. (ed.) *Psychopathology in Animals: Research and Clinical Implications*. New York: Academic Press.

Cooke, D. J. (1980a) The structure of depression found in the general population. *Psychological Medicine*, **10**, 455–463.

Cooke, D. J. (1980b) Causal modelling with contingency tables. *British Journal of Psychiatry*, **137**, 582–584.

Coopersmith, S. (1967) *The Antecedents of Self Esteem.* San Francisco: W. H. Freeman.

Coppen, A. (1967) The biochemistry of the affective disorders. *British Journal of Psychiatry*, **113**, 1237–1264.

Costello, C. G. (1972) Depression: Loss of reinforcers or loss of reinforcer effectiveness. *Behaviour Therapy*, **3**, 240–247.

Costello, C. G. (1978) A critical review of Seligman's laboratory experiments on learned helplessness and depression in humans. *Journal of Abnormal Psychology*, **87**, 21–31.

Cotman, C. W. & McGaugh, J. L. (1980) *Behavioral Neuroscience: An Introduction.* New York: Academic Press.

Coyne, J. C. (1976a) Depression and response to others. *Journal of Abnormal Psychology*, **85**, 186–193.

Coyne, J. C. (1976b) Towards an interactional description of depression. *Psychiatry*, **39**, 28–40.

Coyne, J. C. (1982) A critique of cognitions as causal entities with particular reference to depression. *Cognitive Therapy and Research*, **6**, 3–13.

Coyne, J. C., Aldwin, C. & Lazarus, R. S. (1981) Depression and coping in stressful episodes. *Journal of Abnormal Psychology*, **90**, 439–447.

Crisp, A. H. (1980) Sleep activity, nutrition and mood. *British Journal of Psychiatry*, **137**, 1–7.

Crook, J. H. (1980) *The Evolution of Human Consciousness.* Oxford: Oxford University Press.

Crow, T. J. (1973) Catecholamine-containing neurones and electrical self stimulation. II. A theoretical interpretation and some psychiatric implications. *Psychological Medicine*, **3**, 66–73.

Dahlström, A. & Fuxe, K. (1964) A method for the demonstration of monoamine-containing nerve fibres in the central nervous system. *Acta Physiologica Scandinavica*, **60**, 293–295.

Davis, K. L., Hollister, L. E., Overall, J., Johnson, A. & Train, K. (1976) Physostigmine: Effects on cognition and affect in normal subjects. *Psychopharmacology*, **51**, 23–27.

deCatanzaro, D. (1980) Human suicide: A biological perspective. *Behavioral and Brain Sciences*, **3**, 265–290.

deCharms, R., Morrison, H. W., Reitman, W. R. & McClelland, D. C. (1955) Behavioral correlates of directly and indirectly measured achievement motivation. In McClelland, D. C. (ed.) *Studies in Motivation.* New York: Appleton-Century-Crofts.

Decsi, L. & Nagy, J. (1979) Neurotransmitter organisation of aggressive behavior. *Behavioral and Brain Sciences*, **2**, 216–217.

Depue, R. A. & Monroe, S. M. (1978a) Learned helplessness in the perspective of the depressive disorders: Conceptual and definitional issues. *Journal of Abnormal Psychology*, **87**, 3–20.

Depue, R. A. & Monroe, S. M. (1978b) The unipolar–bipolar distinction in the depressive disorders. *Psychological Bulletin*, **85**, 1001–1029.

Depue, R. A. & Kleiman, R. M. (1979) Free cortisol as a peripheral index of central vulnerability to major forms of polar depressive disorders: Examining stress-biology interactions in subsyndromal high-risk persons. In Depue, R. A. (ed.) *The Psychobiology of the Depressive Disorders.* New York: Academic Press.

Depue, R. A. & Monroe, S. M. (1979) The unipolar–bipolar distinction in the depressive disorders: Implications for stress-onset interactions. In Depue, R. A. (ed.) *The Psychobiology of the Depressive Disorders. Implications for the Effects of Stress.* New York: Academic Press.

Diaz, J., Ellison, G. & Masuoka, D. (1978) Stages of recovery from central norepinephrine lesions in enriched and impoverished environments. A behavioral and biochemical study. *Experimental Brain Research*, **31**, 117–130.

Di Mascio, A., Weissman, M. M., Prusoff, B. A., Neu, C., Zwilling, M. & Klerman, C. L. (1979) Differential symptom reduction by drugs and psychotherapy in acute depression. *Archives of General Psychiatry*, **36**, 1450–1456.

Dixon, N. F. & Henley, S. H. A. (1980) Without awareness. In Jeeves, M. (ed.) *Psychology Survey No. 3.* London: Allen & Unwin.

Dixon, T. & Lucas, K. (1982) *The Human Race.* London: Thames-Methuen.

Dobzhansky, T. (1975) Evolution and man's self-image. In Goodall, V. (ed.) *The Search for Man.* London: Phaidon Press.

Douglas, D. & Anisman, H. (1975) Helplessness or expectation incongruency: Effects of aversive stimulation on subsequent performance. *Journal of Experimental Psychology*: Human Perception and Performance, **1**, 411–417.

Dweck, C. S. (1975) The role of expectations and attributions in the alleviation of learned helplessness. *Journal of Personality and Social Psychology*, **31**, 674–685.

D'Zurilla, T. J. & Goldfried, M. R. (1971) Problem solving and behavior modification. *Journal of Abnormal Psychology*, **78**, 107–126.

Eccleston, D. (1981) Monoamines in affective illness: Is there a place for 5-HT? *British Journal of Psychiatry*, **138**, 257–258.

Eikelboom, R. & Stewart, J. (1982) Conditioning of drug-induced physiological responses. *Psychological Review*, **89**, 507–528.

Ellenberger, H. F. (1970) *The Discovery of the Unconscious. The History and Evolution of Dynamic Psychiatry.* New York: Basic Books.

Ellis, A. (1977a) Psychotherapy and the value of a human being. In Ellis, A. & Grieger, R. (eds) *Handbook of Rational Emotive Therapy.* New York: Springer.

Ellis, A. (1977b) Characteristics of psychotic and borderline psychotic individuals. In Ellis, A. & Grieger, R. (eds) *Handbook of Rational Emotive Therapy.* New York: Springer.

Ellis, A. (1977c) A rational approach to interpretation. In Ellis, A. & Grieger, R. (eds) *Handbook of Rational Emotive Therapy.* New York: Springer.

Ellis, A. & Whiteley, J. M. (eds) (1979) *Theoretical and Empirical Foundations of Rational Emotive Therapy.* California: Brooks-Cole.

Engle, G. L. (1977) The need for a new medical model: A challenge for biomedicine. *Science*, **196**, 129–136.

Erdelyi, M. H. & Goldberg, B. (1979) Let's not sweep repression under the rug: Toward a cognitive psychology of repression. In Kihlstrom, J. F. & Evans, F. J. (eds) *Functional Disorders of Memory.* Hillsdale, N.J.: Lawrence Erlbaum Associates.

Eysenck, H. J. (1970) The classification of depressive illness. *British Journal of Psychiatry*, **117**, 241–250.

Eysenck, H. J. (1979) The conditioning model of neurosis. *Behavioral and Brain Sciences*, **2**, 155–199.

Feighner, J. P., Robins, E., Guze, S. B. et al. (1972) Diagnostic criteria for use in psychiatric research. *Archives of General Psychiatry*, **26**, 57–63.

Ferster, C. B. (1973) A functional analysis of depression. *American Psychologist*, **28**, 857–870.

Ferster, C. B. (1974) Behavioral approaches to depression. In Friedman, R. J. & Katz, M. M. (eds) *The Psychology of Depression: Contemporary Theory and Research.* New York: Winston-Wiley.

Fish, F. (1974) *Fish's Clinical Psychopathology: Signs and Symptoms in Psychiatry* (ed. Hamilton, M.). Bristol: J. Wright.

Folkman, S., Schaefer, C. & Lazarus, R. (1979) Cognitive processes as mediators of stress and coping. In Hamilton, V. & Warburton, D. M. (eds) *Human Stress and Cognition: An Information Processing Approach.* Chichester: Wiley & Sons.

Forrest, M. S. & Hokanson, J. E. (1975) Depression and autonomic arousal reduction accompanying self-punitive behavior. *Journal of Abnormal Psychology*, **84**, 346–357.

Foulds, G. A. (1973) The relationship between the depressive illnesses. *British Journal of Psychiatry*, **123**, 531–533.

Foulds, G. A. & Bedford, A. (1975) Hierarchy of classes of personal illness. *Psychological Medicine*, **5**, 181–192.

Foulds, G. A. & Bedford, A. (1976) Classification of depressive illness—a re-evaluation. *Psychological Medicine*, **6**, 15–19.

Fowles, D. C. & Gersh, F. S. (1979a) Neurotic depression: The endogenous–neurotic distinction. In Depue, R. A. (ed.) *The Psychobiology of the Depressive Disorders: Implications for the Effects of Stress*. New York: Academic Press.

Fowles, D. C. & Gersh, F. S. (1979b) Neurotic depression: The concept of anxious depression. In Depue, R. A. (ed.) *The Psychobiology of the Depressive Disorders: Implications for the Effects of Stress*. New York: Academic Press.

Freud, S. (1917) *Mourning and Melancholia*. In *Completed Psychological Works, Vol. 14.* (standard ed.). (Translated and Edited by Strachey, J.) London: Hogarth Press.

Friedman, A. S. (1970) Hostility factors and clinical improvement in depressed patients. *Archives of General Psychiatry*, **23**, 524–537.

Fuchs, C. Z. & Rehm, L. P. (1977) A self-control behavior therapy program for depression. *Journal of Consulting and Clinical Psychology*, **45**, 206–215.

Garber, J. & Hollon, S. D. (1980) Universal versus personal helplessness in depression: Belief in uncontrollability or incompetence. *Journal of Abnormal Psychology*, **89**, 56–66.

Gatchel, R. J., Paulus, P. B. & Maples, C. W. (1975) Learned helplessness and self-reported affect. *Journal of Abnormal Psychology*, **84**, 732–734.

Gershon, S. & Shaw, F. W. (1961) Psychiatric sequalae of chronic exposure to organo-phosphorous insecticides. *Lancet*, **1**, 1371–1374.

Gibby, R. G., Snr & Gibby, R. G., Jr (1967) The effects of stress resulting from academic failure. *Journal of Clinical Psychology*, **23**, 35–37.

Gilbert, P. (1980) An investigation of cognitive factors in depression. Unpublished PhD Thesis, University of Edinburgh.

Glass, R. M., Uhlenhuth, E. H., Hartel, F. W., Matuzas, W. & Fischman, M. W. (1981) Cognitive dysfunction and imipramine in outpatient depressives. *Archives of General Psychiatry*, **38**, 1048–1051.

Glisson, S. N., Karczman, A. G. & Barnes, L. (1972) Cholinergic effects on adrenergic neurotransmitters in rabbit brain parts. *Neuropharmacology*, **11**, 465–477.

Glisson, S. N., Karczman, A. G. & Barnes, L. (1974) Effects of diisopropyl-phosphoro-flouridate on acetylcholine, cholinesterase and catecholamines of several rabbit brain parts. *Neuropharmacology*, **13**, 623–632.

Goldberg, A. I. (1975) The evolution of psychoanalytic concepts of depression. In Anthony, E. J. & Benedek, J. (eds) *Depression and Human Existence*. Boston: Little Brown.

Goss, A. & Morosko, J. E. (1970) Relation between a dimension of internal–external control and the M.M.P.I. with an alcoholic population. *Journal of Consulting and Clinical Psychology*, **34**, 189–192.

Gray, J. A. (1971) *The Psychology of Fear and Stress*. London: Weidenfeld & Nicolson.

Gray, J. A. (1979) *Pavlov*. London: Fontana (Modern Masters).

Gray, J. A. (1981) Anxiety as a paradigm case of emotion. *British Medical Bulletin*, **37**, 193–198.

Growdon, J. H. & Wurtman, R. J. (1979) Dietary influences on the synthesis of neurotransmitters in brain. *Nutrition Reviews*, **37**, 129–136.

Hall, C. S. & Nordby, V. J. (1973) *A Primer of Jungian Psychology*. New York: Mentor.

Harlow, H. F. & Mears, C. (1979) *The Human Model: Primate Perspectives*. New York: Winston & Sons.

Harré, R. (1980) The notion of causality. *British Journal of Psychiatry*, **137**, 578–579.

Harrison-Read, P. E. (1981) Synaptic and behavioural actions of antidepressant drugs. *Trends in the Neurosciences*, **4**, 32–34.

Harrow, M., Colbert, J., Detre, T. & Bakeman, R. (1966) Symptomatology and subjective experiences in current depressive states. *Archives of General Psychiatry*, **14**, 203–212.

Hartmann, E. & Keller-Teschke, M. (1979) The psychological effects of dopamine-β-hydroxylase inhibition in normal subjects. *Biological Psychiatry*, **14**, 455–462.

Hawkins, L. H. & Barker, T. (1978) Air ions and human performance. *Ergonomics*, **21**, 273–278.

Henderson, S. (1974) Care-eliciting behavior in man. *Journal of Nervous and Mental Disease*, **159**, 172–181.

Henry, G. M., Weingartner, H. & Murphy, D. L. (1973) Influence of affective states and psychoactive drugs on verbal learning and memory. *American Journal of Psychiatry*, **130**, 966–971.

Henry, G. M., Buchsbaum, M. & Murphy, D. L. (1976) Intravenous L-dopa plus carbidopa in depressed patients: Average evoked response, learning and behavior changes. *Psychosomatic Medicine*, **38**, 95–105.

Hilgard, E. R. (1977) *Divided Consciousness: Multiple Controls in Human Thought and Action*. New York: Wiley.

Hill, D. (1968) Depression: Disease, reaction or posture? *American Journal of Psychiatry*, **125**, 445–457.

Hill, E. (1981) Mechanisms of the mind: A psychiatrist's perspective. *British Journal of Medical Psychology*, **54**, 1–13.

Hinde, R. A. (1979) *Towards Understanding Relationships*. London: Academic Press.

Hington, J. N. & Aprison, M. H. (1976) Behavioral and environment aspects of the cholinergic system. In Goldberg, A. M. & Hanin, I. (eds) *Biology of Cholinergic Function*. New York: Ravens Press.

Hippocrates (460–367 BC) As quoted in Zilboorg & Henry (1941).

Hiroto, D. S. & Seligman, M. E. P. (1975) Generality of learned helplessness in man. *Journal of Personality and Social Psychology*, **31**, 311–327.

Hirsch, S. R. & Shepherd, M. (eds) (1974) *Themes and Variations in European Psychiatry*. Bristol: John Wright.

Hirschowitz, J., Casper, R., Garver, D. L. & Chang, S. (1980) Lithium response in good prognosis schizophrenia. *American Journal of Psychiatry*, **137**, 916–920.

Hollister, L. E., Overall, J. E., Johnson, M. H., Pennington, V., Katz, G. & Shelton, J. (1964) Controlled comparison of amitriptyline, imipramine and placebo in hospital depressed patients. *Journal of Nervous and Mental Disease*, **139**, 370–375.

Hollister, L. E., Overall, J. E., Johnson, M. H., Shelton, J., Kimbell, I. & Brunse, A. (1966) Amitriptyline alone and combined with perphenazine in newly admitted depressed patients. *Journal of Nervous and Mental Disease*, **142**, 440–469.

Hollon, S. D. & Beck, A. T. (1979) Cognitive therapy of depression. In Kendall, P. C. & Hollon, S. D. (eds) *Cognitive-behavioral Interventions: Theory, Research and Procedures*. New York: Academic Press.

Holmes, D. S. (1978) Projection as a defense mechanism. *Psychological Bulletin*, **85**, 677–688.

Holmes, D. S. (1981) Existence of classical projection and the stress-reducing function of attributive projection: A reply to Sherwood. *Psychological Bulletin*, **90**, 460–466.

Holt, J. (1969) *How Children Fail*. London: Pelican.

Hong, M. K., Wirt, R. D., Yellin, A. M. & Hopwood, J. (1979) Psychological attributes, patterns of life change and illness susceptibility. *Journal of Nervous and Mental Disease*, **167**, 275–281.

Horowitz, M. J. & Wilner, N. (1976) Stress films, emotion and cognitive response. *Archives of General Psychiatry*, **33**, 1339–1344.

Horowitz, M. J., Wilner, N., Marmar, C. & Krupnick, J. (1980a) Pathological grief and the activation of latent self-images. *American Journal of Psychiatry*, **137**, 1157–1162.

Horowitz, M. J., Wilner, N., Kaltreider, N. & Alvarez, W. (1980b) Signs and symptoms of posttraumatic stress disorder. *Archives of General Psychiatry*, **37**, 85–92.

Horrobin, D. F. & Manku, M. S. (1980) Possible role of prostaglandin E in the affective disorders and in alcoholism. *British Medical Journal*, **280**, 1363–1366.

Isaacson, R. L., Street, W. J., Petit, T. L. & Dunn, A. J. (1977) Neonatal treatment with 6-OH-DA affects brain NE content but not behavior. *Physiological Psychology*, **5**, 49–52.

Isen, A. M., Shalker, T. E., Clark, M. & Karp, L. (1978) Affect, accessibility of material in memory and behavior: A cognitive loop? *Journal of Personality and Social Psychology*, **36**, 1–12.

Iversen, L. L. (1979) The chemistry of the brain. *Scientific American*, **241**, 118–129.

Iversen, S. D. & Iversen, L. L. (1975) *Behavioural Pharmacology*. Oxford: Oxford University Press.

Janowsky, D. S., El-Yousef, M. K., Davis, J. M. & Serkerke, H. J. (1972) A cholinergic-adrenergic hypothesis of mania and depression. *Lancet*, **2**, 632–635.

Janowsky, D. S., El-Yousef, M. K., Davis, J. M. & Serkerke, H. J. (1973) Parasympathetic suppression of manic symptoms by physostigmine. *Archives of General Psychiatry*, **28**, 532–547.

Jung, C. G. (1933) *Modern Man in Search of a Soul*. London: Routledge & Kegan Paul.

Jung, C. G. (1940) *The Integration of the Personality*. London: Routledge & Kegan Paul.

Jung, C. G. (1963) *Memories, Dreams, Reflections*. London: Collins/Fount Paperbacks.

Jung, C. G. (ed.) (1964) *Man and his Symbols*. London: Aldus-Jupiter Books.

Jung, C. G. (1972) *Four Archetypes*. London: Routledge & Kegan Paul.

Kagan, J. (1982) The emergence of self. *Journal of Child Psychology and Psychiatry*, **23**, 363–381.

Kapp, B. S. & Gallagher, M. (1979) Opiates and memory. *Trends in the Neurosciences*, **2**, 177–180.

Karczman, A. G. (1975) Cholinergic influences on behavior. In Waser, P. G. (ed.) *Cholinergic Mechanisms*. New York: Raven Press.

Karczman, A. G. (1976) Central actions of acetylcholine, cholinomimetics and related drugs. In Goldberg, A. M. & Hanin, I. (eds) *Biology of Cholinergic Function*. New York: Raven Press.

Katkin, E. S., Sasmor, D. B. & Tan, R. (1966) Conformity and achievement-related characteristics of depressed patients. *Journal of Abnormal Psychology*, **71**, 407–412.

Keller, M. B. & Shapiro, R. W. (1982) "Double depression" superimposition of acute depressive episodes on chronic depressive disorders. *American Journal of Psychiatry*, **139**, 438–442.

Kelly, G. (1955) *The Psychology of Personal Constructs*. New York: Norton & Co.

Kendell, R. E. (1968) The problem of classification. In Coppen, A. & Walk, A. (eds) *Recent Developments in Affective Disorders: A Symposium*. British Journal of Psychiatry, Special Publication No. 2.

Kendell, R. E. (1974) The stability of psychiatric diagnoses. *British Journal of Psychiatry*, **124**, 352–356.

Kendell, R. E. (1975) *The Role of Diagnosis in Psychiatry*. London: Blackwell Scientific Publications.

Kendell, R. E. (1976) The classification of depression: A review of contemporary confusion. *British Journal of Psychiatry*, **129**, 15–28.

Kendell, R. E. & Brocklington, I. F. (1980) The identification of disease entities and the relationship between schizophrenic and affective psychoses. *British Journal of Psychiatry*, **137**, 324–331.

Kiloh, L. G. & Garside, R. F. (1963) The independence of neurotic depression and endogenous depression. *British Journal of Psychiatry*, **109**, 451–463.

King, D. S. (1981) Can allergic exposure provoke psychological symptoms? A double blind test. *Biological Psychiatry*, **16**, 3–19.

King, R., Rases, J. D. & Barchas, J. D. (1981) Catastrophe theory of dopaminergic transmission: A revised dopamine hypothesis of schizophrenia. *Journal of Theoretical Biology*, **92**, 373–400.

Klein, D. C., Fencil-Morse, E. & Seligman, M. E. P. (1976) Learned helplessness, depression and the attribution of failure. *Journal of Personality and Social Psychology*, **33**, 508–516.

Klein, D. C. & Seligman, M. E. P. (1976) Reversal of performance deficits and perceptual deficits in learned helplessness and depression. *Journal of Abnormal Psychology*, **85**, 11–25.

Klein, D. F. (1974) Endogenomorphic depression: A conceptual and terminological revision. *Archives of General Psychiatry*, **31**, 447–454.

Klerman, G. L. (1979) The psychobiology of affective states: The legacy of Adolf Meyer. In Meyer, E., III & Brady, J. (eds) *Research in the Psychobiology of Human Behavior*. Baltimore, Md.: John Hopkins University Press.

Klinger, E. (1975) Consequences and commitment to aid disengagement from incentives. *Psychological Review*, **82**, 1–24.

Klinger, E. (1977) *Meaning and Void*. Minneapolis: University of Minnesota Press.

Kostowski, W. (1980) Noradrenergic interactions among central neurotransmitters. In Essman, W. B. (ed.) *Neurotransmitters, Receptors and Drug Action*. Lancaster: Spectrum Publications Inc.

Kovacs, M. (1980) Cognitive therapy of depression. *Journal of the American Academy of Psychoanalysis*, **8**, 127–144.

Kovacs, M., Rush, J., Beck, A. T. & Hollon, S. D. (1981) Depressed outpatients treated with cognitive therapy or pharmacotherapy: A one year follow up. *Archives of General Psychiatry*, **38**, 33–39.

Kraepelin, E. (1855–1926) As quoted in Zilboorg & Henry (1941).

Kraupl Taylor, F. (1980) The concepts of disease. *Psychological Medicine*, **10**, 419–424.

Krueger, A. P. & Reed, E. J. (1976) Biological impact of small air ions. *Science*, **193**, 1209–1213.

Lader, M. M. (1975) *The Psychophysiology of Mental Illness*. London: Routledge & Kegan Paul.

Lawick-Goodall, J. V. (1973) The behavior of chimpanzees in their natural habitat. *American Journal of Psychiatry*, **130**, 1–12.

Lawick-Goodall, J. V. (1975) The chimpanzee. In Goodall, V. (ed.) *The Quest for Man*. London: Phaidon Press.

Lazarus, A. A. (1977) Toward an egoless state of being. In Ellis, A. & Grieger, R. (eds) *Handbook of Rational Emotive Therapy*. New York: Springer.

Lazarus, R. S. (1966) *Psychological Stress and the Coping Processes*. New York: McGraw Hill.

Lazarus, R. S. & Averill, J. R. (1972) Emotion and cognition: With special reference to anxiety. In Spielberger, C. D. (ed.) *Anxiety: Current Trends in Theory and Research, Vol. 2*. New York: Academic Press.

Lazarus, R. S. & Launier, R. (1978) Stress related transactions between person and environment. In Pervin, L. A. & Lewis, M. (eds) *Perspectives in Interactional Psychology*. New York: Plenum Press.

Lefcourt, H. M. (1976) *Locus of Control: Current Trends in Theory and Research*. New York: Wiley.

Leff, J. P. (1978) Social and psychological cases of the acute attack. In Wing, J. K. (ed.) *Schizophrenia: Toward a New Synthesis*. London: Academic Press.

Leonhard, K. (1959) Aufteilung der endogenen psychosen. (As quoted by Becker, J., 1974.)

Leshner, A. I. (1978) *An Introduction to Behavioral Endocrinology*. New York: Oxford University Press.

Lewinsohn, P. M. (1974) A behavioral approach to depression. In Friedman, R. J. and Katz,

M. M. (eds.) *The Psychology of Depression: Contemporary Theory and Research.* New York: Winston-Wiley.

Lewinsohn, P. M. (1975) The behavioral study and treatment of depression. In Hersen, M., Eisler, R. M. & Miller, P. M. (eds) *Progress in Behavior Modification, Vol. 1.* New York: Academic Press.

Lewinsohn, P. M., Youngren, M. A. & Grosscup, S. J. (1979) Reinforcement and depression. In Depue, R. A. (ed.) *The Psychobiology of Depressive Disorders: Implications for the Effects of Stress.* New York: Academic Press.

Lewinsohn, P. M., Mischel, W., Chaplin, W. & Barton, R. (1980) Social competence and depression: The role of illusory self-perceptions. *Journal of Abnormal Psychology,* **89,** 203–212.

Lewinsohn, P. M., Steinmetz, J. L., Larson, D. W. & Franklin, J. (1981) Depression related cognitions: Antecedent or consequence? *Journal of Abnormal Psychology,* **90,** 213–219.

Lewis, A. (1967) *Inquiries in Psychiatry: Clinical and Social Investigations.* London: Routledge & Kegan Paul.

Lewis, A. (1971) "Endogenous" and "exogenous". A useful dichotomy? *Psychological Medicine,* **1,** 191–196.

Lewis, P. R. & Shute, C. C. D. (1967) The cholinergic limbic system: Projections to hippocampal formation, medial cortex, nuclei of the ascending cholinergic reticular system and the subfornical organ and supra-optic crest. *Brain,* **90,** 521–540.

Lipton, M. A. (1972) The neurobiology of mood and psychoses. In McGaugh, J. L. (ed.) *The Chemistry of Mood, Motivation and Memory.* New York: Plenum Press.

Lloyd, G. G. & Lishman, W. A. (1975) Effect of depression on the speed of recall of pleasant and unpleasant experiences. *Psychological Medicine,* **5,** 173–180.

Loeb, A., Feshbach, S., Beck, A. T. & Wolf, A. (1964) Some effects of reward upon the social perception and motivation of psychiatric patients varying in depression. *Journal of Abnormal Psychology,* **68,** 609–616.

Loftus, E. F. & Loftus, G. R. (1980) On the permanence of stored information in the human brain. *American Psychologist,* **35,** 409–420.

Loudon, J. B. (1977) Private communication.

Lyketsos, G. C., Blackburn, I. M. & Tsiantis, J. (1978) The movement of hostility during recovery from depression. *Psychological Medicine,* **8,** 145–149.

Maas, J. W. (1975) Biogenic amines and depression. *Archives of General Psychiatry,* **32,** 1357–1361.

Maas, J. W. (1979) Neurotransmitters and depression: Too much, too little, or too unstable. *Trends in the Neurosciences,* **2,** 306–308.

Maas, J. W., Koslow, S. H., Davis, J. M., Katz, M. M. et al. (1980) Biological component of the NIMH clinical research branch collaborative program on the psychobiology of depression: I. background and theoretical considerations. *Psychological Medicine,* **10,** 759–776.

MacCulloch, M. J. & Waddington, J. L. (1979) Catastrophe theory: A model interaction between neurochemical and environmental influences in the control of schizophrenia. *Neuropsychobiology,* **5,** 87–93.

MacKarness, R. (1976) *Not all in the Mind.* London: Pan Books.

Mackie, A. J. (1981) Attachment theory: Its relevance to the therapeutic alliance. *British Journal of Medical Psychology,* **54,** 203–212.

Mackintosh, N. J. (1974) *The Psychology of Animal Learning.* London: Academic Press.

Mackintosh, N. J. (1978) Conditioning. In Foss, B. M. (ed.) *Psychology Survey, No. 1.* London: G. Allen & Unwin.

MacLean, P. D. (1977) The triune brain in conflict. *Psychotherapy and Psychosomatics,* **28,** 207–220.

Mahoney, M. J. (1974) *Cognition and Behavior Modification.* Cambridge, Mass.: Ballinger.

Mahoney, M. J. & Arnkoff, D. B. (1978) Cognitive and self-control therapies. In Garfield,

S. L. & Bergin, J. W. (eds) *Handbook of Psychotherapy and Behavior Change*, 2nd ed. New York: Wiley & Sons.

Mandell, A. J. (1979) On a mechanism for mood and personality changes of adult and later life: A psychobiological hypothesis. *Journal of Nervous and Mental Disease*, 167, 457–466.

Mandell, A. J. (1980) Toward a psychobiology of transcendence: God in the brain. In Davidson, J. M. & Davidson, R. J. (eds) *The Psychobiology of Consciousness*. New York: Plenum Press.

Mandler, G. (1975) *Mind and Emotion*. New York: John Wiley.

Marzillier, J. S. (1980) Cognitive therapy and behavioural practice. *Behaviour Therapy and Research*, 18, 249–258.

Mason, S. T. & Iversen, S. D. (1979) Theories of the dorsal bundle extinction effect. *Brain Research Reviews*, 1, 107–137.

Matson, J. L. & Zeiss, R. A. (1979) The buddy system: A method of generalised reduction of inappropriate interpersonal behaviour of retarded psychiatric patients. *British Journal of Social and Clinical Psychology*, 18, 401–405.

McCarley, R. W. (1982) REM sleep and depression: Common neurobiologic control mechanisms. *American Journal of Psychiatry*, 139, 565–570.

McCarley, R. W. & Hobson, A. J. (1977) The neurobiological origins of psychoanalytic dream theory. *American Journal of Psychiatry*, 134, 1211–1221.

McClelland, D. C., Atkinson, J. W., Clark, R. H. & Lowell, E. L. (1953) *The Achievement Motive*. New York: Appleton-Century-Crofts.

McC.Miller, P. & Ingham, J. G. (1976) Friends, confidants and symptoms. *Social Psychiatry*, 11, 51–58.

McKinney, W. T. (1977) Animal behavioral-biological models relevant to depressive and affective disorders in humans. In Schulterbrandt, M. S. and Raskin, A. (eds) *Depression in Childhood: Diagnosis, Treatment and Conceptual Models*. New York: Raven Press.

McReynolds, P. & Guevara, C. (1967) Attitudes of schizophrenics and normals toward success and failure. *Journal of Abnormal Psychology*, 72, 303–310.

Melges, F. T. & Bowlby, J. (1969) Types of hopelessness in psychopathological processes. *Archives of General Psychiatry*, 20, 690–699.

Mendels, J. & Cochrane, C. (1968) The nosology of depression: The endogenous-reactive concept. *American Journal of Psychiatry*, 124, 1–11.

Mendels, J. & Frazer, A. (1974) Brain biogenic amine depletion and mood. *Archives of General Psychiatry*, 30, 447–451.

Menninger, K. (1963) *The Vital Balance: The Life Processes in Mental Health and Illness*. New York: Viking Press.

Meyer, A. (1866–1950) As quoted by Zilboorg & Henry, 1941, and Lewis, 1967.

Meyersburg, H. A. & Post, R. M. (1979) A holistic developmental view of neural and psychobiological processes: A neurobiologic-psychoanalytic integration. *British Journal of Psychiatry*, 135, 139–155.

Miller, N. E. & Weiss, J. M. (1969) Effects of somatic or visceral responses to punishment. In Campbell, B. A. & Church, R. M. (eds) *Punishment and Aversive Behavior*. New York: Appleton-Century-Crofts.

Miller, W. R. (1975) Psychological deficit in depression. *Psychological Bulletin*, 82, 238–260.

Miller, W. R. & Seligman, M. E. P. (1973) Depression and the perception of reinforcement. *Journal of Abnormal Psychology*, 82, 62–73.

Miller, W. R. & Seligman, M. E. P. (1975) Depression and learned helplessness in man. *Journal of Abnormal Psychology*, 84, 228–238.

Mills, I. H. (1976) The disease of failure of coping. *The Practitioner*, 217, 529–538.

Milner, P. (1971) *Physiological Psychology*. New York: Holt, Rinehart & Winston.

Mineka, S. & Suomi, S. J. (1978) Social separation in monkeys. *Psychological Bulletin*, 85, 1376–1400.

Minkoff, K., Bergman, E., Beck, A. T. & Beck, R. (1973) Hopelessness, depression and attempted suicide. *American Journal of Psychiatry*, **130**, 455–459.

Mischel, W., Ebbesen, E. B. & Zeiss, A. R. (1973) Selective attention to the self: Situational and dispositional determinants. *Journal of Personality and Social Psychology*, **27**, 129–142.

Mischel, W., Ebbesen, E. B. & Zeiss, A. (1976) Determinants of selective memory about the self. *Journal of Consulting and Clinical Psychology*, **44**, 92–103.

Montagu, A. (1976) *The Nature of Human Aggression*. New York: Oxford University Press.

Mowrer, O. H. & Viek, P. (1948) An experimental analogue of fear from a sense of helplessness. *Journal of Abnormal Psychology*, **43**, 193–200.

Myers, R. E. & Swett, C., Jr (1970) Social behavior deficits in free-ranging monkeys after anterior temporal cortex removal. A preliminary report. *Brain Research*, **18**, 551–556.

Neisser, U. (1967) *Cognitive Psychology*. New York: Appleton-Century-Crofts.

Neisser, U. (1976) *Cognition and Reality? Principles and Implications of Cognitive Psychology*. San Francisco: Freeman & Co.

Nelson, J. C. & Charney, D. S. (1981) The symptoms of major depressive illness. *American Journal of Psychiatry*, **138**, 1–13.

Nisbitt, R. E. & Wilson, T. D. (1977) Telling more than we can know: Verbal reports on mental processes. *Psychological Review*, **84**, 231–259.

Olds, J. & Milner, P. M. (1954) Positive reinforcement produced by electrical stimulation of the septal area and other regions of rat brain. *Journal of Comparative and Physiological Psychology*, **47**, 419–427.

Overall, J. E. & Zisook, S. (1980) Diagnosis and the phenomenology of depressive disorders. *Journal of Consulting and Clinical Psychology*, **48**, 626–634.

Overmier, J. B. & Seligman, M. E. P. (1967) Effects of inescapable shock upon subsequent escape and avoidance learning. *Journal of Comparative and Physiological Psychology*, **63**, 28–33.

Parker, G. & Lipscombe, P. (1981) Influences on maternal overprotection. *British Journal of Psychiatry*, **138**, 303–311.

Parkes, C. M. (1970) The first year of bereavement. *Psychiatry*, **33**, 444–467.

Parkes, C. M. (1972) *Bereavement: Studies of Grief in Adult Life*. London: Tavistock.

Paykel, E. S. (1971) Classification of depressed patients: A cluster analysis derived grouping. *British Journal of Psychiatry*, **118**, 275–288.

Paykel, E. S. (1978) Contribution of life events to causation of psychiatric illness. *Psychological Medicine*, **8**, 245–253.

Paykel, E. S. (1979) Recent life events in the development of the depressive disorders. In Depue, R. A. (ed.) *The Psychobiology of the Depressive Disorders: Implications for the Effects of Stress*. New York: Academic Press.

Paykel, E. S. & Tanner, J. (1976) Life events, depressive relapse and maintenance treatment. *Psychological Medicine*, **6**, 481–485.

Paykel, E. S. & Henderson, A. J. (1977) Application of cluster analysis in the classification of depression: a replication study. *Neuropsychobiology*, **3**, 111–119.

Paykel, E. S., Weissman, M. M. & Prusoff, B. A. (1978) Social maladjustment and severity of depression. *Comprehensive Psychiatry*, **19**, 121–128.

Pearce, J. M. & Hall, G. (1980) A model for Pavlovian learning: Variations in the effectiveness of conditioned but not of unconditioned stimuli. *Psychological Review*, **87**, 532–552.

Peck, D. & Whitlow, D. (1975) *Approaches to Personality Theory*. London: Methuen.

Pedder, J. R. (1982) Failure to mourn and melancholia. *British Journal of Psychiatry*, **141**, 329–337.

Perez De La Mora, M. & Fuxe, K. (1977) Brain G.A.B.A., dopamine and acetylcholine interactions. I. Studies with oxotermorine. *Brain Research*, **135**, 107–122.

Perris, C. (1966) A study of bipolar (manic depressive) and unipolar (recurrent depressive) psychoses. *Acta Psychiatrica Scandinavia*, **42**, (Suppl. 194), 1–189.

Plato (427–347 BC) As quoted in Zilboorg & Henry (1941).

Plotkin, H. C. & Odling-Smee, F. J. (1981) A multiple-level model of evolution and its implications for sociobiology. *Behavioral and Brain Sciences*, **4**, 225–268.

Popper, K. R. & Eccles, J. C. (1977) *The Self and its Brain*. New York: Springer International.

Postle, D. (1980) *Catastrophe Theory: Predict and Avoid Personal Disasters*. London: Fontana.

Prange, A. J., Jr, Wilson, I. C. & Lynn, C. W. et al. (1974) L-Tryptophan in mania: Contribution to a permissive hypothesis of affective disorders. *Archives of General Psychiatry*, **30**, 56–62.

Price, J. S. (1972) Genetic and phylogenetic aspects of mood variations. *International Journal of Mental Health*, **1**, 124–144.

Prusoff, B. & Klerman, G. L. (1974) Differentiating depressed from anxious neurotic outpatients. *Archives of General Psychiatry*, **30**, 302–309.

Rachman, S. J. (1978) *Fear and Courage*. San Francisco: Freeman.

Rachman, S. (1981) The primacy of affect: Some theoretical implications. *Behaviour Research and Therapy*, **19**, 279–290.

Rahe, R. H. & Arthur, R. J. (1978) Life change and illness studies: Past history and future directions. *Journal of Human Stress*, March, 3–15.

Raimy, V. (1975) *Misunderstandings of the Self*. San Francisco: Jossey Bass.

Ramsay, R. W. (1979) Bereavement: A behavioral treatment of pathological grief. In Sjöden, P. O., Bates, S. & Dockens, W. S., III (eds) *Trends in Behavior Therapy*. New York: Academic Press.

Rao, R. V. A. & Coppen, A. (1979) Classification of depression and response to amitriptyline therapy. *Psychological Medicine*, **9**, 321–325.

Raskin, A., Schulterbrandt, J. G., Raetig, N. & McKeon, J. J. (1970) Differential response to chlorpromazine, imipramine and placebo: A study of sub groups of hospitalized depressed patients. *Archives of General Psychiatry*, **23**, 164–173.

Raskin, A. & Crook, T. H. (1976) The endogenous-neurotic distinction as a predictor of response to antidepressant drugs. *Psychological Medicine*, **6**, 59–70.

Rasmussen, K. L. R. & Reite, M. (1982) Loss-induced depression in an adult Macaque monkey. *American Journal of Psychiatry*, **139**, 679–681.

Raw, M. (1978) Depression: The long journey up. *Psychology Today*, May, 24–28.

Rehm, L. P. (1977) A self control model of depression. *Behavior Therapy*, **8**, 787–804.

Rehm, L. P. (ed.) (1981) *Behavior Therapy for Depression*. New York: Academic Press.

Rehm, L. P., Fuchs, C. Z., Roth, D. M., Kornblith, S. J. & Romano, J. M. (1979) A comparison of self control and assertion skills treatments of depression. *Behavior Therapy*, **10**, 429–442.

Reite, M., Short, R., Seiler, C. & Pauley, J. D. (1981) Attachment, loss and depression. *Journal of Child Psychology and Psychiatry*, **22**, 141–169.

Reus, V. I., Weingartner, H. & Post, R. M. (1979a) Clinical implications of state-dependent learning. *American Journal of Psychiatry*, **136**, 927–931.

Reus, V. I., Silberman, E., Post, R. M. & Weingartner, H. (1979b) δ-amphetamine: Effects on memory in a depressed population. *Biological Psychiatry*, **14**, 345–356.

Rippere, V. (1979) Scaling the helpfulness of antidepressive activities. *Behaviour Research and Therapy*, **17**, 439–449.

Rippere, V. & Adams, N. (1982) Clinical ecology and why clinical psychology needs it. *Bulletin of the British Psychological Society*, **35**, 151–152.

Risch, S. C., Cohen, R. M., Janowsky, D. S. et al. (1981) Physostigmine induction of depressive symptomatology in normal human subjects. *Psychiatry Research*, **4**, 89–94.

Robins, E., Muñoz, R. A., Martin, S. & Gentry, K. A. (1972) Primary and secondary affective disorders. In Zubin, J. & Freyhan, F. A. (eds) *Disorders of Mood*. Baltimore, Md.: Johns Hopkins University Press.

Rollins, N. (1974) The new Soviet approach to the unconscious. *American Journal of Psychiatry*, **131**, 301–304.

Roth, R. H. & Bunney, B. S. (1976) Interaction of cholinergic neurons with other chemically defined neuronal systems in the CNS. In Goldberg, A. M. & Hanin, I. (eds) *Biology of Cholinergic Function*. New York: Raven Press.

Roth, S. & Kubal, L. (1975) Effects of noncontingent reinforcement on tasks of differing importance: Facilitation and learned helplessness. *Journal of Personality and Social Psychology*, **32**, 680–691.

Rotter, J. B. (1966) Generalized expectancies for internal versus external control of reinforcement. *Psychological Monographs*, **80** (Whole no. 609).

Rotter, J. B., Seeman, M. & Liverant, S. (1962) Internal versus external control of reinforcement: A major variable in behavior theory. In Washburne, N. F. (ed.) *Decisions, Values and Groups, Vol. 2*. Oxford: Pergamon Press.

Rounsaville, B. J., Klerman, G. L. & Weissman, M. M. (1981) Do psychotherapy and pharmacotherapy for depression conflict? *Archives of General Psychiatry*, **38**, 24–29.

Rush, A. J., Beck, A. T., Kovacs, M. & Hollon, S. D. (1977) Comparative efficacy of cognitive therapy and pharmacotherapy in the treatment of depressed outpatients. *Cognitive Therapy and Research*, **1**, 17–37.

Rutter, M. (1975) *Helping Troubled Children*. Harmondsworth: Penguin Books.

Rutter, M. (1981) *Maternal Deprivation Reassessed*, 2nd ed. Harmondsworth: Penguin Books.

Ryle, A. (1982) *Psychotherapy. A Cognitive Integration of Theory and Practice*. London: Academic Press.

Sadd, S., Lenauer, M., Shaver, P. & Dunivant, N. (1978) Objective measurement of fear of success and fear of failure: A factor analytic approach. *Journal of Consulting and Clinical Psychology*, **46**, 405–416.

Sarason, I. G. (1972) Experimental approaches to test anxiety: Attention and uses of information. In Spielberger, C. D. (ed.) *Anxiety: Current Trends in Theory and Research, Vol. 2*. New York: Academic Press.

Scadding, J. (1980) The concepts of disease: A response. *Psychological Medicine*, **10**, 425–427.

Schildkraut, J. J. (1965) The catecholamine hypothesis of affective disorders: A review of supporting evidence. *American Journal of Psychiatry*, **122**, 509–522.

Schildkraut, J. J. (1975) Depressions and biogenic amines. In Hamburg, D. A. & Brodie, K. H. (eds) *American Handbook of Psychiatry, Vol. 6*, 2nd ed. New York: Basic Books.

Schildkraut, J. J. (1976) The current status of biological criteria for classifying the depressive disorders and predicting responses to treatment. *Psychopharmacological Bulletin*, **10**, 5–25.

Schildkraut, J. J., Orsulak, P. J., Schatzberg, A. F. et al. (1978a) Toward a biochemical classification of depressive disorders: I. Differences in urinary excretion of M.H.P.G. and other catecholamine metabolites in clinically defined, subtypes of depressions. *Archives of General Psychiatry*, **35**, 1427–1433.

Schildkraut, J. J., Orsulak, P. J., Labrie, R. A. et al. (1978b) Toward a biochemical classification of depressive disorders. II. Application of multivariate discriminant function analysis to data on urinary catecholamine and metabolites. *Archives of General Psychiatry*, **35**, 1436–1440.

Schless, A. P., Schwartz, L., Goetz, C. & Mendels, J. (1974) How depressives view the significance of life events. *British Journal of Psychiatry*, **125**, 406–410.

Schwartz, G. E. (1978) Psychobiological foundations of psychotherapy and behavior change.

In Garfield, S. L. & Bergin, A. E. (eds) *Handbook of Psychotherapy and Behavior Change*, 2nd ed. New York: Wiley.

Schwartz, R. M. & Gottman, J. M. (1976) Toward a task analysis of assertive behavior. *Journal of Consulting and Clinical Psychology*, **44**, 910–920.

Segal, H. (1975) *Introduction to the Work of Melanie Klein*. London: Hogarth Press.

Seligman, M. E. P. (1971) Phobias and preparedness. *Behavior Therapy*, **2**, 307–320.

Seligman, M. E. P. (1974) Depression and learned helplessness. In Friedman, R. J. & Katz, M. M. (eds) *The Psychology of Depression: Contemporary Theory and Research*. New York: Winston-Wiley.

Seligman, M. E. P. (1975) *Helplessness: On Depression Development and Death*. San Francisco: Freeman & Co.

Seligman, M. E. P. & Mater, S. F. (1967) Failure to escape traumatic shock. *Journal of Experimental Psychology*, **74**, 1–9.

Seligman, M. E. P., Maier, S. F. & Solomon, R. L. (1971) Unpredictable and uncontrollable aversive events. In Brush, F. R. (ed.) *Aversive Conditioning and Learning*. New York: Academic Press.

Seligman, M. E. P., Abramson, L. Y., Semmel, A. & Baeyer, C. V. (1979) Depressive attributional style. *Journal of Abnormal Psychology*, **88**, 242–247.

Shapiro, D. A. (1980) Science and psychotherapy: The state of the art. *British Journal of Medical Psychology*, **53**, 1–10.

Shaver, P. (1979) Personal communication.

Shaw, B. F., Steer, R. A., Beck, A. T. & Schut, J. (1979) The structure of depression in heroin addicts. *British Journal of Addiction*, **74**, 295–303.

Sherwood, G. G. (1982) Consciousness and stress reduction in defensive projection: A reply to Holmes. *Psychological Bulletin*, **91**, 372–375.

Shevrin, H. & Dickman, S. (1980) The psychological unconscious: A necessary assumption for all psychological theory? *American Psychologist*, **35**, 421–434.

Siegle, S. (1979) The role of conditioning in drug tolerance and addiction. In Keehn, J. D. (ed.) *Psychopathology in Animals: Research and Clinical Implications*. New York: Academic Press.

Silberman, E. K., Reus, V. I., Jimerson, D. C., Lynott, A. M. & Post, R. M. (1981) Heterogeneity of amphetamine response in depressed patients. *American Journal of Psychiatry*, **138**, 1302–1307.

Sitaram, N., Nurnberger, J. I., Gershon, E. S. & Gillin, C. J. (1982) Cholinergic regulations of mood and REM sleep: Potential model and marker of vulnerability to affective disorder. *American Journal of Psychiatry*, **139**, 571–576.

Sklar, L. S. & Anisman, H. (1981) Stress and cancer. *Psychological Bulletin*, **89**, 369–406.

Slater, J. & Depue, R. A. (1981) The contribution of environmental events and social support to serious suicide attempts in primary depressive disorder. *Journal of Abnormal Psychology*, **90**, 275–285.

Solomon, R. L. (1980) The opponent-process theory of acquired motivation: The cost of pleasure and the benefits of pain. *American Psychologist*, **35**, 691–712.

Starkman, M. N., Schteingart, D. E. & Schork, M. A. (1981) Depressed mood and other psychiatric manifestations of Cushing's syndrome: Relationship to hormone levels. *Psychosomatic Medicine*, **43**, 3–18.

Staude, J. R. (1981) *The Adult Development of C. G. Jung*. Boston: Routledge & Kegan Paul.

Stein, L. (1968) Chemistry of reward and punishment. In *Psychopharmacology: A Review of Progress 1957–1967*. Washington, D.C.: US Government Printing Office.

Stein, L. (1972) Noradrenergic reward mechanisms, recovery of function and schizophrenia. In McGaugh, J. L. (ed.) *The Chemistry of Mood, Motivation and Memory*. New York: Plenum Press.

Stengel, E. (1971) *Suicide and Attempted Suicide*, 2nd ed. Harmondsworth: Penguin Books.

Stern, S. L., Rush, J. A. & Mendels, J. (1980) Toward a rational pharmacotherapy of depression. *American Journal of Psychiatry*, **137**, 545–552.

Stolk, J. M. & Nisula, B. C. (1979) Genetic influences on catecholamine metabolism. In Depue, R. A. (ed.) *The Psychobiology of the Depressive Disorders: Implications for the Effects of Stress*. New York: Academic Press.

Storm-Mathisen, J. & Fonnum, F. (1972) Localization of transmitter candidates in the hippocampal region. In Bradley, P. B. & Brimblecombe, R. W. (eds) *Biochemical and Pharmacological Mechanisms Underlying Behavior. Progress in Brain Research, Vol. 36*. Amsterdam: Elsevier Publishing Company.

Storr, A. (1973) *Jung*. London: Fontana.

Suomi, S. J., Eisele, C. D., Grady, S. A. & Harlow, H. F. (1975) Depressive behavior in adult monkeys following separation from family environment. *Journal of Abnormal Psychology*, **84**, 576–578.

Suomi, S. J., Seaman, S. F., Lewis, J. K., Delizio, R. D. & McKinney, W. T., Jr (1978) Effects of imipramine treatment of separation-induced social disorders in rhesus monkeys. *Archives of General Psychiatry*, **35**, 321–325.

Surtees, P. G. & Kendell, R. E. (1979) The hierarchy model of psychiatric symptomatology: An investigation based on present state examination ratings. *British Journal of Psychiatry*, **135**, 438–443.

Sutherland, G., Newman, B. & Rachman, S. (in press) Experimental investigations of the relations between mood and intrusive unwanted cognitions. *British Journal of Medical Psychology* (in press).

Sutherland, S. N. (1976) *Breakdown: A Personal Crisis and a Medical Dilemma*. London: Weidenfeld & Nicolson.

Synder, S. (1975) Biology. In Perlins, S. (ed.) *A Handbook for the Study of Suicide*. Oxford: Oxford University Press.

Szasz, T. (1974) *Ideology and Insanity*. New York: Penguin.

Tarrier, N., Vaughn, C., Lader, M. H. & Leff, J. P. (1979) Bodily reactions to people and events in schizophrenics. *Archives of General Psychiatry*, **36**, 311–315.

Tart, C. T. (1980) A system approach to altered states of consciousness. In Davidson, J. M. & Davidson, R. J. (eds) *The Psychobiology of Consciousness*. New York: Plenum Press.

Teasdale, J. D. & Bancroft, J. (1977) Manipulation of thought content as a determinant of mood and corrugator electromyographic activity in depressed patients. *Journal of Abnormal Psychology*, **86**, 235–241.

Teasdale, J. D. & Rezin, V. (1978a) Effect of thought-stopping on thoughts, mood and corrugator EMG in depressed patients. *Behaviour Research and Therapy*, **16**, 97–102.

Teasdale, J. D. & Rezin, V. (1978b) The effects of reducing frequency of negative thoughts on the mood of depressed patients—tests of a cognitive model of depression. *British Journal of Social and Clinical Psychology*, **17**, 65–74.

Teasdale, J. D. & Fogarty, S. J. (1979) Differential effects of induced mood on retrieval of pleasant and unpleasant events from episodic memory. *Journal of Abnormal Psychology*, **88**, 248–257.

Teasdale, J. D. & Taylor, R. (1981) Induced mood and accessibility of memories: An effect of mood state or of induction procedure. *British Journal of Clinical Psychology*, **20**, 39–48.

Tennant, C. & Andrews, G. (1978) The pathogenic quality of life stress in neurotic impairment. *Archives of General Psychiatry*, **35**, 859–863.

Tennant, C. & Bebbington, P. (1978) The social causation of depression: A critique of the work of Brown and his colleagues. *Psychological Medicine*, **8**, 565–575.

Tennant, C., Smith, A., Bebbington, P. & Hurry, J. (1979) The contextual threat of life events: The concept and its reliability. *Psychological Medicine*, **9**, 525–528.

Tennant, C., Bebbington, P. & Hurry, J. (1981a) The short-term outcome of neurotic disorders in the community: the relation of remission to clinical factors and to "neutralizing" life events. *British Journal of Psychiatry*, **139**, 213–220.

Tennant, C., Bebbington, P. & Hurry, J. (1981b) The role of life events in depressive illness: Is there a substantial causal relation? *Psychological Medicine*, **11**, 379–389.

Tennant, N. & Thompson, I. E. (1980) Causal models and logical inference. *British Journal of Psychiatry*, **137**, 579–582.

Tennen, H. & Eller, S. J. (1977) Attributional components of learned helplessness and facilitation. *Journal of Personality and Social Psychology*, **35**, 265–271.

Thompson, P. J. & Trimble, M. R. (1982) Non-MAOI antidepressant drugs and cognitive functions: A review. *Psychological Medicine*, **12**, 539–548.

Thornton, J. W. & Jacobs, P. D. (1971) Learned helplessness in human subjects. *Journal of Experimental Psychology*, **87**, 367–372.

Tucker, D. M. (1981) Lateral brain function, emotion and conceptualisation. *Psychological Bulletin*, **89**, 19–46.

Tucker, D. M., Stenslie, C. E., Roth, R. S. & Shearer, S. L. (1981) Right frontal lobe activation and right hemisphere performance: Decrement during depressed mood. *Archives of General Psychiatry*, **38**, 169–174.

Ursin, H. (1980) Personality, activation and somatic health: A new psychosomatic theory. In Levine, S. & Ursin, H. (eds) *Coping and Health*. New York: Plenum Press.

Valzelli, L. (1977) Social experience as a determinant of normal behavior and drug effect. In Iversen, L. L., Iversen, S. D. & Synder, S. H. (eds) *Handbook of Psychopharmacology, Vol. 7.* New York: Plenum Press.

Vaughn, C. E. & Leff, J. P. (1976) The influence of family and social factors on the course of psychiatric illness: A comparison of schizophrenic and depressed neurotic patients. *British Journal of Psychiatry*, **129**, 125–137.

Wachtel, P. L. (1977) *Psychoanalysis and Behavior Therapy: Toward an Integration.* New York: Basic Books.

Warburton, D. M. (1979) Physiological aspects of information processing and stress. In Hamilton, V. & Warburton, D. M. (eds) *Human Stress and Cognition: An Information Processing Approach.* Chichester: John Wiley.

Warheit, G. J. (1979) Life events, coping, stress and depressive symptomatology. *American Journal of Psychiatry*, **136**, 502–507.

Weiner, B. (1972) *Theories of Motivation: From Mechanism to Cognition.* Chicago: Rand McNally.

Weiner, B. (ed.) (1974) *Achievement Motivation and Attribution Theory.* Morristown, N.J.: General Learning Press.

Weiner, B., Heckhausen, H., Meyer, W. U. & Cook, R. E. (1972) Causal ascriptions and achievement motivation. *Journal of Personality and Social Psychology*, **21**, 239–248.

Weiner, B., Nierenberg, R. & Goldstein, M. (1976) Social learning (locus of control) versus attributional (causal stability) interpretations of expectancy of success. *Journal of Personality*, **44**, 52–68.

Weiner, B., Russell, D. & Lerman, D. (1978) Affective consequences of causal ascriptions. In Harvey, J. H., Ickes, W. J. & Kidd, R. F. (eds) *New Directions in Attribution Research, Vol. 2.* Hillside, N.J.: Lawrence Erlbaum Press.

Weiner, B., Russell, D. & Lerman, D. (1979) The cognition-emotion process in achievement-related contexts. *Journal of Personality and Social Psychology*, **37**, 1211–1220.

Weingartner, H., Miller, H. & Murphy, D. L. (1977) Mood-state-dependent retrieval of verbal associations. *Journal of Abnormal Psychology*, **86**, 276–284.

Weingartner, H., Cohen, R. M., Murphy, D. L., Martello, J. & Gerdt, C. (1981) Cognitive processes in depression. *Archives of General Psychiatry*, **38**, 42–47.

Weinstein, M. S. (1969) Achievement motivation and risk preference. *Journal of Personality and Social Psychology*, **13**, 153–172.

Weintraub, M., Segal, R. M. & Beck, A. T. (1974) An investigation of cognition and affect in the depressive experiences of normal men. *Journal of Consulting and Clinical Psychology*, 42, 911.

Weiss, B. L., Foster, F. G. & Kupfer, D. J. (1976) Cholinergic involvement in neuropsychiatric syndromes. In Goldberg, A. M. & Hanin, I. (eds) *Biology of Cholinergic Function*. New York: Raven Press.

Weiss, J. M., Stone, E. A. & Harrell, N. (1970) Coping behavior and brain norepinephrine level in rats. *Journal of Comparative and Physiological Psychology*, 72, 153–160.

Weiss, J. M., Glazer, H. I. & Pohorecky, L. A. (1976) Coping behavior and neurochemical changes. An alternative explanation for the original "learned helplessness' experiments. In Serban, G. & Kling, A. (eds) *Animal Models in Human Psychobiology*. New York: Plenum Press.

Weiss, J. M., Glazer, H. I., Pohorecky, L. A., Bailey, W. H. & Schneider, L. H. (1979) Coping behavior and stress-induced behavioral depression: Studies of the role of brain catecholamines. In Depue, R. A. (ed.) *The Psychobiology of the Depressive Disorders*. New York: Academic Press.

Weissman, M. M. (1979) The psychological treatment of depression. *Archives of General Psychiatry*, 36, 1261–1269.

Weissman, M. M., Klerman, G. L. & Paykel, E. S. (1971) Clinical evaluation of hostility in depression. *American Journal of Psychiatry*, 128, 261–266.

Weissman, M. M. & Klerman, G. L. (1977a) Sex differences and the epidemiology of depression. *Archives of General Psychiatry*, 34, 98–111.

Weissman, M. M. & Klerman, G. L. (1977b) The chronic depressive in the community: Unrecognized and poorly treated. *Comprehensive Psychiatry*, 18, 523–532.

Wetzel, R. D. (1976) Hopelessness, depression and suicide intent. *Archives of General Psychiatry*, 33, 1069–1073.

Whitlock, F. A. & Siskind, M. (1979) Depression and cancer: A follow-up study. *Psychological Medicine*, 9, 747–752.

Wilber, K. (1982) The pre/trans fallacy. *Journal of Humanistic Psychology*, 22, 5–43.

Winokur, G. (1973) Diagnostic and genetic aspects of affective illness. *Psychiatric Annals*, 3, 6–15.

Wollheim, R. (1971) *Freud*. London: Fontana.

Wolpe, J. (1971) Neurotic depression: Experimental analogue, clinical syndromes and treatment. *American Journal of Psychotherapy*, 25, 362–368.

Wolpe, J. (1979) The experimental model and treatment of neurotic depression. *Behaviour Research and Therapy*, 17, 555–565.

Wolpe, J. (1981a) The dichotomy between classically conditioned and cognitively learned anxiety. *Journal of Behavior Therapy and Experimental Psychiatry*, 12, 35–42.

Wolpe, J. (1981b) Commentary on the report of the behavior therapy conference. *Journal of Consulting and Clinical Psychology*, 49, 604–605.

Wright, J. & Mischel, W. (1982) Influence of affect on cognitive social learning person variables. *Journal of Personality and Social Psychology*, 43, 901–914.

Youngren, M. A. & Lewinsohn, P. M. (1980) The functional relation between depression and problematic interpersonal behavior. *Journal of Abnormal Psychology*, 89, 333–341.

Zajonc, R. B. (1980) Feeling and thinking: Preferences need no inferences. *American Psychologist*, 35, 151–175.

Zeeman, E. C. (1977) *Catastrophe Theory: Selected Papers 1972–1977*. Reading: Addison-Wesley. (See especially Duffing's equation in brain modelling, pp. 293–300.)

Zilboorg, G. (in collaboration with Henry, G. W.) (1941) *History of Medical Psychology*. New York: W. W. Norton & Co.

AUTHOR INDEX

Abraham, K., 24
Abramson, L. Y., 68, 90, 92, 96, 164
Adams, D. B., 153
Adams, N., 213
Akiskal, H. S., 2, 13–18, 70, 100, 106, 167, 176
Altman, J., 109
Amsel, A., 65
Anderson, G. H., 213
Andrews, G., 174, 179
Anisman, H., 92, 102, 103, 111, 114, 115, 118, 122, 125, 130, 154, 181
Antelman, S. M., 104
Anthony, E. J., 26
Aprison, M. H., 109, 110
Arieti, S., 25, 46, 57, 69, 96
Arnkoff, D. B., 68, 77
Arthur, R. J. 179
Atkinson, J. W., 21
Averill, J. R., 151, 175

Bagshaw, V. E., 14
Baldessarini, R. J., 102
Bandura, A., 52, 93, 97, 112, 145, 164
Barker, T., 213
Basch, M. F., 39
Bebbington, P., 174–177, 180
Beck, A. T., 5, 10, 18, 28, 41, 43, 44, 46, 47, 53, 65, 68, 72, 77–89, 93, 96, 97, 112, 134–138, 164, 191
Becker, J., 8, 10, 45, 47, 57, 58, 96, 97, 104
Bedford, A., 13, 14, 16
Bemporad, J., 46, 57, 69, 96
Benedek, T., 26
Bibring, E., 44, 45, 84, 88, 96, 97, 134
Bignami, G., 111
Birney, R. C., 94, 95
Bishop, S., 19
Blackburn, I. M., 19, 86, 87, 157, 189, 190
Blakemore, C., 2
Blaney, P. H., 58, 68, 86, 88, 89
Blatt, S. J., 18, 98, 143, 196
Blumenthal, M. D., 17
Bonham, K. G., 189, 190
Bowlby, J., 37–44, 52, 74, 85, 88, 99, 116, 119, 133, 142, 144–146, 159, 168
Bowman, M. K., 9
Braden, W., 192
Brady, J., 122
Breslow, R., 189
Brockington, I. F., 10

Bronowski, J., 131
Brown, G. W., 43, 79, 84, 86, 97, 174, 176–178, 181, 182
Bunney, B. S., 104
Bunney, W. E., 102
Burns, D. D., 103
Buxton, D. A., 110
Byrne, D. G., 18

Caggiula, A. R., 104
Carlton, P. L., 109, 110
Carney, M. W. P., 11
Carroll, B. J., 15, 105, 153
Charney, D. S., 12
Clarke, A. D. B., 43, 119
Clarke, A. M., 43, 119
Cochrane, C., 11
Cohen, M. B., 46, 96, 198
Cohen, R. M., 191
Colotla, V. A., 119
Cooke, D. J., 12, 174
Coopersmith, S., 98
Coppen, A., 13, 102, 103
Costello, C. G., 61, 62, 88, 89
Cotman, C. W., 102
Coyne, J. C., 58, 86, 168, 174, 182
Crisp, A. H., 213
Crook, J. H., 48, 98, 143, 163, 185, 217, 221
Crow, T. J., 103

Dahlström, A., 103
Davis, J. M., 102
Davis, K. L., 105, 106, 191
deCatanzaro, D., 1, 139, 220
deCharms, R., 96
Decsi, L., 153
Depue, R. A., 12, 13, 15, 89, 153, 195
Diaz, J., 181
Dickman, S., 39, 40, 85
DiMascio, A., 87
Dixon, T., 48, 219
Dobzhansky, T., 185
Douglas, D., 92
Dweck, C. S., 91, 92
D'Zurilla, T. J., 97

Eccles, J. C., 2
Eccleston, D., 104
Eikelboom, R., 122, 123

246

SUBJECT INDEX

hypothalamus, pleasure areas, septum
Brain state instability model, 199–212
see also catastrophe theory

Catastrophe theory, 18, 156, 201–212
  and conflicting motivation(s), 201–212
Catastrophizing, 139–141
Catecholamines, 14, 102, 153, 155, 177, 181
  and classification of depression, 14
  and theories of depression, 102–104, 107
  see also 5-hydroxytryptamine, noradrenaline
Classical conditioning, 70–76, 122–126, 133, 212
  of anxiety, 70, 71, 75
  of depression, 73, 74, 76, 122–126, 212
Cognition
  and automatic thoughts, 80, 81, 85, 99
  and the negative cognitive triad, 70, 80, 82, 84, 166
  and primitive thinking, 81, 82
  see also information processing
Cognitive distortion(s), 41, 57, 59, 66, 68, 79, 81, 83, 84, 99, 184, 187, 190
Cognitive schemata, 82–85, 99, 115, 135, 139, 145, 165, 191, 209
  see also attitudes, beliefs, cognition
Cognitive therapy, 86, 87, 99, 100
Commitment
  to incentives, 63, 65
Complex(es), 77
Contextual threat, 174, 177
Coping, 108, 110–116, 127–129, 132, 133, 164–174, 179, 180
  failures in, 110–116, 127–129
  and neurochemical change, 108, 110–116
  strategy, 95, 190
  style, 179
Cortisol, 15, 153, 158
  and dexamethasone, 15, 17, 105, 107
Counterconditioning, 71, 74
  of dysphoria, 74
Current concern(s), 63, 191
  and cognitive processes, 63

Death
  and depression, 158–160, 185, 220
Defensive exclusion, 41, 43, 168
Dementia praecox, 3, 4, 6, 24
Despair, 119, 120, 131, 193
Dexamphetamine, 211
Dexamethasone
  see cortisol
Dependency, 27, 31, 34, 46, 57, 60, 133, 158, 160–163, 172
Depression
  and Beck Inventory, 86, 100
  and character (personality) disorder, 12, 17, 82
  and classification issues, 2–20
  dimensional versus categorical, 10, 11, 70
  endogenomorphic, 12, 16
  endogenous, 5–9, 12, 195
  exogenous, 5–9, 16, 70, 102, 167, 176
  hierarchical model, 13, 14, 16, 31
  manic-depressive, 3, 5, 24, 25
  neuropsychological approach, 214

neurotic, 3, 8, 9, 12, 14–16, 67, 70, 71, 167, 176
  primary-secondary, 13, 17
  and psychogenesis, 6, 7, 9, 70
  psychotic, 3, 6, 8–10, 12, 14, 16, 29, 149
  reactive, 7, 9
  unipolar-bipolar, 13, 15, 17
Depressive programs, 217–220
Development, 32
  of behavior, 55
  critical stages of, 32, 122
  personal, 122
  see also cognitive schemata, positions
Diet, 213
Discontinuity of affect, 200–212
Discrimination learning, 55, 217, 218
Disease
  concepts of, 2–8
  cancer, 1
  Cushing's, 19, 128, 153
Disengagement, 65, 66, 119–121, 129, 131, 159, 169, 206, 207
  failure of, 67, 68, 168
Dominance behavior, 163
  and frustration, 66, 154
  and protection, 184, 185
  and social hierarchy, 133, 140, 163, 171
  and social rank, 121, 143
  and submissive interactions, 98, 147, 152–154, 198, 219
  see also aggression
Dopamine (DA), 102–103, 106, 114
  L-dopa, 128
Dorsal bundle, 117–119, 122, 127
Drugs, 37, 60, 86, 160, 191
Dualism, 2, 3, 7, 8, 21, 101, 215

Ego, 44–47
  states, 44–47
  ideals, 45, 134
  see also psychoanalytic
Emotion
  expressed emotion and schizophrenia, 60
  see also warm glow
Energy, 27, 28, 36, 161
Equipotentiality, 61, 73, 74
Evolution, 21, 47, 48, 60, 61, 131, 221
  and abandonment, 149–152, 198
  and archetype, 32, 33
  and attachment theory, 37–39, 159, 163
  Darwin's influence, 21
  and life events, 176
  and threats to survival, 135, 139, 149
  and self-esteem, 98
Exploration, 38, 55, 57, 218
Exposure, 72, 75, 76
Extinction, 64, 214, 215
  events, 68
  of incentives, 63
  resistance to, 53, 54, 73

Failure, 64, 92, 94, 95, 172, 205
  and attribution of, 92
  fear of, 94, 95, 172, 205